DADDY HA
GOODBYE

A STORY OF HOPE

(handwritten inscription and signature)

David J. Brown

Published by David J. Brown Books, LLC

DAVID J BROWN BOOKS, LLC
http://www.davidjbrownbooks.com

Paperback ISBN: 9781725974487

Cover Illustration by Emilia Kolarova, updated by Angie Simonson. All rights reserved – used with permission.

Library of Congress Control Number: 2015910464

PRINTED IN THE UNITED STATES OF AMERICA

Reader Praise and Reviews of
DADDY HAD TO SAY GOODBYE

Note from the author:

My agent was appalled when I submitted book reviews from legitimate readers and friends. According to the agent, only people of prominence, fame, and stature should be used for book reviews. I very much enjoyed the gasp and rapid eye blinking when I said, "You are fired!"

David J. Brown takes me to the depths of my marrow.

This read is like listening to an audio book. I can clearly hear the characters' voices and the pulse of their lives. It will cause the most casual of readers to examine their moral compass.
- RW Clark

Powerful

Resilient, the one word that leaps from the pages of this solid book. My reading this book took me on an adventure of soul searching of both Flanagan and myself. Only when you finish this great book will you truly understand why "Daddy Had to Say Goodbye."
- Sean Carrigan

Thank you David for writing this book.

…re-living moments most couldn't and shouldn't have to understand. I know what courage it took to write this book, and brother, in my eyes, you continue to be a hero!
- Kevin Roberts

Incredible story, get the Kleenex ready.

I'm greatly impressed with the author's ability to capture the voice of that young child, then the voice of the teenager, and the man he became. I am further overwhelmed with Mr. Brown's ability to repeatedly break the "Fourth Wall" and to so cleanly get away with it. Simply masterful! A beautiful story from a beautiful soul. Thank you for using your painful experiences to help others.
- J.K. Swift

Daddy Had to Say Goodbye is not just a game changer, it's a life changer!
This writer is a true warrior in this battle called life and I find inspiration through him and his writing. Many of us in the First Responder business know and understand the truth and pain you shared. Sadly, very few of us can admit it, to ourselves or to others. I applaud your amazing bravery to write for all of us. Mr. Brown is an incredible human who continues to save lives.
- R.S. Crown

Unfathomable suffering…extraordinary courage
The author and his character Clinton Flanagan deserve a lifetime achievement award. So very brave, so very strong. A true champion to all people. I adore this man and his story, I someday hope to meet him.
- Susan Kiker

It is not only my pleasure to personally know David, but to highly recommend his book for your library.
I've known David for many years. He has always spoken exactly what is on his mind. His honesty and no nonsense approach to life is well documented in this book.
- Ryc Lyden

Powerful, useful and heart-rending story
This book is a success from the front cover all the way through. Its title alone is powerful; can tear the buyer up while pulling her/him into the text. If this is fiction, I believe that the facts have only been adjusted to highlight the author's messages. I highly recommend this book.
- Thomas J. Aron

Lifesaving. Heart and soul.
David, I love the book, just don't know how to put in to words how just reading this book saved my life! I feel like a new man, thank you so much.
-Edward Conrad

Tears from the introduction to the last page.
Laughter, giggles and smiles throughout. From this book I was taught how to understand and how to forgive. I read the ebook but had to have a copy for my private library. I strongly suggest you buy several copies for your friends and family. They will want to borrow it and you may never see it again.
- Connie Duncan

Finally... the real truth.
This book should be a mandatory read for all First Responders during their certification process. Teachers and social workers would greatly benefit from this book as well. It shows the heartbreaking truth of child abuse and neglect and how it carries over to adulthood. It shows the struggles of a man who has been through these terrible things but never loses his ability to feel empathy and love for others in his career as a paramedic and police officer. So much in this book I could identify with. So honest, so compelling. It will make you want to hug everyone near you.
- Karen Jones

The honest truth, a real gut punch.
Great book into the underbelly of public servants, addiction, and destructive self-talk. We all have a story. It's not completely unique however, it may be unique to you. Broaden your horizons and put yourself in someone else's shoes. Great read! Thank you for your courage Mr. Brown!
- John Jones

Highly recommend!
Being a medic I can relate to this book. The author has a very kind heart. I couldn't put it down.
- Anna Rogers

A must read! Buy it for yourself/buy it for a friend.
Daddy Had to Say Goodbye is a compelling read from start to finish. I highly recommend this book for those who have experienced child abuse, depression, alcoholism, P.T.S.D., and difficult life challenges. The brightness of this writing is that all people can overcome the challenges in life and find true happiness regardless of your circumstances. The author has such insight into life as he takes you on a journey from his childhood to his current life's circumstance. The accounts in this book touched my heart, made me laugh and helped me understand life more fully. Our world needs more people like David Brown! Buy the book!!
- Amazon Customer

This story is inspired, in part, by true events. In certain cases, locations, incidents, characters and timelines have been changed for dramatic purposes. Certain characters may be composites, or entirely fictitious.

A special thank you to my dear friend, Lydia Lombardo,
who gifted me her editing services.
Forever in my heart, dear Lydia!

Thanking my web site designer and artist
Angie Simonson of:
Main Idea Creative Marketing and Design
www.maincreativeidea.com

INSPIRED BY A TRUE STORY

DEDICATION

To my most darling little boy. As of this writing, you are a grown man. Your presence on earth has always made me want to be a better man.

This book is meant to tell you of the many hardships of the heart and the challenges of life. To hopefully counsel you in your life. To lend hope and clarity to those who struggle to find some sense of normalcy in their own shattered lives.

ACKNOWLEDGMENTS

With honor and remembrance for the millions of 'Friends' of Bill W.'

With respect and admiration for the 'Defenders' of our great nation.

With reverence and humble gratitude for our 'First Responders,' worldwide.

To all those many who quietly suffer from PTSD. There can be no shame for your surviving when others didn't. Don't let your memories darken your heart and kill you. Talk about it, you are not alone. You needn't hurt or suffer alone. Your silence is . . . Deadly!

WITH THANKS

To the women that loved me . . . for as long as they could.

To those people that love me today . . . no matter what.

Within all fiction, lies a bit of truth.

Within all truth, lies a bit of fiction.

Our perceptions are the deciding factors.

David J. Brown

INTRODUCTION

The small bodied 8-year-old boy sat at the edge of his bed, waiting for God to come. To kill him. With his small hands in his lap, and chin on his tiny chest, he prays that the end will come soon. Staring down at his black 'poor-box' shoes from St. Helens Catholic Church, he was determined not to cry. "If God doesn't come to get me soon, then Daddy will kill me and Daddy will kill me even more-harder and even more-worser." With morbid resignation he smiles and finds comfort in knowing that either way, today would be the end. "Nobody can ever hurt me again. I will never have to wonder why Daddy beats me up so bad or why God hates me so bad." Little Clinton Flanagan was ready for God to come and to put him in hell.

No child should ever know and understand fear. Not the fear of monsters under the bed or something bad happening but the paralyzing fear of what has already happened; will happen again, and it will happen soon. This is inspired by the true life story of a beaten child that became a bully; a bully that becomes a batterer.

This is a story of unfathomable pain and suffering.

This is a story of immense struggles.

This is a story of faith.

This is a story of hope.

This is a story of victory.

This is also, and most importantly, a story of freedom!

Chapter 1 "TIME FOR THE TRUTH"

Clinton Flanagan stood as he lived; rigid and alone. He knew the years had been good to him. He stood as a diplomat would in a receiving line, greeting world leaders. He held himself with the stoic posture of a Marine and displayed the gentleness of a Priest. His deeply tanned, smooth skinned face, chiseled jaw line and rugged good looks had not betrayed him. His full head of well-groomed salt and pepper hair complemented his tailored suit, that did nothing to hide his deeply muscled chest and shoulders which were offset by his lean waist. The many people that he had not seen in thirty years were amazed with how well he had aged. The huge line of family friends snaked around the vast Friendship Hall of the mortuary to offer their condolences to Clinton Flanagan; he was the oldest surviving member of his family. The absent son that had returned to preside over his Mother's funeral. He was all but giddy on the inside.

More importantly, this was the final day that Flanagan would have to live his life as a fraud. His gracious manors, his engaging smile, and warm eyes, well hid his marrow deep pain. The pain which had destroyed his spirit and left him a deeply troubled and broken man. At the end of this day Flanagan would never have to again ask why. It would no longer matter.

Flanagan stood behind the podium, alongside his Mother's open, gleaming, white casket, as he delivered her eulogy. He eloquently spoke of his Mother's warmth and her many acts of kindness. He showered her remembrances with praise and glory. The 200 plus extended family members and friends hung on every soothing and melodic word delivered by the dutiful son. Protecting his Mother's image was the order of the day. The actual truth of his Mother was only his to know. Flanagan was not mourning the loss of his Mother. He was mourning his battered childhood that caused him to be a shattered man.

Clinton Flanagan's Mother died in late May of 2009. That same week Flanagan turned 61 years old. He wasn't able to see his

1

Mom for the last 3 years. Flanagan had lived in Wyoming and his Mother had lived in Wisconsin. They talked on the phone every week, on Sunday night. For the last 20 years his Mother had been ready to die. Her lifetime of heartache, sorrow, and shame, took her will to live. His Mother just sat in her chair waiting to die. She spoke of dying in every phone conversation. She never complained of her physical pain, or even of her heartache. She would just say "I'm ready to go." Flanagan had driven to Wisconsin so he had plenty of 'think time' to review his Mother's life. The tragedy was not about his Mother's passing. He was grateful for God's mercy. It was just simply time for her.

The tragedy was the way in which his Mother had lived. She was a 'throw away' child who grew to suffer even more all throughout her life. And yet, she never gave up. He saw his Mom as a 4' 4" tower of strength and a true study of character.

When Flanagan arrived at his Mom and Phil's house, his Stepdad greeted him with a handshake and a hug. Mom and Phil were married for 31 years. He was a great guy; you just couldn't ask for a better Stepdad. Flanagan called him 'Pops.' As he stood in front of Pops, he saw a big framed man, yet his hug was as weak as a kitten. He could feel Pops emptiness and grief. Clint didn't think Pops would live through the summer, and it broke his heart.

Pops and he walked into the house and into the living room where Pops pointed at Mom's chair and said, have a seat. Flanagan balked, as he thought, "That is Mom's chair. No one ever sat in Mom's chair. It was Mom's Chair. The chair, in which Mom died in, just two days ago." Whenever Flanagan thought of his Mom, he always saw her sitting in her old green, worn, cloth chair and now, the chair is empty. Flanagan always had the uncanny, if not spooky ability, to sense a person's spirit or presence and know what is in their soul. Flanagan had four premonitions in his life, and they all came true. The events were catastrophic and life-changing, but those stories come later.

Flanagan sat in his Mother's chair for the next ten days. From that very first moment and all throughout the next ten days, he could not feel his Mother's presence or her soul. In truth, he knew that his Mother's spirit had left her many years ago and he briefly cried. Those few tears turned into a smile as he marveled in his Mother's strengths. Mom loved her family, held hopes for everyone, never spoke harshly of anyone, and yet, his Mom's own heart was emptied by her life's many tragedies. And then it hit him. "I am my Mother." Flanagan's own sorrows, from many of his life's tragedies are embedded in his marrow, the emptiness he carries' is deep inside him and it has never let him go. He can find no joy in his own heart, and like his Mother, he too, is just waiting to die.

Clinton Flanagan's earliest memories are of despair and fear. He knew he had to stay quiet and stay out of the way. He couldn't say that he was hungry, cold, or scared, he could only listen for the monsters while laying all day under his bed. His Daddy was mean to him and said loud, bad words to him. His Mommy cried a lot, and shook kind of funny when she smoked her cigarettes. Big, mean men, came to their apartment and said they wanted money. The Police came a lot, to stop his Dad from beating up his Mom and there was always his Mom's blood splattered on the linoleum floor and walls.

They didn't always have food. Sometimes they got a big box of powdered milk, big green cans of peanut butter that they had to stir up to make the oil on top go away, big hunks of stinky yellow cheese and a monster size bag of puffed rice cereal. He didn't like eating that food, because it made him know that they were poor. The wintertime was really cold. The Flanagan family's apartment was only four small rooms with an oil burning stove in the kitchen. Sometimes they didn't have money for fuel oil and the toilet water would freeze. Clinton's and his brother's bedroom was next to the bathroom and there was only a sheet covering the doorway, instead of a door.

It was Clinton's job, to break the ice from the toilet with a little kid's baseball bat and put it in the bathtub. He got to do that job a lot. He could never see out the windows as they were covered with frost on the inside. He would try to scrape the ice away with his fingernail but it hurt and made him cold. The finger nail scraping never worked as the window would just freeze up right away again. He could never see the light outside and it made him feel like he was locked-up inside a box. On the really cold nights his Mother put her, 'monkey fur coat' over him, it was heavy and made it hard for him to breathe, but he did feel a little bit safe and maybe, just a little bit loved.

Clinton will always remember with fondness, the dark blue Ford Custom station wagon with the big red and white Salvation Army badge on the doors parked in front of their apartment building. He was embarrassed and ashamed that everyone knew that they were poor and they had no food. The Salvation Army people were nice to the boys. The man would give them a box of food. The ladies always gave the boys some Tootsie Rolls, and the boys felt important. They said they were good boys. To this day the only charity he supports, is the Salvation Army. He gives when he can. Clint goes to their Soup kitchens at Thanksgiving and Christmas when they give out free turkey dinners, he washes pots and pans. During Christmas time, he spends several nights ringing bells over the red kettle in front of Kmart. It's his way of quietly saying, 'thank you.'

The doctor came to their apartment a lot because his big brother, Donnie, was real sick. Sometimes his Mom took the boys on the bus to see the doctor. Donnie was in the hospital a lot too. Mom and Clinton walked to the Drug Store to buy Donnie a gift, then they rode the bus to the hospital to make Donnie feel better. He never got better. Mommy would sit on the couch and cry and her hands shook a lot. Clinton would try to pat her and say it would be alright. Then she would hit him in his face. He never stopped trying to pat her to say it would be okay. Each time he would try to comfort his Mother, she would slap his face; it stung really bad and he got real dizzy. She would always say "I wish you were never born! I wish you were dead!"

Daddy came home drunk every night. Clinton would lay

4

awake and hide under his covers waiting and listening for Dad's car door to slam. The car door slamming made him want to climb inside his skinny old lumpy mattress so Daddy couldn't get him. He had to stay awake to make sure that Daddy didn't hurt Mommy too bad, in case he had to try to call the police. Dad slapped Mom's face a lot of times and her nose and lips bled a lot. When he begged his Daddy to stop hitting his Mommy, Clinton's Daddy would grab him real hard and slap him in his head and throw him into the wall. It hurt, really bad, and he got dizzy. Clinton always had a headache and he could not see very well, after they repeatedly hit him. His ears buzzed all the time. After every time they hit him, they told him to go to his room and he knew there would be no supper that night. Each time, he pulled the covers over his head and tried not to cry too loud, but the blood in his nose and throat made it hard for him to breathe. All of this happened before Clinton was six years old.

Even at this young age, he knew they didn't mean to hurt him, their hearts were just real sad. Clinton thought, "All these bad things that happened to us are all my fault and if I just could be a better boy, then everyone wouldn't be so sad and so mean to me."

Donnie, (who was two years older than Clinton), got even sicker. The doctor said he was going to die, real soon. Mom said no, he wasn't. They took Donnie to the University Hospital. Donnie had to live there all by himself. Clinton and his parent's would drive 150 miles one-way, every Sunday to go see him. They would bring Donnie a new toy. The back seat and trunk were full of stinky, dirty old tires and Daddy would have to stop a lot of times to change tires. The old car would break too. Dad would put more water in it when the steam went away and they would go again for a little while.

Clinton couldn't go with them in the winter because if the car broke down, he might freeze. Clinton missed eating those cheese sandwiches from wax paper and those stinky old dirty tires. He missed Donnie too. Clint would think of Donnie lying in his hospital bed, real fat with a big, great big head. His eyes and skin

5

were yellow. His arms were all bruised and had tape marks from all the needles from the yucky medicine they made him have. They put tubes in his arms with hanging bottles of blood and a bunch of other funny colored stuff. The Doctors and Nurses scared Clinton, he hated them, he wanted to beat them up for hurting Donnie, but even more, he knew they were going to do all that same stuff to him too, someday. It made Clinton want to hug his big brother, to cry, to run away, and to die.

Clinton thought, "If I were a better boy, maybe Donnie would get better." The hospital would call their house and tell Mom and Dad that they were giving Donnie, 'The Last Rights.' And they better come down right away. It seemed as though those calls were always late at night when everyone was asleep and it was snowing real hard and the wind was noisy. Mom and Dad would wrap Clinton in his blanket and take him to someone's house so they could go to Minneapolis, to see Donnie before he died. Clinton would wake up real scared, he didn't know where he was. He didn't know or remember any of those people. He just wanted for his Mom and Dad to come back and get him. He couldn't let himself eat any of the people's food because it belonged to them and they needed it.

Sometimes when Daddy was at work and Mommy was asleep on the couch, from taking too many pills, Clinton would sneak into their bedroom closet, and look at Donnie's new toy that they were going to bring him on the next Sunday. He would look at the pictures on the box and get mad at Donnie because he always got new toys and he didn't have any. Not even one. One time, Clinton found a box with a picture of a real pretty, blue and white, seaplane on it. It was the kind that you could put in the bathtub, wind it up, and it would go all by itself.
The box was real heavy. Clinton wanted Donnie to die. Then maybe he could have that sea plane that went all by itself in the bathtub. Clinton prayed to God that Donnie would die. He knew he was being a bad boy and that God was going to punish him really bad. So Clinton just sat on his bed and waited for God to

6

punish him. God didn't punish him that day. But he knew he was going to sometime, someday. He knew he was doomed.

Mommy said she was going to have a new baby. At first Clinton hated that baby and wanted it to die in Mommy's tummy. When the baby came out, Clinton liked him a lot. The new baby was real little. His name was Peter, but Clinton called him, 'Petey.' Clinton was scared that Mom and Dad were going to beat up the new baby like they did him, so he had to take care of him so they couldn't hurt him. Mommy and Daddy were real nice to the new baby, but they were not nice to Clinton. Daddy would say to him, "You little bastard, get your stupid ass to your room." A lot of times, Mommy still said, "I wish I never had you, I wish you were dead." He went to his bed, pulled the covers over his head, and tried not to cry too loud. Clinton was still only six years old.

Something changed when Petey was born. Mom and Dad, stopped calling Clinton, Clinton. They started to call him Clint. It made Clinton feel sad that they took away his name just because they got a new, better little boy. Clinton thought that his new name Clint, made him junk. His perception was that he wasn't good enough to have a whole name anymore. Clinton decided that when he got bigger and when Mom and Dad couldn't beat him up any more, he would make his name back to Clinton.

Donnie was still in the hospital and still getting a new toy on every Sunday. Petey was always getting a lot of attention. Clint, was getting none. He wanted both of his brothers dead. He started to think of ways to kill Petey, but he was scared of getting caught and getting beat up, really bad again. So Clint prayed to God, that he would make them both die so he could get a new toy every week and Mommy and Daddy would be real nice to him and give him all that attention. This time, he knew God was going to put him in Hell. All those times that he was sent to his room for the day, he would dream of someday that he could be a Daddy and be nice. He planned to give his babies kisses, read them stories, give them ice cream, and buy them nice toys to have.

Clint had an old, long handle, wooden mixing spoon with a

big crack in it, to play with. It was his only toy. The spoon was his friend, it was his fire truck, his airplane, his bulldozer, his gun, and he loved it. It was all he had. He always sat in the corner, on the floor (he wasn't allowed to sit on the couch, Mom was usually sleeping on it from her pills) with his back up against the wall so nobody could hit or kick him when they walked by and he wouldn't get in trouble. He had to stay quiet. He was scared, he was always scared, every day.

Donnie was starting to get better. They would take him out of the hospital for two hours but he couldn't run or climb a tree. Daddy had a 'Brownie Star Flash Camera.' He took a lot of pictures of Donnie but never of Clint.

Clint was in the first grade and missed a lot of school because he had Impetigo really bad in his ears and nose and his arms, with a lot of icky puss and blood. The teacher didn't like him because he didn't talk or read, he just sat there. At the end of that school year, Clint had to go with Mom and Dad to see the teacher. The teacher told them that Clint was slow and had to stay in the first grade for another year. Clint's Dad called him a dummy and slapped him in the back of the head. Clint sat on his bed and told himself "I will never, ever, hit my kids, no matter what! I will be a good Daddy!"

During that summer Clint found a safe place to hide by his house. It was a big swamp of Alder brush, tall stink weeds and cattails. There were trails that the kids ran through all day on their way to the rope swing that was tied to a big old Maple tree. He didn't think the kids liked him because he was stupid, had funny looking eyes, and couldn't hear very well. So he hid in the brush and weeds all day, as the kids ran through the trails. Always wishing he could play with them.

He would dream of some day when he could be a Daddy. Clint never dreamed of what he wanted to be when he grew up, not a fireman, a soldier, a teacher, no, he just wanted to be a good Daddy that wanted to take his babies to the circus. Summer was over and he went back to the first grade.

And much like the year before, he didn't talk and he didn't read.

Donnie got real sick, again. The hospital would call late at night to tell them that Donnie was going to die, right now. Mom and Dad put Clint in somebody's house just like before, they took Peaty with them for the 150-mile ride to Minneapolis. Clint hated Donnie, Petey and Mom and Dad. Then, Clint made the biggest sin in the entire world. He prayed to God, that Donnie would die and Mom, Dad and Petey, would get killed in a car accident so he could go to the orphanage and maybe get adopted. Maybe, somebody would want him.

That same call from the hospital came often through the fall and winter. Clint would be at somebody's house, with the covers over his head, saying the same prayers. It was a bad sin but he hated them, they made him cry.

Spring came again and Clint's Mom, Dad and he, had to go see the teacher. The teacher said Clint might be retarded and next year would have to go to the 'Opportunity Class,' where there were other, slow kids like him. Dad got real mad and swore real loud at the teacher and pushed her real hard and she fell on the floor.

That summer was like the one before. Clint hid in the brush and stink weeds all day, except for the times he tried to play baseball with the other boys. When they picked sides, he was never picked. Donnie had come home to live from the hospital and he heard Mom and Dad talking about Clint going to the, 'Opportunity Class.' So Donnie told all the neighborhood boys that Clint was a retard and an 'Oppy.' They called him an 'Oppy' and a queer. At first it made him real sad and he cried a lot, then he got mad. Real, real mad, and he wanted to kill them. Clint would hide in the swamp and plan how to kill each one of them. He stopped dreaming about being a good Daddy, he stopped trying to be a good boy so God would help them. He only wanted to kill people.

The only dream young Clint ever had, was replaced with fantasies of hacking people to death. For a little kid he was really smart. He acted like he really liked all the kids so they would, in

9

turn, like him, so when it came time, it would be easier to sneak up on them, to kill them. Clint got a knife from his Dad's hunting box and cut half-way through the rope swing tied to the big ole Maple tree, so some kid would swing and the rope would break and he would fall a long way down and break his neck and die. The bigger kids saw the rope was cut and their Dad's put up a new rope. Clint then made a bunch of wood spears with sharp points, with his Dad's hunting knife and hid them in the Alder brush and weeds so when a kid came by on any trail, he could stab them and they would die.

Then, summer vacation was over. Donnie and Clint went to St. Helen's Catholic School so Clint wouldn't have to go to the 'Oppy Class.' They had to wear a white shirt with a black bow tie, black pants and black shoes. The first day of school the Nuns sent them home because their Dad bought them black 'engineer' boots instead of shoes. Boots were only allowed in the winter but not 'hoodlum engineer boots,' not ever! They didn't know that rule. It made Clint sad because they were poor and Dad didn't have the money to buy them shoes too. It means that he couldn't go to Catholic school. He would have to go to the 'Oppy Class' but he couldn't do that. So he knew, at 8 years old, that he would have to kill himself. It was sad but kind of okay because "nobody could ever be mean to me, anymore - no matter what!"

That day the boys hid in Barkers Park so the cops wouldn't get them for being truant. Clint knew "We can't go home because Dad would get real mad and hit me in my head. If my nose bleeds I will get hollered at and get called a, God damn sissy." Donnie never got hit or beat up because he could die. The next day the boys, walked the ten blocks to St. Helens School but went to hide in the bushes in Barker Park until school was over. Father Parish, the St. Helens boss priest, found them and made them come in his car. Father Parish drove them to the J.C. Penney store and bought Donnie and Clint, new black shoes. He gave the lady at the J.C. Penney Store a piece of big paper instead of money. The boys, knew it came from the 'poor box' money and that made them feel

10

poor, poor and stupid. Father Parish said they could do work at the church to pay for the new black lace-up shoes. The boys swept the front and back sidewalks and steps every school morning.

They wore their "hoodlum" boots on their way to school and put on their shoes, which they kept in the janitor's closet. The boys never told their Dad about the J.C. Penney shoes.

All students had to attend church before school each day. In just a few short days Clint fell in love with church, religious lessons in school, and God. He realized that praying to God for good things for other people would make him a good boy so he wouldn't have to kill those mean boys, and maybe they would have more food and it wouldn't be so cold in their apartment in the winter. Even maybe, "Daddy wouldn't beat Mommy and me up so much."

The school was old, but really nice. It smelled real nice. The floors were wood, they were kind of creaky but real nice and shiny. There were real big statues of God, Jesus, Mary and the 12 Apostles in the hallways, and they were beautiful. The statues were so tall that when he looked up to see their faces, he almost fell over backwards.

Clint thought the Nuns knew, that he was a sad little boy because they gave him soft, little nice pats on his head. Sometimes they gave him root beer barrels and smiled at him and said he was a good boy. Clint liked them a lot. On Saturdays he walked to church and said the Rosary and did the Stations of the Cross. Church made him happy and he felt safe. He would rather go to church than play dumb old baseball or football and have to see those mean boys that would never pick him to play with them.

Every boy at St. Helens School had to play basketball on the grade teams and Clint hated it. He thought he was too short and he didn't know how to play. It made him feel stupid. Clint joined the Cub Scouts because he liked the uniforms the boys wore on 'Scout Day' each week. If he could look just like them, then he wouldn't look poor all the time and he might get to be happy. A neighbor lady gave him an old, kind of faded Cub Scout shirt with no patches sewn on it. It had dark spots on it where the patches used to be. It looked kind of funny but Clint was proud of it. He was a Cub Scout!

Clint shoveled sidewalks to buy the pack numbers and patches for his, new-used shirt and a new scarf. He went door-to-door to ask for odd jobs (even into other neighborhoods) to earn money so he could buy those patches that would make him look like a 'real' Cub Scout. He thought that he would look important. He would get to look just like all the other boys! The Cub Scout Den Mother was a real nice lady at first, but then she and the boys got mad at him, and then even the Scout Master started to hate him too. Clint was trying to be a good boy and pretended he was like all the other boys. Almost.

Each week, the cub scouts took turns bringing a pack of cookies to the Den Mother's house for the meeting. Clint could never eat a cookie, because he knew when it was his turn to bring cookies that he couldn't come to the meeting. They were poor and his Dad would holler at him, call him bad names, and send him to his room with no supper if he dared to ask his Dad for cookie money. So, Clint didn't ask him. He would put on his Cub Scout shirt on meeting day, go to school, but instead of going to the Den Mother's house after school, he would find an old empty abandoned building to hide in so nobody could see him cry.

Cub Scouts were supposed to have the pack numbers and arrow points, and merit awards patches sewn on their shirts. Clint earned the money to buy his patches and he took a bus downtown to the Surplus store where they sold Cub and Boy Scout stuff. The bus driver said he was too young to ride the bus by himself. Clint told the bus driver that his Mom was real sick and he had to go downtown to get her medicine for her. The bus driver let him on the bus. He was a nice man.

All his Mom ever did was smoke cigarettes. Her hands shook all the time. She took pills and slept a lot on the couch. He could never wake her up. When she was awake she talked and walked funny. She was like a monster on the TV. Every time his

Mom was awake he would ask her to sew on his patches that he bought with his own money. She would always say "Yah, ask me later. But if you ask me again then the answer, is no." She didn't say that very nice. She kind of screamed it at him. Days, weeks and even months went by and there were no patches on his used old Cub Scout shirt.

There was a monthly Scouts meeting at school at night. It was for awards for all the Cub Scout packs in the area. There were a lot of packs and a lot of Moms and Dads. But his Mom and Dad never came to see him get his awards. When he did get a merit patch award he would show it to his Dad, and his Dad would ask real hard "Where the hell did you get the money for that?" Clint stopped showing his Dad his awards and patches.

Each Cub Scout pack got points for each parent that was there that night and more points for all the patches sewn on and a real, full uniform with the Cub Scout shirt, belt, hat and pants. The pack with the most complete uniforms and most patches that night, got a special trophy and candy bars. His pack could never win because of him. Everyone hated him. He didn't want to quit, but he knew they didn't want him. He didn't get mad or want to kill anyone. He just put his Cub Scout shirt, his scarf, and his unsown patches in the trash.

Clint went to church, said the Rosary, prayed at the Stations of the Cross, and prayed even more, so they could have more food. He felt like he could never join anything ever again. He wasn't any good at anything. Nobody liked him and it made him sad to always have to go away. So he just went to school and church and he didn't talk to anyone. It seems he spent most of his time just sitting on his bed or laying under his bed looking up at the springs and mattress above him on their bunk beds. He would just have to wait until he got older to have some babies so he could be nice to them and never, ever make them feel bad or cry and maybe then, he could be happy.

In their bedroom there was no door. There was a little shelf on the green wall where Donnie had an old brown, 'Philco' radio with dirty old yellow knobs, but it played pretty good music. He really liked Elvis Presley, Johnny Rivers, Dion and those kind of guys. He would have to have the volume real low and just sing in his head because Mom would holler at him if he sang out loud because she was on the phone, or sleeping, or watching TV, or Petey was sleeping. He couldn't go outside because Mom grounded him all the time, so when she woke up, she could go to the neighborhood ladies houses and play 'Yahtzee.' He knew that he didn't do anything wrong. She was just being mean to him, so she could go and play 'Yahtzee' and he would have to babysit Petey. Sometimes the neighbor ladies would come to their apartment to play 'Yahtzee' and they would bring cookies and potato chips and cinnamon rolls. He could smell the cinnamon rolls but they never asked him, if he wanted any. Their tiny bedroom was just ten feet away from the kitchen table, most of the time they never knew he was there. Those ladies talked about their husbands, talked about their kids, and buying them footballs and bikes and clothes. They mostly talked about movie star guys and their doctors and all the pills they were taking. The ladies said they got extra pills from different doctors.

Clint hated those neighbor ladies because they wouldn't give him any of their snacks and he didn't have a football or bicycle, and they took a lot of pills like his Mom did. He hated their kids too, as they always had new bikes, baseball mitts and bats, and new, really nice clothes. He hated everyone because of what they had and he didn't have, it told him that he was poor and not as good as they were. He felt junkie. He was just a crummy little kid and nobody liked him. Sometimes he would go a long time, not thinking about being a good Daddy. Those times he just wished that he were dead. It was getting fall time and the weeds and cattails were dying again for winter and he lost his hiding place. He found an old shed with a dirt floor and with smelly burnt motor oil, soaked into the ground. It stunk really badly but it kept him out of the wind. Snow came in from the roof, but not too bad. He made it his winter hiding place where no one could see him.

The only time he ever really got to ride in the car was when Dad would take them all Partridge hunting in the fall. It wasn't real hunting. His Dad would just drive really slowly down some old potholed, swampy logging roads. When they saw a partridge in or on the side of the road, Dad would get out of the car and shoot it with his 12-gauge single-shot shotgun. Dad never missed. Dad shot a lot more partridge than he was supposed to. The boys hid the birds under their blankets, in the back seat, so the Game Warden wouldn't see them. Game Wardens stopped them some times, but they never saw the extra birds under the blankets with them.

Clint was always scared the Game Wardens would get them and make him go to jail. Dad would drink a lot of beer when they were partridge hunting. Dad would get the car stuck in the mud almost every time. He swore a lot. They would have to find logs and big rocks to put in the tire tracks and jack up the back of the car to put the logs and rocks under the tires so they could get out of the swamp. It wasn't much fun because Dad was always mad. The best part of partridge hunting was when it got dark and it was time to go home. Dad would put on the car radio and they all listened to 'The Lone Ranger' and 'Johnny Dollar.' Clint liked that a lot. Sometimes they saw a deer on the road and Dad would put a rifle slug in his shotgun and kill the deer. Clint had to hold the lantern while Dad cut off the deer's front and back legs (they had to hurry real fast because it was against the law to kill deer in the early fall). Clint was always scared that the Game Wardens would come and put him in reform school. They put the big deer legs in the trunk. It kind of made him sad and happy at the same time. The deer was pretty. He didn't want his Dad to kill him, but it meant they had meat to eat for a little while, so he was like, happy-sad.

Dad worked on the railroad in the summer and was a butcher in the winter. After they killed a deer they drove to the butcher shop and cut it up real fast. Sometimes Dad sold some of the dear meat to their landlord to pay rent to him, or for money so they could buy other kinds of food.

15

Chapter 2 "CHRISTMAS COPS"

It was almost Christmas, Clint's Mom and Dad took the boys downtown to the big department store to see Santa Claus. When Clint sat on Santa's lap and Santa asked him what he wanted for Christmas, Clint told Santa "I don't want for my Daddy not to hit me in my head anymore and call me stupid." There were a lot of people in the Santa Claus line. It got real quiet. Some ladies started to cry and took their children away. Clint's Dad just stood there and didn't say anything, but his face looked funny. Santa looked real hard at Dad. Santa gave Clint a candy cane. They went home.

The next day his Daddy went away and didn't come home for a long time. The landlord said his Dad was in the 'dryer.' Clint didn't know what the, 'dryer' meant. He missed his Dad, but at least he wasn't hitting him in his head anymore and he liked that.

It was the day before Christmas Eve, his Mom was crying a lot because they didn't have any food or a Christmas tree. His Dad was still gone away. Clint and Donnie felt bad for Mom so they snuck into the landlord's shed and found an old, rusty saw. It was snowing real hard so they walked to a man's house that lived in the 'slew' (like a swamp). The man had a lot of Christmas trees growing in his front yard. The boys found a real nice tree and cut it down with the landlord's saw. It stopped snowing and they were happy, as they dragged the tree home. It would help their Mom to stop crying so hard. They told their Mom that "a nice man came by and gave us this tree." Their Mom, knew they were lying but they didn't look at her. They acted busy putting the tree stand on.

They heard a bunch of men coming up the stairs and they knocked on their door real hard. It was the Police! There were two cops, a man who said he saw the boys cutting down the tree and the man who owned the house where they cut the tree down from. The men saw Mom crying and asked if the boys cut down the man's tree. The boys said "Yes." One of the policemen took Donnie and Clint to the police car and made them sit in the front

17

seat. The policeman showed them the button to turn on the red lights. The policeman let Donnie push the button and the red lights came on. They could see the red lights reflecting off the snow and other cars really good as it was getting dark outside. Then the policeman showed Clint the button for the siren and told him to push it. Clint got scared and was afraid to, as he might get into trouble. The policeman said it would be ok to turn on the siren for just a little bit. He turned the siren on and it made them laugh. The policeman showed them the radio and he talked to a man and told the man to say hi to Donnie and Clint. The man said, "Hello gentlemen" in a real big voice. Then a whole bunch of men kept saying Merry Christmas Donnie and Clint, for a real long time.

The men kept saying, "Squad #...Hi boys, I'm Officer..." a lot more times. Donnie and Clint felt important. They also got to work the spotlight. They saw a cat and put the spotlight on him and the cat jumped up in the air and ran away real fast. They laughed real hard. The policeman laughed real loud. The other policeman came to the police car with those other two men. The first policeman told them to get out of the car. Both of the policemen shook the boy's hands. So did the other two men. The man who owned the tree said he was not mad at them and they could keep the tree because they picked out the very best tree to cut down. The other man shook their hands too and gave them each $5.00 and told them to buy a nice Christmas present for their Mommy.

Donnie and Clint went in the house and their Mom was pretty much done crying. She gave them a big hug and said "I love you boys" and gave them a kiss on their cheeks. It was the first time that his Mom gave him a hug, a kiss and said "I love you" that he could ever remember. Right then Dad called them and said he was going to get on a Greyhound bus in the morning and be home before lunchtime. Their Mom told their Dad that a real nice man gave them a beautiful Christmas tree. Their Dad said he would put it up when he got home so they could decorate the tree. Their Mom told the boys that they could not tell their Dad about using

18

the landlord's saw, cutting down the tree, or the police coming to get them. The boys said ok.

The next day their Dad came in the door and had a big smile, kissed each of the boys and told them to go out and play. When they came back home from playing their Dad and Mom had them sit on the couch. Daddy said that he was never going to drink any kind of alcohol ever again. Daddy said he was never going to hit Clint ever again or say bad words to him. Dad said he was sorry for being so mean to him. Dad gave him a nice hug and told him he loved him. He gave him kisses all over his face and head. Dad was crying. The family decorated the tree. It was the most fun Clint ever had.

Somebody called their house and said there were some boxes on the bottom of their stairs. It was Christmas Eve day. There were four big boxes of food and three great big boxes that were taped closed. Their Dad told the boys to go play and he would carry the boxes up the stairs. Their Dad came out to the street and told them to get into the car. Their Dad drove them to the movies. The boys had never been to the movies before. Their Dad got them popcorn and Milk Duds and said to wait out front of the movie house and he would pick them up after the movies. The boys, saw "Smith Family Robinson." When the movie was over they were scared that their Dad wouldn't come to get them.

It reminded them of the many times that Dad would come home late at night, really, really drunk. He would wake them up and tell them to pack clothes and food for several days because they were going on a fishing or hunting trip. He would tell the boys' to, "Wake me up at 6:00 am" and they would pack everything and stay up all night so they could wake Dad up at 6:00 am. But every time they tried to wake Dad up he would say, "Wake me up at 7:00 am." At the 7:00 am wakeup he always said, "Wake me up at 8:00 am." When their Dad finally woke up, he told them to put everything in the car and for them to wait in the car for him. When their Dad finally came out of the house Donnie and Clint got really excited about going on a fishing trip with Dad.

19

Each time and every time, Dad would say he had to stop at the Tavern Bar, (the neighborhood bar and his hangout) to cash a check and he would be right out. After two hours of sitting in the car Donnie would make Clint go into the bar to tell Dad it was 10 o'clock and they were ready to go fishing. Dad was drinking beer and playing bumper pool. He would tell him to go back out to the car and he would be right out. Two hours later Donnie would make him go back in the bar and tell Dad that they were hungry and wanted to walk home. Dad would get mad and call him a, "God damn sissy." Donnie and he walked home. They didn't get to go fishing. That sure made them sad.

But this time Dad was there! The boys walked out of the movie house and Dad was parked right in front. It was cold outside but Dad's car was real warm. Donnie and he were happy that Dad didn't forget them. Dad talked to the boys on the way home. He never did that before. He asked them how they liked school and if they were having fun on Christmas vacation. They kept looking at each other and didn't know what to say. Their Dad said "Me and Mom want to talk to you boys when we got home." Donnie and Clint looked at each other and they got scared. They both thought that they were going to get a divorce and Dad would have to go away.

When they got home, Mom gave them a hug hello. It was such a weird day, that Clint just wanted to go to bed and hide under the covers. There were three great big Christmas stockings hanging from the top of the windowsill with their names on them and they were full of a lot of stuff all wrapped up. There were a whole bunch of presents under the Christmas tree too. The presents were wrapped real pretty with neat, shiny wrapping paper and ribbons and bows with each of the boy's names on them. Clint was pretty sure that all those boxes that were at the bottom of the stairs somehow came from the Policeman that came to get them the day before.

Young Clint thought for the first time that maybe he wanted to be something when he grew up, other than a Daddy.

Maybe he will want to be a Cop! He remembered the past, when the cops came to their house because Dad was beating up Mom. He would have to crawl across the kitchen floor to get to the phone to call the police to come and make Dad stop hitting Mom. Sometimes the cops would take his Dad to jail but most of the time the cops would take Dad to the truck stop across the street and give him a lot of coffee. After a long time, they came back from the truck stop and the cops would wait for Dad to shave and put on his work clothes. Dad went to work early on those times that the cops came. The cops always called Mom, 'Ma'am.' They were nice to her. Sometimes the cops brought Dad home because he was too drunk to drive. Clint could hear them coming up the stairs and Dad was usually swearing. He remembered the sound of the grocery bags clinking; the leather of the cops' gun belts creaking like cowboys getting in the saddle of their horses. He could also hear the cops' night sticks clacking and their keys jingling. He knew the cops must have found Dad stuck in a snow bank drunk driving, so the cops gave Dad a ride home and they brought the groceries home so they wouldn't freeze. The cops had to carry the groceries because Dad was too drunk to carry them up the stairs. Clint thought it would be kind of neat to someday call ladies "Ma'am" and give drunk guys a ride home. Yup, he might want to be a Policeman someday.

That night Mom made them pancakes, the boy's favorite, but a rare treat. Dad had a real funny soft voice, kind of like he was whispering loud. He didn't look at anyone, he just kept his head down and was rubbing his eyes a lot. He wasn't eating his pancakes. Dad said he was sorry for being so mean to the boys and Mom. He said he wasn't ever, ever going to hit anyone, anymore. He wouldn't swear as much and he wouldn't holler at them and call them bad names either.

Dad said he was going to go to Alcoholics Anonymous and never drink beer and stuff again. He said he was not going to the bar ever again, and he would come right home from work and play ball with them. He said he was going to take them hunting and

21

fishing a lot more times, go to church, go to teacher conferences and even go to Clint's Cub Scout stuff. Clint didn't say anything about his quitting Scouts, a long time ago.

After dinner they got to open their Christmas presents. They never saw so many presents before. It was the most fun ever. The great big Christmas stockings had each of their names spelled on them with glitter. They had socks, mittens, t-shirts, underwear, two toothbrushes and two tubes of toothpaste. But mostly they were filled with candy. But the best things, were envelopes full of movie tickets, for the next year of Saturday afternoon movie shows. There were 52 matinee movie tickets to the "South-Shore Theater." And just as he had thought, the outside of the envelope said "From all of your friends at the Stanford Police Dept." (Yup, I'm going to be a Cop). Donnie and he both got the same crummy old white shirt, black pants and those dumb ole engineer boots to wear to Catholic School for the rest of the year. They got a pair each of C.C.M. hockey skates (the very best hockey skates in the whole world) and a bunch of board games. They were pretty happy kids. On Christmas morning the tree was full of neat stuff! Hockey sticks, pucks, sleds, boxing gloves, new jackets, an erector set and a science set with a real microscope. They got the same kinds of stuff that all the other kids got for Christmas! They went and told all of their friends what they got. Their friends were not impressed because they even got more stuff. It made the boy's feel a little sad but they didn't care. They got good stuff and they were going to the movies each Saturday for a whole year!

The boy's first day back to school after Christmas vacation, Clint got into the most trouble of all of his whole life. They were out at recess. There was a pretty big hill that all the kid's used pieces of cardboard to slide down the hill on. The hill was real icy. Donnie was a mean kid. He grabbed the kids and threw them down the hill real hard. A Nun came over and grabbed Donnie by the hair and told him to sit down and she was going to push him down the hill and see if he liked it. Donnie told the sister (in penguin clothes) that "I can't sit on the ground and slide down the hill, because our Dad will get real mad at me if my new clothes get hurt." Donnie tried to get away from the nun but she held on tight to his hair and kept pulling him around and shaking him. The nun got real mad and slapped Donnie's face real hard. Clint hollered real loud for her to stop hitting Donnie because he was still sick and he could die. She slapped him again and all little Clint knew, is that he was going to kill her. Clint hit the Nun in the belly as hard as he could. She 'woofed' air out and fell down. He pounced on her and punched her in the face a lot of times. Another Nun got him off of her and he kicked the beat-up nun a lot of times. The boys ran home. Clint did not remember anything else. The priest came to their house the next day. The Priest said Clint used a lot of dirty words when he was beating up the Nun. He said they could never go to school there again and they could not go to church there either. He gave the boys the J.C. Penny 'poor box' shoes that were kept in the janitor's closet. The boys went back to the public school and Clint didn't have to go to the 'Oppy Class.'

Their first day back at the Elementary School, the lady principal took them into her office and made them sit down as she stood in front of them with her arms crossed. She didn't say anything at first. She just tapped her foot and looked at them real hard. He could tell she was trying to tell them she didn't like them, or want them there. She was trying to scare him but he wanted to smile at her just before he told her to go fuck herself and punch her in the belly then beat her up, just like he did the Nun. It made him feel good when he thought about beating up the Nun. The good feeling did not come from the idea that he was protecting Donnie or even that it was a Nun he beat up. The good feeling came that he got to beat up a lady and he hated ladies. Nuns were supposed to be sacred so he got to beat up God and ladies at the same time.

The Principal Lady, told Donnie and him that if either one of them were rude or disrespectful to any teachers or staff, they would be in a lot of trouble. If they used bad words or pushed around or beat up any of the students, even if they started it, she was going to call the police and make them take the boys to reform

23

school for the rest of their lives. Donnie did a loud burp and they both started laughing.

All of the kids found out about Clint and the Nun. A couple of girls said he was going to hell so he told them to go to hell back. It was fun. The teachers did not talk to him and the kids were afraid of him. Donnie and he weren't allowed in the lunchroom at lunchtime. They had to go sit in the gym. When there was a school assembly or a play or Christmas show in the gym, they had to go sit in the lunchroom by themselves. They weren't allowed to go to gym class either because they were too mean.

Clint felt kind of sad that no one liked him. When the teachers made them go away from the other kids (because they were bad), he would always think about starting the school on fire. He would daydream about all the kids screaming and crying so they would know how he felt. It would be the most fun to tie up the principal lady to a chair and watch her burn up. He did pull the fire alarm once and the teachers and the firemen thought it was him. But he told them it wasn't him. And there wasn't anything they could do because they couldn't prove it. It made him feel good that he got to lie to them and they knew he was lying and they still couldn't do anything about it. He got to be smarter than the big people were.

There were two things Clint really liked to do in school that winter. But he made sure that no one ever knew it.

Clint still wanted to be a Cub Scout and when he got bigger, he really wanted to be a Boy Scout, but he knew he never could be either of those because no one liked him. He would sneak to the library and read the, 'Boys Life' magazine that came to the school every month. 'Boys Life' magazine was a Cub Scouts and Boy Scouts magazine. He liked to look at all the neat stuff you could buy with the Cub Scouts and Boy Scouts of America name on it. He kind of wondered how it would feel to have a complete uniform and all that other stuff. It made him sad. His biggest secret was that he wanted to be those boys in the pictures of the magazine, standing with their Dads. The Dads always had their hands on their son's shoulders and the Dads were looking down at their sons with a big smile on their faces and the boys were looking up at their Dads smiling back. He wanted to feel like that boy. He knew he could never be that 'smiling boy,' because his Dad, hated him.

Clint liked the Jeff White series of books. Jeff White was some kind of a Game Warden guy in Alaska or Canada. He was always alone in the woods and nobody bothered him. He would fall through the ice on a lake or a river, get caught in a big blizzard and was about to freeze to death, get attacked by grizzly bears and mountain lions and wolves and he would always fight his way out, no matter what. He was never scared. Clint wanted to be like Jeff White and always win and never be scared either.

To check a book out of the school library you had to write your name on a piece of paper inside the cover and the librarian would stamp the due date next to your name. He never checked out a book from the library. He stole them, but always brought them back. He was afraid that if a kid saw his name on the book they would think he was a sissy and would not be afraid of him anymore. When he finished a book he would sneak it back into the library and steal the next book in the series.

The last day of school was also Clint's birthday. His teacher told him he would go on to the fourth grade the next year. He tried to be happy about that, but the way she smiled at him, told him that she was happy to get rid of him. It was the first time she ever smiled at him and he wanted to beat her up.

Chapter 3 "THROWN AWAY"

Clint Flanagan skipped on his way home from school. It was now summer vacation! He would get to go on to the next grade and it was also, his Birthday. His Mom gave him some money and told him to go to the A & W Drive-In (five blocks away) and buy a gallon jug of root beer and bring it back home for his birthday party. He carried that heavy brown glass jug of root beer, like it was a trophy. He smiled with the thought that he got to have a whole jug of root beer at his house. He hoped the neighbors saw him walking with it, so they would think that he was just like them.

They got to eat pancakes for supper but had to drink that yucky powdered milk from the brown box that said 'U.S. Govt. Surplus' in big black letters. He hated that dumb ole brown box of powdered milk. It meant that they were poor and it made him feel like he was crummy. The boys got to drink the A & W root beer with their cupcakes. Clint got a kite and a baseball, for his birthday presents.

The next day, his Dad woke him up early and told him to hurry and get dressed. Dad said there was no time for breakfast and told him to go and get in the car. When he got in the car he saw the old brown and tan striped suitcase in the back seat (with an old, big belt strapped around it to keep it closed). He got scared and did not talk as they drove all the way through town. When they got to the Forks River (City limits), he asked Dad where they were going. Dad told him to stop asking questions and said he would know when they got there.

Clint's Dad didn't have to tell him. The grim look on his face, the direction they were going and the feeling in his belly told him, "We are going to Grandma's, so she can kill me, or maybe Dad is going to kill me and bury me with all my clothes. I know someone is going to kill me."

It was cold and windy as they drove along the South Shore of Lake Superior. The big whitecaps and the mean looking gray colored water gave him the shivers. Dad turned off the highway and they drove up the long dirt driveway to Grandma's house.

They pulled up to the back door and all of Grandma's big dogs in the kennels were barking and jumping to get out and bite him.

Dad told him to get out of the car. Dad got out and opened the back door and took out the suitcase and put it on the ground. Dad looked at him real hard and said, "You are going to stay here with Grandma and Jim and I don't want to hear of any bullshit from you." Dad got in the car and backed down the driveway.

Clint stood there and worked real hard not to cry. Dad never waved good-bye. He didn't say when he would be back. He just drove away.

Clint picked up the clunky ole suitcase, walked up the cement steps and knocked on the back door. He stood there for a long time and knocked on the door several times but no one answered. He sat on the cold cement stairs and shivered. He tried to think about what he did to get sent to Grandma's. "What did I do? Was I so bad that I don't even know when I was being bad? Is that why Daddy didn't even say good-bye to me?"

Clint had been to his Grandma's house twice before. In the front of her house was the highway and Lake Superior, where big ships went by. In the back were the dog pens, chicken coops, and a garage. Just up the hill was the railroad tracks. The boys were told to never, ever, go by the pens or coops or the railroad tracks. So he just sat there and cried for a long time. Clint was pretty sure that Mom, Dad, Donnie and Petey, were going to move away and Grandma was going to kill him or put him in the orphanage just like she did his Mom.

Clint hated his dumb ole fat Grandma with her big jiggly fat arms and her stupid funny red hair. He thought about the times she came to their apartment to visit Mom in her dumb ole pink and black Nash Rambler with her stupid ole red hair and great big fat lips with red lipstick on her teeth. She was ugly! At their apartment Grandma would say, shut up to them and "Kids are to be seen and not heard." She always used a mean voice at them and made her face all squeezed up and she looked like a witch. Grandma and Mom would smoke cigarettes, drink coffee and trade pills. Dad hated her and called her a whore. Donnie and Clint called her 'Jiggles', when they were really sure that she couldn't hear them.

Grandma drank whiskey a lot and got married a lot of times. She would always steal her husband's money, divorce them and take their houses and stuff. She was a mean and bitchy crazy person and his Dad and Donnie and he, hated her.

Clint liked Grandma's new husband Jim. Jim was a railroad engineer and drove the trains that went by the house. The trains went really fast. There were no neighbors around, just the forest and the highway and the big lake.

Clint had sat on the steps for a long time waiting for Grandma to come home. It was still cold and windy and he was hungry. He looked at the junky ole poor people's suitcase and wondered if there was maybe his jacket in there. He opened the suitcase, found his jacket and put it on, but his legs and butt were still cold. He put some pants on the cold cement step to keep his butt warm and put his shirts on his legs. He felt a lot better and he stopped shivering after a while. He also found a paper bag with a small bag of potato chips and a Hershey bar. He ate everything.

Clint looked at the dog pens and noticed that all the dogs had stopped jumping at the fence and had stopped barking. He was still pretty scared but he was warmer and not hungry any more. There were eight 'Boxer' dogs standing in a row looking at him, so he just started talking to them. Their nubby tails wiggled and their heads would turn from side to side at the same time. They seemed like they were really listening to him. He would turn his head to one side and they all did the same. It made him kind of laugh and he thought maybe they liked him.

Clint became tired of just sitting there on those cement steps. He stood up and slowly walked to the dog pens. He got about half way there when they started to snarl at him. He sat on the ground and kept talking to them. After a few minutes they started to whine and hop around. He got back up and slowly walked to them while he kept talking. They all backed up a little bit but their nubby little tails started to wag. He put his fingers through the chain link fence and they came up to him and started to lick his fingers. The dogs kept pushing each other out of the way, to get pets and lick his fingers. He could tell that they were going to be friends and it made him kind of happy. It started to get dark and he could hear the wolves starting to howl. He got scared and went back to sit on the steps to be safe.

Clint could hear cars zooming by on the highway all day long. Suddenly he heard a car slow down and turn on the dirt driveway. It was Grandma in her dumb ole pink and black Nash Rambler. She stopped fast and there was a lot of dust. Grandma was drunk and staggered as she walked past him to the dog pens. She told him to turn on the garden hose and fill the dog's water bowls. It was the first time he had ever been inside the dog pens and he was scared. The dogs backed away a little bit when he gave them water, but when Grandma filled their food bowls they backed up a long way from her. Clint realized the dogs liked him more than they did Grandma. Clint and the dogs all hated her. It made him feel good that the dogs wanted to be his friends.

Grandma unlocked the back door, told him to get his suitcase and pointed at a door next to the entry-way and said, "You sleep in there, now get to bed!" Grandma smelled like whiskey and with all of her stinky perfume, it made him feel like he had to vomit. He was hungry but he was afraid to tell her.

Clint felt even smaller than he was, as he sat on the bed in the dark and wondered when Grandma was going to come in and kill him. After a while, he heard a car drive up. He heard the door open and heard Jim's voice and he let out a deep sigh because Jim liked him, so he didn't think Jim would let Grandma kill him that night.

Jim woke him up the next morning and told him breakfast was ready. It was the very best breakfast he had ever had, in his whole life. After breakfast Jim took him out to the dog pens and

29

showed him how to feed and water the dogs. Jim said it was his job to do that twice a day. Jim told him who each dog was. Clint asked Jim why they didn't have their names on their houses. Jim told him that these were purebred dogs and they got sold to rich people, mostly from California. Clint had to change the straw in the dog houses every two days, he had to change the wood chips in the kennel once a week and had to shovel poop each night, at the last feeding. Jim gave him an old watch to wear so he knew when it was time to feed them and the chickens. The dogs liked Jim a lot and they licked his hands. He pet each one and scratched their heads, then Jim let Clint do it too. The dogs were a little bit scared of Clint, but still let him pet them. He also had to put each dog on a leash and walk them on the path that went around the whole property. He had to go around five times with each dog.

There was one doghouse that had a big bolt on the top and the bottom of the door, with a heavy, thick, chain link fence on it. The other dogs just had chicken wire on their doors. Jim said that only he or Grandma could ever open the door because that dog was kind of mean, real big and he was the prize stud. The big stud dog never got to go for a walk like the rest of the dogs because he could break the chain and run away. Jim told him, he wasn't ever supposed to put his fingers in his door. There was two holes in the side of his dog house with a pipe inside that went to his dog dish and another for water. He poured the dog food into the hole to feed him. His name was 'South Harbor Speculation.' But Clint called him 'Spec.' Spec didn't act too mean to him. After Clint walked all the dogs for their five times each, he would sit next to Spec's door for the same amount of time and talk to him. Clint thought Spec wanted to be nice, but he was sad that he never got to play with the other dogs or out to go out for walks. He just had to sit in his house all day. Clint got mad at Grandma and Jim for being so mean to Spec.

Clint loved those dogs a lot. They were his real friends; they were his only friend's in his whole life.

One day a lady came to the house in a fancy, brand new

Cadillac car. The lady went into the house for a little while and came back out with Grandma. Grandma had a dog leash in her hand and went into the kennel. She took a dog named Sandy out and put the dog in the rich lady's car. The lady drove away with his friend Sandy. He asked Grandma where she was taking their dog. Grandma told him to shut up and mind his own business. He knew he would never see his friend Sandy, ever again.

Jim came home from work that day and took him fishing. They got fishing poles from the garage, a tackle box, a big net and Jim got out a minnow bucket from the car. They walked across the highway, climbed over some big boulders and stood on the beach to fish. Jim gave him some red licorice and pointed at the big ships going by and told him what country they were from. Jim knew all the flags on the ships and what kind of cargo they were coming to load. Jim was nice to him. He had a nice voice. He had really big muscles. Clint was never afraid that Jim would hit him or holler at him. Clint felt safe with him. Jim was his friend. Clint asked Jim if the next time he drove his train by, if he would honk the horn at him. Jim told him the next time would be at 11:10 in the morning the next day.

Clint was standing on the hill the next morning waiting for Jim's train to come by. When he saw the big headlight on the front of the engine of the train he realized it was coming slower than normal. Jim stopped the train right in front of him and said "Hop aboard young man." Jim let him clang the bell and toot the horn. He got to sit on the engineer's seat and they went to Gold Bay. They got off of that train and got on another train but they had to ride in the caboose. They stopped in South Harbor and Jim and him and the new train driver went to a restaurant and had a Coke, hamburger and fries. It was fun. It was the first time Clint ever got to eat at a restaurant. After the restaurant, they walked to the Ben Franklin store and Jim bought a real nice, Swiss Army Knife. They got back in the caboose and the trainman took them home. Jim helped him walk the dogs and when they were done, they sat on the cement stairs and drank some Kool-Aid.

Jim reached into his pocket and took out his new Swiss Army Knife. He opened all the different blades and told Clint what they were for. Jim closed all the blades and told him to open his hand. Jim put the brand new Swiss Army Knife and a penny in Clint's hand and told him the knife was for him. Jim said that on his next day off they would go fishing and he would teach him how to whittle sticks with his new knife. Jim said he could carry the knife in his pocket but he could never take it out and open the blades unless he was with him. Clint had to promise Jim that he would never open the blades unless, he said he could. Clint promised Jim and they shook on it.

Clint's other job was to let the chickens out each morning, feed them and clean the coup. He wasn't allowed to pick the eggs because Grandma said he was too clumsy. One rooster was a real mean guy. His name was Henny Penney and Clint hated him because he always tried to bite him. Henny Penney would try to sneak up on him. One day he was feeding the chickens when Henny Penney bit his leg and he wouldn't let go. It hurt really badly and his leg was bleeding. Clint picked up a stick and tried to hit him so he would let go of his leg.

Grandma came running out of the house screaming at him. She grabbed his arm and started to beat him with a big hairbrush. Clint wanted to fight her back but he knew she would win him. He took the beating without crying, he just stood there without making a sound. When she was done beating him, he stared real hard at her so she knew he wanted to kill her. Grandma called him a "Retarded son of a bitch" and went back into the house. Grandma came back out and got in her pink and black car and drove away. Every day Grandma drove somewhere and was gone for about four hours. When she came back home she was always drunk and smelled like whiskey and stinky perfume.

After Grandma was gone, Clint went into the dog pen. They were barking real loud when Grandma was beating him up. The dogs gave him a lot of licks. Spec was making some funny sounding noises so he went to talk to him. His eyes were wet, like he was crying. Clint sat there with him and felt sad and mad. He told Spec that he thought about not going to sleep that night. He told Spec that he was going to sneak out of bed in the middle of the night and set the house on fire, and how much fun it would be for them to hear that crummy, mean ole' bitch screaming as she was on fire. Spec made a sound and looked like he was smiling. So, Clint promised all the dogs that he was going to kill ole' 'Jiggles' and they all seemed really happy.

Jim came home and asked what happened to his face. Clint told him he fell down but he could tell that Jim didn't believe him. Jim cooked them some fish that they caught two days before.

Grandma came home after dark and she was really drunk and was swearing real loud. Jim told Clint to go to bed. He sat on his bed and could hear them arguing. Jim said he was tired of her always bring drunk and if she ever hit Clint again that he was going to break both her arms. Hearing that made him happy. But he was still afraid of her.

Lying in bed he realized he couldn't set the house on fire and make that crummy ole' 'Jiggles' dead because Jim might get hurt and he liked Jim a lot. He was afraid that Grandma was going to get him that night because she kept telling Jim that she "hated that stupid little bastard Grandkid." Clint took out his new Swiss Army Knife and opened up the big blade. He went to sleep on top of the covers with the knife in his hand. If Grandma came in his room to kill him, he was ready to stab her in the guts.

Clint was feeling bad that night because Grandma was being mean to Jim because he stood up for him. It made him feel real lonely. Everyone hated him but Jim and the dogs.

That night, Clint thought a lot about Spec, he thought he was a lot like him. He wasn't bad. He was just lonely and because he seemed crabby, everyone thought he was mean. He was just sad because he couldn't play with the other dogs and he never got pets or got walked around the yard five times like everyone else. Spec thought nobody liked him so he didn't like them either.

The next day, after ole' 'Jiggles' drove away to drink whiskey, he took the big chain leash and had a talk with Spec. Clint made Spec promise him that he would not bite him or try to run away. Spec was just like all the other dogs. He pulled a little harder and wanted to go faster but he was good. Clint liked to sneak Spec out when Grandma went to drink whiskey.

Clint spent most of each day hiding out in the dog pens so Grandma couldn't get him. It was always cold and windy living next to Lake Superior. He liked to snuggle with the dogs and feel warm and safe.

Grandma sold more of the dogs and got new ones. Every time he watched Grandma put a leash on a dog and put it in the back seat of someone's car, he wanted to kill her. He felt so sad that he would go and hide in the woods. He thought about letting all the dogs out so they could run away. But then he would think about all the cars on the highway, or maybe the bears or wolves getting them. So then he thought about being real mean to the dogs and hit them with sticks and kick them, so they would get mean to him and he could hate them, so when they had to go away and he wouldn't have to be so sad and cry.

But, he could not be mean to them. They were his friends. He would just have to get used to being sad.

One day in the mid-summer, he was having a nap in the kennels with the dogs. He had put down new woodchips and straw that morning so it was still kind of prickly. They were all sleeping pretty good when he heard the back porch screen door slam and heard Grandma screaming his name. He could tell that she was really mad at him and he was going to get a beating. He stood up as Grandma came into the kennels. She grabbed his hair and his arm and pulled him out of the pens. The dogs got real mad at her and he wanted them to bite her and kill her and eat her. But they just growled and barked. They were afraid of her too.

Grandma pulled him by his hair across the back yard and into the house. She smelled like whiskey really bad.

She pulled him into the bathroom and pointed to the sink

screaming "Look at what you did." She was screaming that over and over. She was crazy and her eyes were all bugged out like they might explode. In the sink was a broken bottle of stinky perfume. He kept saying that he didn't do that but she just kept shaking his head with her hand pulling on his hair and punching him in his ribs and his back. He wanted to punch her in the belly like he did the Nun but Grandma was way bigger than him and she would fight him back and kill him.

She grabbed his arm and twisted it real hard and it hurt a lot. She pulled him by his twisted arm into the kitchen, dragged him to the gas stove, turned on the burner to high and held his right hand in the flames. He still remembers the smell of his hand burning to this very day.

Clint didn't remember how he got away from her or how he got across the highway without getting hit by a car. He kind of woke up sitting on a rock with his hand in the water of Lake Superior. The water was so cold that it hurt his hand. When he took his hand out of the water, then the other hurt came from the flames and it was worse. His hand was real pink and had a funny gray/black color and was bubbly looking, and it itched real, really bad.

He saw Grandma standing in the yard across the highway. He thought she was coming to kill him. It was too far away to see her face. But he knew it was full of hate and she was going to kill him that day.

There is an old saying, that you heard all your life growing up on the lake. "Lake Superior never gives up its dead." The water is so cold that people drown from the cold and just sink to the bottom. He thought about swimming out "Until the cold gets me and I can just sink to the bottom and Grandma can't get me." He realized Mom and Dad would feel sad, if they could never find him to bury him. So he didn't do that. Cars were zooming by on the highway. "Maybe I will just run out in front of a car and get killed." He couldn't do that either because he thought how bad the man would feel driving the car that just killed a little nine-year old boy. He thought he would run up the shoreline a long way so Grandma couldn't see him, cross over the highway, sneak through the woods to the dog kennels, let all the dogs out so Grandma couldn't be mean to them or sell them, any more.

Maybe he could climb up the hill, get on the train tracks and wait for a train to come by and kill him.

He couldn't do that either because what if the dogs got killed too? And what if the train driver was Jim? He was really stuck with what to do. He just knew that he wasn't going to let 'Jiggles,' kill him. He would rather kill his own self.

Clint didn't know what happened next. He didn't remember the rest of the summer. He never asked. No one ever told him. When he looks at his hand 51 years later, the scars are still visible. When it gets cold, his right hand aches as it has for many, so very many years.

This is just another broken spoke in the wheel as to how a child can be so severely damaged.

Chapter 4 "GETTING EVEN"

Clint made himself pretend that he never went to his Grandma's. That she never hurt him and Jim and the dogs were not real. He would just pretend that he played baseball every day with his friends and that he was really good at baseball. He would pretend that Dad and Mom took them on picnics and to the carnival at Pine Point and a bunch of other neat places.

From these first nine years of his young life, Clint knew that he didn't belong anywhere and no one wanted him. And because he knew that everyone hated him, he had to hate them back and he had to hate them first. God stopped being real and even if there was a God, God hated him too. Clint had to hate God even more, so God couldn't hurt him back. He was going to find a way to show God, that he was even more-meaner, than him.

Late that summer, Clint snuck into St. Helens Catholic Church where he used to go before he got kicked out. He knows the Church really well. He took some dog poop in a bag and put it on the floor and on the priest's seat in the confessional. He took a pee in the holy water stand where people dipped their fingers to make the sign of the cross. He wanted to go on the Alter and tear up the bible the Priest used. But he got scared and couldn't do it. He thought the devil was going to get him if he went on the Alter. He found a bunch of U.N.I.C.E.F. collections boxes that the church kids took, 'trick-or-treating' and asked for contributions. The kids brought the boxes back to the church and the Nuns counted the money and sent it to U.N.I.C.E.F. to feed starving little kids in Africa.

Clint went out on Halloween and collected for U.N.I.C.E.F. He got three boxes filled with coins and bills. (The boxes were a little bigger than a school lunchroom carton of milk.) He went into the bathroom of a gas station, tore open the boxes, put the money in his pockets, threw the boxes in the trash and went to the Corner Dairy Bar. He ordered a Cherry Coke and quietly said out loud, "Fuck you God. And fuck those starving little kids in Africa."

He had a big kid buy him a pack of cigarettes and he played pinball machines (with a lit cigarette hanging from his mouth like the big kids do,) with the U.N.I.C.E.F. money he stole. He told himself that, "Love and compassion for my fellow man was a bunch of bullshit. That crap was for suckers! No one cares about me so I didn't care about them. Nobody is ever going to get me, ever again! Everything is a lie. God was a lie, the Priest and Nuns were liars, the people that went to church were liars and Mom and Dad are liars too!"

Clint has always been ashamed to admit what he did at the church and how he stole from U.N.I.C.E.F. He has, in the last few years confessed these sins to a Catholic priest. The Priest forgave him and helped him contact U.N.I.C.E.F. and he made complete financial amends, with interest.

Chapter 5 "THE PUNISHER"

The fall and winter of 1957 were uneventful. School was crummy. He didn't beat up any kids during the school days. He waited until nights and weekends to beat them up, so he would not get in trouble at school. Dexter Park was one block away, if you cut through yards and between houses. In the summer, Dexter Park had three baseball fields where big men played softball. In the winter, the city had two guys' use fire hoses to flood the ground after it froze to make an ice skating rink. The rink was bigger than a football field and had lights on it so you could skate on it all night. And, it was free. Clint would put his skates on at home, put rubber blade guards on them and walk to the rink.

Clint would spend every minute he could at the rink. The place was always crowded. There were Moms and Dads with little kids that were just learning to skate. There were always a bunch of girls all over the place holding hands and getting in the way and trying to act like figure skaters and falling on their asses. Clint was real proud of his C.C.M. high backed, hockey skates that he got the Christmas before from the Cops. Those skates made him feel like he was flying. But mostly it made him feel like he was better than everyone on the ice. It was like he had some kind of magic radar.

He would skate really fast and coast by kids even bigger than him, when they were going as fast as they could. There were no skating lanes and people were all over the place. Somehow he could tell when some dummy was about to cut in front of him or fall down. He would skate as close to them as he could and do some kind of trick to just brush against them and look back at them and tell them with his eyes that they were stupid and he could have taken them out if he wanted to, and it would be their fault. He liked that feeling of power. If the same kid got in his way again, he would put him on his ass, hard. If it was a kid he never saw before, he would memorize the color of his jacket his face and size and body shape, so if he ever cut him off again, a few days or even weeks later, he knew he owed him one. It was crazy. But every day he looked for those kids. It was like he was hunting them. When he got to put them down, it felt like he was shooting them, like a rabbit. It felt good. As strange as it may sound, he felt less angry the harder and longer he skated. When a kid got in his way he saw them as stealing his rhythm and sense of peace and he wanted to kill them for that. When he skated all his fear left him, he didn't feel the bruises on his head or ribs from his Mom and Dad hitting him. He forgot that he was poor. He didn't have to think about lying in bed later that night and shivering under the covers because they didn't have any money for fuel oil. There would be frost on the inside of their windows because there was no heat in their apartment, other than what came from all the burners on the gas stove.

Clint always brought his hockey stick and puck with him. He hid them in the towering snowbank by the fence, where he walked into the rink. He would have to climb over the great big snow banks made by the snowplows that cleared the ice. When he got tired of zooming around free skating he would get his stick and puck. He would go into some other kind of mind zone. It was just his skates, his stick, his puck and him. He never saw the ice. He was a part of it. It was his safe place. He didn't see or hear anyone else. The rink had light posts along the fence line that went all around the Park. The Park was one and one half blocks long and a full block wide. The light posts also had loud speakers on them. And the guy who ran the big brick, warming house played rock and roll music. It was fun to skate to the music but it made him feel funny to like dance on skates and he didn't want anyone to think he was a queer.

At the far end of the monster skating rink were two hockey rinks with sideboards, bleachers, benches and painted lines on the ice and goal nets. They looked just like the hockey rinks that you saw on TV. He could out skate and out stick handle most every kid on the hockey teams. He didn't want to play on an organized hockey team. They were a bunch of rich kids that had full uniforms that matched and they always had brand new sticks and wore CCM logoed helmets, gloves, padded shorts and shin guards under their fancy colored socks that matched their jerseys and shorts. He hated that they all made him feel poor. All Clint had was a worn out old car coat with a plaid shirt and a pair of too short corduroy pants. He had an old pair of choppers (leather mittens) with holes in them and his fingers were always cold. The one thing he hated even more than the rich kids were the coaches always hollering and telling you what to do and those stupid referees always blowing their whistles and telling you, you can't do this or that. He didn't like those rules. He had his own rules. If you screwed with him, he was going to hurt you. Those were all the rules he needed.

The best part of every night was when the hockey games were over. The hockey kids came on the public ice to free skate with their fancy uniforms on to show off to the girls. Those pricks were all conceited and skated around like they were bored as they showed how good they could stick handle a puck. It made Clint smile. He would say to himself, "Now, Fucker, you're mine!"

Clint would pick up his puck and put it in his pocket, go after the closest kid, steal his puck away, do a fast stop and turn to face him and tell him to come and get it. Most all of the kids knew he was looking for a fight. A few times a kid would try to get his puck back and Clint would punish him for it. He would hook his skate and dump him. If he got back up, he would spear him in the ribs with his stick. But what he enjoyed the most was getting ahead of him, stopping fast and shooting a slap shot at him as hard as he could. He was always amazed that he was shorter and skinnier than most all the kids, but he was really strong, and the kids knew that. They knew even if they kicked his ass, he would get up and keep getting up every time they knocked him down. The more they hit him, the harder he would fight back. He didn't like to fight kids his own size. He knew he would hurt them too bad. The big kids that won fighting him were afraid that they would have to kill him to make him stop. He picked a lot of fights with big kids that he knew they were going to kick his ass and he didn't care. He just wanted to show them and everyone else that he could take a punch, that he could take a beating, and that he was tough. But mostly they would know that someday, that little kid with a bloody nose and a busted lip staggering in front of him, would beat him. He could see the fear in their eyes, the next time they saw him. He could tell that the big kid was wondering if Clint was going to start a fight with him again. And if today, was the day that Clint would win the fight and destroy him. When he saw that question in a kids eyes, he felt powerful. He knew he owned him. He would do a quick fake like he was going to throw a punch. The kid would flinch and back up real fast from being afraid and Clint would glare at him like a crazy dog and then grin. Just to let him know that his day was coming, maybe even today! He loved doing that.

Clint had an old man friend. His name was Mac. He owned, "Mac's Shoe Repair Shop." Mac also sharpened everyone's skates and all the hockey player's skates too. Clint loved going into Mac's little shop. It was full of all kinds of old looking green and brown machines to fix shoes. It smelled really good. Like new leather and shoe polish. (Clint still loves to slip into a shoe repair shop today, just to fill his nostrils with that heavenly smell. He thinks of Mac each time. He would look up and say a thanks to him for his friendship and his kindness and then he'd whisper "I love you ole friend.)"

Mac was funny looking, and even an ugly guy. He was real short and fat. He had a birth defect with one leg that was four or more inches shorter than the other. His shoe on his left foot was a big block of wood that he made. Kind of like a real thick sole. Mac walked with a big limp and dragged his left foot behind him.

A lot of kids called him names. They would say "I'm going to the 'Gimps' or the 'Crips' to get my skate's sharpened." Clint would go crazy. He would holler at them "I will fucking kill you, if you guys ever call Mac or anyone else who was crippled, names again." A few times a kid would smart off to Clint after he had warned them. Each time he would hit that kid so hard that he would knock him down with the first punch. He would get so mad that he couldn't even breathe. He would stand over them and shake for a long time. He couldn't even think. He was like a zombie that you saw in the monster movies. He was always surprised that he did that; that he hit him so hard that he knocked him down. It was like it wasn't even him that did that. Then he always got afraid that the kid was dead. No sooner did that thought leave and he thought, "Fuck him, I hope he is dead. He deserves it."

Clint liked Mac and he went out of his way to be his friend. He felt sorry for him. He knew he didn't like being ugly and crippled. Mac knew that kids' made fun of him. Clint knew Mac was very sad about his life.

Mac charged 30 cents to sharpen skates. One day Clint needed to get his skates sharpened but he didn't have the 30 cents. He went to Mac's shop to ask him if he would let him polish shoes in trade for his skates to be sharpened. Mac showed him how to put polish on shoes and how to use the buffers and how to apply the sole and heal dressings. Clint loved doing that. He loved the smell. He loved the machines. He loved to make the shoes and boots shine even better than when they were new. He also loved Mac's praise. Mac hired him to polish shoes for 10 cents a pair. Clint went there every day after school, instead of hiding in the shed with the cold and stink of burnt motor oil on the dirt floor.

After a while, he asked Mac to teach him how to sharpen skates and Mac did teach him. Clint wasn't allowed to use the medium grinder, as it was easy to overheat a skate blade and warp it. He was only allowed to use the fine, extra fine and buffing wheels. Mac put the skates in big wooden boxes with signs reading; medium, fine, extra fine, de-burr and polish, on each box.

Mac had to leave the shop to go home to take care of his sick wife a lot. So he gave Clint a key so he could let himself in and sharpen the skates and polish the shoes when Mac had to go home. All the shoes and skates were tied together in pairs with a string tag with the people's names on them.

When Clint had to let himself in, he went to the 'medium grind' skate box and looked for the kid's names that he hated for being assholes; especially the smart asses that talked down to, or

43

bad about Mac. He would intentionally hold those skate blades hard on the medium grinding wheel to make them real hot so the heat would warp the kid's skates so they would fall on their ass all the time.

Some of the hockey kids were kind of poor but not as poor as him. Other hockey kids weren't very good skaters and the good skaters always made fun of them. Clint made a special effort to perfectly sharpen and polish the kind-of poor and not so good skater kid's skates. He even put shoe polish on them to make them look new so they would feel better.

Clint never used the buffing wheel (but he was supposed to) on an asshole's or girl's figure skates. He left the sharpening burrs on them to kind of give them the finger and tell them they are not as good a skater as they think they are.

One day after school, Mac wasn't there and he had to use his key to get in to sharpen skates. He looked through the medium grind box, and found the biggest prick's skates he could find. He held them on the medium grit wheel for a long time. Suddenly the wheel motor stopped. He looked up and Mac was standing there with his hand on the power box lever. Clint could smell the heat from the skate blade against the grinding wheel. Mac looked at him and shook his head. Clint knew that he just got caught.

Mac walked over to him and looked at the kid's name on the tag. He half smiled and said "I don't like the mouthy little prick either. But when a customer pays for a job, you do the best job you can. You treat each customer as they were your best friend." Clint promised Mac that he would not do it again. He even de-burred the blades of everyone's skates; even the girls. That is except for the rich kids. Fuck them!

One day, Mac told him that he had sold all his equipment to a guy, and as soon as spring came, he was going to retire. It hurt Clint really bad. He thought he would work for Mac for the rest of his life. He knew he would never be happy, ever again.

Chapter 6 "SMELT FISHING AND DROWNING"

Suddenly, one day, ice-skating was over. The ice was melting and it was going to be spring soon. Smelt season was about to start and Clint loved smelt fishing. Smelt are little silver colored fish about four to six inches long. They taste really good, deep fried, but it takes a lot of them to make a meal, because they are real skinny. The smelt live in the Great Lakes and when the ice goes out of the rivers, the smelt swim up the river to spawn. The rivers run fast and hard and the water is cold during the ice break up. The best time to smelt fish is after midnight and it is really cold. You have to wear long underwear and jeans with your insulated hip boots.

You never want to go too deep in the water, so that the water goes over the top of your hip-boots. Some guys wear chest waders and could go out a lot further in the water but it was dangerous because if the water filled your chest waders, you would float away into the strong current and all the water in your waders would sink you, and you would drown even before hypothermia set in. Even on a weeknight, there were hundreds of people in the mouth of the rivers trying to catch smelt with their dip nets. A lot of people were drunk and there were bonfire parties all over the riverbanks. There were six big rivers in less than 20 minutes from the city limits. The Flanagan's liked to smelt fish on the Forks River. One night, his Dad, Donnie and he, were smelting and a man just up river, ahead of them, fell and his chest waders filled up with water and the current got him and as he came rushing by. Clint's Dad dove for him and caught the guy. But Dad could not hold on to him because of the fast current. Dad swam back to where he was out of the current and could stand up. The man was screaming for help but nobody could catch him. Donnie and Clint shined their six-volt lantern lights on the man, so did a lot of other people. Some man between the guy in the water and where the Flanagan's were, fell in also and the current got him too. They watched both of the men fight to get out of the current but they

45

never made it. They saw them both splashing and screaming for help as the river carried the men out into the lake. They watched both of the men go under and drown. Everyone there got real quiet. Quiet like when you were in church. All you could hear was the bonfires crackling on the beach and a few people coughing somewhere. No one said a word. Several people had their heads bowed and it was still. Suddenly, Clint didn't even feel the cold.

People everywhere started to say the Lord's Prayer real soft. When the prayer was over, it was quiet for a few more minutes and no one moved. All at once it seemed that everyone got out of the river and started to walk along the gravel shore to the parking lot. There were a lot of cops there asking what happened. Dad told the boys to follow him and stay close. A cop was coming up to them because some men pointed at Dad when the cop asked them what happened. Dad told the cop the man's name that he grabbed but couldn't hold on to. Dad told the cop that he worked with him on the railroad and drank beers together at the Tavern Bar. Dad told the cop that the man was 25 years old and had two little kids, Dad looked real sad. They didn't talk on the way home. They drove the 15 miles' home through the city. Donnie and he just sat in the back seat and looked out the windows. Dad just looked straight ahead as he drove the car.

When they got home, Dad went and changed his clothes and told Mom that he didn't want to talk and he was going to the Tavern Bar. At first Mom looked mad. Then she looked puzzled. Dad said "The boys will tell you" as he walked out the door.

They told Mom what happened and she started to cry. They all started to cry. Mom was saying how sad it was for the man. That he knew he was going to drown and how sad it was for his wife and their little kids. Then Mom said "Poor Bud." (Dad's nickname was Bud). Then Mom grabbed her jacket and said that she was going to the Tavern Bar to take care of their father and walked out the door. Mom walked to the Tavern Bar all by herself, in the dark. Clint laid in bed that night and thought about that man but mostly how he wished he could have some beers too, so he could not be so sad and he could feel better, just like his Dad. He felt bad for Dad too. He tried to save his friend's life but couldn't and he had to watch his friend and the other man die. If Dad wasn't such a good swimmer, he would have drowned too. It gave Clint the shivers.

The very next night another man drowned on the same river, the same way. The police closed the smelt fishing down. A few days later the Fire Department and the Coast Guard put up a big net to catch people that were washed out, and had a fire department boat in the water 24 hours a day, until the end of smelting season. The Flanagan's did not go smelting again and Dad never talked about that night and his friend drowning. Clint felt sad about those two men and he felt sad for his Dad, too. But he didn't have anyone to talk to about it. He just had to feel sad, all by himself.

A month later fishing season opened on the inland lakes. Everyone went fishing on opening weekend. The Flanagan family was too poor to have a boat, so they always had to fish from the shore. They went fishing on every opening day, that is, if they had gas money for the car and they could buy minnows.

Dad took Mom, Donnie, Petey and him, fishing to a lake where there was a big dam and the water was very deep and you could see down a long way. You could catch Northern and Walleye Pike, Bass and Crappies. The fish were not hungry that day and Clint got bored. It was no fun just to sit there and wait for a fish to come by. He walked down the hill to the spillway where they let the extra water out of the dam so it wouldn't get too full. He wanted to catch some frogs and crawdads. There was a great big pool of water that was round shaped and about the size of Dexter Park, if it was round. There were a couple of places that had big pipes with water coming out, with wooden slats over them that you could stand on. The water that came out was swirly and made a lot of bubbles and had a light mist. Clint stood there and watched the bubbles pop and with the sunlight they had colors like silver, green and blue. Some special bubbles were gold and red too.

Usually they were the biggest bubbles. He stood there like he was hypnotized wondering where the bubbles came from and where they went when they popped.

It was a cold, windy day but at least, the sun was out. Clint was wearing a big, heavy wool, knee-length coat that was way too big for him. He got real dizzy watching the water swirl and the bubbles pop and he fell into the deep pool. He sank down pretty fast with that heavy wool coat on. He didn't feel the cold from the water. He felt really warm. He liked the feeling of floating under the water as he sank even deeper. He wondered if the two men he saw drown last month could have felt this good. Then he remembered them screaming for help and splashing and trying to swim. Nope. They were scared and he wasn't. He didn't try to swim. He just felt really happy. He knew he was going to die and the Devil or God or even Dad couldn't get him. He saw real big lights that were the same colors as the bubbles, the colors were beautiful and he was having fun.

Suddenly he felt big hands grabbing him all over, pulling on his arms, his hair and his jacket. He tried to get away from those grabbing hands that pulled him out of the spillway.

Earlier Clint saw two men fishing, one down from him and one across the other side of the pool. He was real mad at those two guys for diving into the pool to save him. He wanted to beat them up, as they were rubbing his arms and chest and legs. He choked and vomited out water and hated them for wrecking his fun. The two men took him up the hill and told his Dad what happened. Dad apologized to the men for having to get all wet to save him. Then the men left. Dad used a real mean and scary voice as he grabbed Clint with both of his big hands by the front of his coat and dragged him to a big rock and said "Get your stupid little ass on that rock and don't you God Damn move until I tell you to." Mom didn't say anything. Clint just sat on that cold, big ole' rock and shivered for a long time with his lips trembling and his jeans frozen to his legs. His feet were so cold that they burned like his hand did, when Grandma burned it.

Mom and Dad did not talk to him on the way home. When they did get home he took off his wet clothes and went to bed to try to warm up. He laid under the bed covers and shivered for a long time and cried for a little bit. Dad had become a lot nicer form AA and not drinking. But his Dad, still didn't care about him.

"Why didn't they even try to help me warm up like those two men did? Why did they make me just sit on that big ole, cold rock? They just wanted to punish me. They wanted me to die. Why didn't they know or care that maybe I jumped in the water so I could drown because I feel so lonely and unwanted? They didn't know or care that I was sinking to the bottom of that big deep pool and it was fun for me. They didn't know that I never even tried to stroke or kick my feet to get out of the water. That was the most fun ever, even more fun that the Cops Christmas movie passes and my C.C.M. hockey skates. Getting to drown was the best thing ever!"

"I am invisible and if I were dead, no one would ever miss me." As Clint was falling asleep, he decided that he would never cry or feel bad again. He was now going to "make up a special kind of hate, just for them."

Somehow, drowning became a big part of Clint's life. In his early teens a bunch of the guys went to Pine Point to body surf the monster waves by the canal. Some of the guys went into the water next to the pier. Clint thought it was too dangerous with the strong undertow. He went further down the beach with some of the other guys. When they came back to the pier, there were a lot of cops, firemen and Coast Guard guys in boats. He could see the Coast Guard divers in the water and a few on the beach with their diving suits and air tanks and masks.

The guys told them that Rudy went out too far and was screaming for help. The guys thought he was just screwing around. They saw Rudy go under and he never come back up. The guys just sat there and didn't talk as they watched the divers. It was starting to get dark and the boss Coast Guard guy said they were done for the day and would come back the next day at first light.

The boys had all ridden the bus together to get to Pine Point and the pier. The cops gave them all a ride home. He didn't tell his Mom about what had happened. He just went to bed and felt sad for Rudy, being left all alone in the dark night and cold water. The boys all got up early the next day and rode the bus to the Pine Point before daylight. None of them talked on the bus or when they got to the pier. They didn't talk as they stood next to the water as they watched the drag boats and divers look for Rudy. They found Rudy's body. The boys were standing on the beach when the divers carried him out of the water. Rudy looked like he was sleeping. They put him on a stretcher, covered him all up in white sheets (like a mummy) and put him in the back of an ambulance.

The next day, Clint's Mom said that she read in the paper that a boy named Rudy from their neighborhood had drowned. She asked if Rudy was one of his friends. Clint said "Yes, he was." But he never told her that he was with him that day or that he saw him when they took him out of the water. He knew she wouldn't care, so why bother?

A few days later, he put on his Catholic school white shirt, black pants and his 'poor box' J.C. Penney shoes and walked to the church for Rudy's funeral. He never saw anyone in a casket before. It scared him. There were a lot of people crying but he didn't. He saved it up for the way home as he walked through all the alleys so no one could see him cry.

Clint went home and changed his clothes and went to the tree swing and sat in the bushes, wondering if when he dies if his Mom and Dad would have a funeral for him. He wondered if anyone would come and if anyone would cry for him. He didn't think that even Mom or Dad would cry and that, made him cry.

Chapter 7 "WHAT LOVE FELT LIKE"

It was mid-summer and Clint was 10 years old now. He sure hated being nine years old. It was bad for him. Really bad. He hoped being 10 years old would be a lot better. But it was not, it was even worse! Mom said she was going to have another baby. All that meant to Clint was, that they were going to have less food. Mom would ground him for no reason so he would have to take care of the new baby (like when Petey got born) when she took too many pills or was playing Yahtzee with those old bitch neighbor ladies'. He was going to hate this new baby, really bad!

Young Clint didn't like girls but he started to like women. There was a next door neighbor lady who always came out of her house to say "Hi" to him when he was playing in the side yard. She was real pretty. She hung out her laundry every day to dry. She had a lot of real pretty underwear, he knew where the underwear was supposed to go, but he never saw them on a lady. He could see her underwear on the clothesline from his bedroom window. He would sit on his bed and watch out the window staring at her underwear for a long time. It made him feel real, real funny inside. He stared out the window a lot.

Sometimes he would feel real brave and pretend that he was going to the shed and walked by her pretty underwear real slow and sneak peeks at her pretty, lacey underwear. He felt kind of dirty and bad. But it was exciting. One day, as he was doing his underwear peek stroll, the neighbor lady opened her back door and asked him if he could come in to her house to help her lift a heavy box. It was a small box and not very heavy. As they put down the box, her bathrobe fell open exposing both of her breasts. She just stood there bent over with her breasts hanging out and she was smiling at him.

She walked over to him, took off her robe, took his hands and put them on each breast and she kissed him, first soft and then hard. He felt so weak that he thought he was going to pass out and fall down. The room was spinning faster and faster. He never saw

51

or felt a woman's breast before. It was like hitting the bottom of a real fast, roller coaster and he thought he was going to throw up.

They played like that almost every day until the leaves started to fall. The lady had a little boy who was just starting to walk. She also had a husband. He was a way lot bigger than him. Clint knew that someday the husband would find out and come to kill him. But, he didn't care because he was in love.

The lady kissed him so nice and petted him soft like a kitten. She held him to her soft, warm, pretty breasts.

That first experience with a woman, set the course for the next thirty years of his life. The few people he has told this story to, had damned the women and called them child molesters. Clint never felt that he was a victim or any kind. It was the entire opposite. Those ladies' rescued him. Their loving warmth and tenderness worked for him. He found that thinking of those lady's and being with them, was intoxicating for him. His rage and hatred left him. He wasn't lonely or sad any more. He no longer wanted to kill people or himself. He felt safe and had his first true reason, to be happy.

Clinton's being poor and not very smart was no longer a worry. It wasn't the physical aspect or sex that was so alluring and satisfying. It was the emotional high. Sex became his drug. It made him a giant and he wanted to be an even bigger giant.

Clint's first heartbreak came when the neighbor lady told him she was going to have a new baby and she could not play with him anymore. It was the saddest he had ever felt. He wanted to beg and plead for her to keep loving him but he did not. He asked the neighbor lady if she knew of some other lady who was as pretty and as nice as her, who would like him the way she did.

The neighbor lady wrote down a phone number of a rich lady who wanted to hire a young boy to do odd jobs and shovel snow. The neighbor lady said that the rich lady would pay him money for doing a good job and give him nice kisses and hugs just like he got from her.

That made his sadness all go away. He ran into the house and called the rich lady. The rich lady told him to get on the 6:20 am bus on Saturday and take it all the way to the bus stop near her house. She said she would be there to pick him up in a white Cadillac. He was really excited to get to ride in a Cadillac. He had never done that before.

Clint was at the bus stop at 6:00 am so he wouldn't miss the bus. The only thing he could remember about the bus ride, was the bus was going too slow and stopping too much. He wanted to kill those people that were getting on and off the bus and he mostly wanted to kill the bus driver for stopping and going too slow.

When he got off the bus where the lady told him to, he saw a white Cadillac with the prettiest lady he had ever seen, sitting behind the steering wheel. When he got into her car, she looked even prettier, even prettier than the movie stars on TV. She smelled real pretty too.

Clint could tell her clothes cost a lot of money. She had perfect white teeth and a nice voice. But he could tell if she got mad at you, her pretty smile and nice voice would go away, real fast!

On the way to her house, the lady told him to come to her house every Saturday at the same time and she would be at the bus stop at the same time. She said a taxi would take him home and she would pay for it and she would pay him twenty-five dollars each Saturday. He was dumb struck to think he would get to see such a pretty lady that smelled so good, get to ride in a taxi for free and get twenty-five whole dollars every Saturday and even get to ride in a brand shiny new white Cadillac.

The lady was nice but kind of bossy when she told him what to do. He had to pick up a bunch of sticks out of the yard because the yard guy wasn't coming back until spring. Then he was supposed to clean and sweep the boathouse and she was going to have the maid take all the cars out of the great big garage so he could sweep the floors. He was to ring the bell at the big front entrance that had two doors when he was finished.

Clint worked real hard and had a big pile of sticks that he picked up from all the big trees. He worked real fast to clean the boathouse and car garage. The boathouse had two big power boats with big engines. Clint had never seen a garage for boats with a dock inside. He had never seen inside a big car garage with a white cement floor. The driveway was as wide as a highway and there were five cars parked in the driveway when he went to sweep out the garage. There were two foreign cars that he had never seen before but they looked, kind of racecar like.

The lady looked like she fit perfectly in the mansion with all the cars and boats and nice stuff. He thought the lady was in her late 20's. She walked with the grace of a deer.

When he had finished his work, he rang the doorbell. The maid answered the door. The lady was standing next to the maid. The maid told him to come in. The lady nodded at the maid and the maid walked away real fast. He saw that nod of her head to mean, "Go away." The maid looked kind of scared. He thought the lady had nodded at her a lot of other times before.

The lady reached out and took his hand. She walked him to a shoe bench in the foyer and told him to sit down. She untied his sneakers and made a face as she took them off. She unzipped his jacket and took it off of him. The lady told him to call her, "Mrs. G.," as she took his hand and walked him up some big curved wooden shiny stairs into a big bedroom and into a great big bathroom. The bathroom had a long counter with two sinks and mirrors on the walls and above the sinks that went the whole length of the countertop. There was a telephone on a little desk and the shower was all glass. The shower was as big as Clint's whole living room and it had showerheads everywhere. Mrs. G. turned on the shower and told him to get undressed and to take a shower as she left the room and closed the door behind her.

Clint was kind of scared. He had never seen a shower before, just their clunky ole scratched up bathtub with feet on it. Mrs. G. was a lot different than the neighbor lady. The neighbor lady was always smiling and touched him soft and petted him and called him sweetheart, darling and honey. He didn't think that Mrs. G. will be soft or smile or call him nice names.

Mrs. G. came back into the bathroom and said he had 30 seconds to rinse off. He was kind of embarrassed to come out of the shower. Mrs. G. was standing there with a big white towel that was the size of a blanket. Mrs. G. would not let him have the towel. She dried him off herself and rubbed him like a massage might be like. Mrs. G. wrapped him in the towel, took his hand and walked him into the bedroom. She took him to the giant bed with the bedcovers pulled back and told him to lie down. He did as she told him. She put an extra pillow behind his head and pulled the covers up on him. He will never forget the smell of the sheets and how soft they were. Mrs. G. smiled at him as she bent down and kissed his mouth real soft. As she stood up he realized she was wearing a fancy dress now. As she walked away, he saw she had on black shiny stockings and black shiny high heels. When she let him in and took off his sneakers, she had on a blouse and slacks. Mrs. G. poured something from a glass pitcher into a glass with ice. She walked around the room and lit candles that were everywhere, and lots of them. Mrs. G. pulled the curtains closed, turned off the lights and walked over to him with the glass. She told him that it was vodka and 7-Up. She said it might taste funny at first, but he would like the way it made him feel. She handed him the glass and propped up the pillows like he was sitting up in bed. He only had one crummy old, lumpy pillow at his house. He only saw that many candles at church and he never tasted vodka and 7-Up and mostly he never saw a lady like a movie star who kissed his lips.

Clint wasn't scared anymore. Now, he was excited. His lower parts told him that. He took a drink and it gave him the shivers. She told him to take a bigger sip and it would taste a lot better. He drank the whole big glass down and it did taste better and he felt really good all of a sudden. His lower part felt good too and he could feel it get bigger. Mrs. G. walked to the dresser, turned on some music and stood at the foot of the bed and kind of danced with her hips swaying as she took off her earrings and necklace. Then she unzipped her dress and let it fall to the floor. She stood there with her black lacey underwear, her garter belt, her black stockings and her shiny black high heels. She turned around real slow for him to look at her. She walked over to him kind of dancing to the music, took his glass, filled it half full and brought it back to him. She stood next to him at the side of the bed and took off her bra and told him "We are going to do this every Saturday and I am going to teach you how to be a man."

The next thing Clint remembered, he was laying on his back and she on her side kissing his neck and his ear. She rubbed his chest as she told him he was the most beautiful boy she had ever seen and when he grows up he was going to be the most handsome man in the world and no woman would be able to resist him.

Clint loved living in those moments. His whole life went away and he got to be someone else. He was with a movie star lady that liked him. She called him baby and he felt powerful. Mrs. G. suddenly got out of bed real fast, put on a bathrobe and told him to get dressed and go downstairs to the family TV room, and the maid would serve him lunch. The lady walked into the bathroom and closed the door hard. He heard the lock click kind of loud. She must have read his mind. He wanted to go in there and do it all over again. It hurt his feelings the way she closed the door and latched it. He felt like she didn't like him anymore.

He dressed and went down the big curled stairs to the family TV room. The maid came into the TV room carrying a tray of food and set it down on the coffee table. She stood there in her gray maid uniform with a white apron and asked "Sir, is there anything else I can get you?" He said "No, thank you" but he was really embarrassed for the maid to have to call him Sir, but he did feel a bit important.

He watched TV and ate the lunch. The maid came back in the room and told him to go and sit on the shoe bench in the foyer and his taxi would be there soon. The taxi came. The maid gave him twenty-five dollars for his work and walked him out to the taxi and gave the driver some money. The maid told him to remember to get on the same bus next Saturday at the same time. The maid called him "young sir." She said to him, "Young Sir, you mustn't tell anyone about your upstairs time. You must never tell. If you do, you can never come back here."

The next week it had snowed for two days. The lady picked him up just like before but in a different new car and she was wearing a different perfume too. Mrs. G. told him that he did a good job last week and she expected him to do a good job today too. He had to shovel a lot of snow and it took him a long time and he was hungry. He rang the bell and the maid let him in. Mrs. G. again nodded at the maid and she went away, and as last week Mrs. G. took him to the shoe bench in the foyer, sat him down, untied his boots, pulled them off, walked him by the hand, and took him up the big wooden curved stairs and told him to get in the shower.

Everything was the same as the week before except Mrs. G. had on a red dress after his shower with red stockings and red high heels. Mrs. G. looked and smiled ever prettier than before. Her different colored dress, red stockings and shoes made him feel special like she was wearing them just for him.

He didn't feel like a little kid anymore. He felt like he was older and smarter. He drank his first drink real fast and as Mrs. G. started to unzip her dress to the music, he asked if he could have another vodka and 7-Up, full to the top. Mrs. G. stopped dancing, frowned at him, made a huff sound, came over to him, took his glass and filled it to the top. She brought the drink to him, kissed his mouth and said "You are so handsome, anything for you, baby, anything you want." That made his lower part grow. She danced back to the foot of the bed, unzipped her dress and let it fall to the floor. She stood still for a minute and blew him a kiss and she had a big smile.

This time, Mrs. G. had on red underwear that was a way lot nicer than the neighbor lady had. It was real pretty and shiny. As

Mrs. G. started to dance, she took off her bra and tossed it to him. She rubbed her hands all over her body and this time she put her fingers in her mouth and put spit on her nipples as she danced. The candlelight on her wet nipples made him dizzy.

When she took all her clothes off, she pulled back the covers and laid on top of him, kissing his face and neck everywhere, she ran her fingers through his hair and called him precious and baby a million times. When they had sex, she whimpered like a little puppy. Clint felt like a king. When they were done, she laid her head on his chest and purred like a kitten. He petted her hair and he told her he loved her. When he said that, she jumped up off the bed, told him to get dressed and went into the bathroom and locked the door. He guessed it made her mad because he said "I love you" and at that moment he decided that he would never say that to anyone, ever again!

Clint went down to the TV room and ate his lunch. When he finished his lunch, the maid came in with Mrs. G. and they both had big shopping bags in their hands. Mrs. G. nodded to the maid. The maid set down the bags, picked up his lunch tray and went away. The bags were marked that they came from real fancy named stores that people had to have a lot of money to go into. Mrs. G. took out a real expensive down jacket and had him stand up to try it on. It fit him perfectly. There were two shirts, two pair of jeans and one pair of cotton lined, corduroy pants. There was a pair of sneakers and new boots with thick wool socks. Two pairs of gloves, one for dress with the jacket and a pair of new choppers and wool lined mittens. As Mrs. G. was showing him all these new clothes, she said he had to wear these new clothes to her house and he could not wear his own clothes there, ever again.

As she gave him the $25.00, she told him to tell his Mom that she bought those clothes for her nephew but they didn't fit him so she gave them to him. She told him to never tell anyone about their upstairs fun. She then pointed to the foyer and said "Take your new clothes and go sit on the shoe bench, until your taxi arrives." He wanted to touch Mrs. G. and kiss her, but she went up the big curved wooden stairs.

Clint sat on the shoe bench and put his new coat on his lap so the maid could not see how much he loved Mrs. G. He sat in the back of the taxi with his mind spinning. He knew he was being bad. He knew he was dancing with the devil, but he didn't care. The lady touched him soft and he was in love with her. He knew she was using him for a toy, but he loved her.

The next few Saturdays were the same except for the different color dresses, nylons, high heels and underwear. He started to understand the dynamics of their upstairs time.

After his shower, he became the boss. As soon as she got up and went into the bathroom, she became the boss again. So it was, for several months, that Mrs. G. picked him up at the bus stop and every time she acted kind of strange, like she didn't know him. When she told him what to do for his chores, she used a stern voice, like a school teacher.

One Saturday, as he was getting dressed after his outside and upstairs chorus, Mrs. G. came out of the bathroom and told him to give the maid his phone number so she could call his Mom and ask her if it was okay if he could come to her house tonight to sit the dogs. Clint said "I didn't know you had dogs." Mrs. G. said, "I do not have any dogs, but it will be our secret." Mrs. G. kissed his lips and said "I will see you tonight baby and it will be a very special, night for you."

The maid called his Mom when he was sitting on the shoe bench. The maid said that the taxi would pick him up at 7:00 and another taxi would take him home before midnight. The maid said, "Thank you Ma'am" to his Mom.

That night the taxi was at his house at 7:00. He got into the taxi and the driver gave him an envelope and said he was to open it now and read the letter. Clint opened the envelope and found $25.00 inside and a letter from Mrs. G. It said the maid would let him in, when he rang the bell. It said he was to call her, Ma'am. He was not to directly look at her and to act shy and uncomfortable when she introduced him to her husband and he must call him, Sir. The letter also said that after they left for the party, the maid would leave too. He was to take a shower and put the clothes on that were in the cabinet under the second sink in the Master Bathroom. There was a big, red lips mark on the bottom of the page, like she kissed the paper with lipstick on. He smiled all the way to Mrs. G.'s house. The taxi driver opened the door for him and told him that he was a very lucky young man. Clint felt really important.

Clint was shocked when he saw the lady and her husband walk down the curved wooden stairs holding hands. She was breathtaking and she belonged on a magazine cover. But what shocked him even more, was her husband. He was really old. His head was bald and real shiny. He had short grey hair on the sides. He was tall and slender, even skinny. He had a lot of wrinkles around his eyes and his chin and neck. The lady introduced Clint to her husband. They shook hands. His handshake was firm but his skin was soft and old. He was wearing a shiny tuxedo with a frilly white shirt and black fancy bow-tie with small black, round buttons, and gold cufflinks on his crisp, starched shirt cuffs. The crease on his pants was sharp. His eyes were smart looking (like he knew all the secrets in the world). Clint could tell that he was in charge of a lot of people. He stood and walked like he was important, like the mayor or someone.

When they and the maid left, he kind of felt small in the great big house all alone. He went upstairs to take a shower, like the letter said. He saw the big glass picture that was always on the dresser and a tall glass of ice on the counter in the bathroom. There was a note that said. "Pour yourself a drink, baby. I will be back soon. I love you!" There was a big kiss mark on the note. Just like on the bottom of the letter the Taxi driver gave him.

The note scared him. He thought "What if Mr. G. had to use the bathroom and saw the note? He will kill me!" Clint poured a full glass of mixed up vodka and 7-Up and drank it down fast, as he thought about looking at Mr. G.'s smart eyes that said he knew all the secrets in the world. "Did he already know about me and

Mrs. G.?" The thought of that, gave him worse shivers than drinking the vodka and 7-Up. He took his shower and got out the new clothes from under the sink.

Clint put on the clothes as he poured himself another drink. He stood in the front of all the mirrors and stared at himself. He looked older and smarter. He looked like he was rich. He liked looking that way. He had on a white shirt with a starched collar and cuffs, shiny silver/gray slacks, a silver and black diamond pattern V-neck sweater and brand new, black loafers with tassels on them. The fabric of the shirt and slacks were real smooth and looked expensive. The crease on the slacks was just as sharp as Mr. G.'s tuxedo pants. The shoes smelled even better than the shoes he polished at Mac's shoe repair store.

He stood and posed in front of the mirrors for a long time, looking at himself holding the drink glass. He liked what he saw. He felt grown up. He felt like he was in in charge of everything.

Clint had never seen the whole house. There were a lot of rooms with big heavy wooden doors. Each door had big brass flipper door knobs. One room had two great big wooden doors, and each door had a flipper door knob. All the doors were a red and brown color. He went into the room with the two red and brown wooden doors. In that room was a giant desk the same color of the doors with a really big red and brown leather chair with brass tacks on it. It looked like the kind of chair that the President or the Pope would sit in. He knew he had to sit in that chair. He had never seen a chair with wheels on it and it spun around too! As he sat down in the chair he put his drink glass on the desk.

He spun around and around in the husband's chair. There were a lot of wood bookcases all the same color as the doors and desk. All the books were the same color and the bindings were lettered and numbered in gold. It made him feel important being in that room. On one side of the room were all the books that could make you smart. The other wall was full of built in wood gun cabinets full of all kinds of shiny nice guns. At the back of the room was a big bar that took up the whole wall. He took his empty glass off the desk and went to get some vodka. The whole back wall had mirrors on it with glass shelves filled with liquor. All kinds of liquor. He wanted to find vodka but he didn't know how to spell vodka. First he looked at all the clear colored bottles where the first letter started with a V. Clint found a clear colored bottle that had a V on it, took off the cap and smelled it. It smelled pretty bad but he thought it to be the right one. He didn't know how to mix a drink or how much vodka and 7-Up to put in it. He poured three quarters vodka and the rest was 7-Up.

It tasted real strong, like pine needles smelled like. Mrs. G.'s vodka and 7-Up tasted a lot better. But this drink made his belly warm up a lot faster. He walked around and looked at all the guns with his already almost half empty vodka and 7-Up. He liked the shivers that came from the vodka.

There were a whole bunch of wooden doors on the upstairs. One big bedroom had a big silver pistol on the nightstand. It gave him the creeps. Another room was filled with glass cases of dolls that looked like real baby's, and a whole bunch of funny colored over-sized Easter eggs cut in half, with little people and animals inside of them. All the cabinets were full of that stuff. He thought it looked dumb.

Clint decided that he had seen enough of the upstairs. As he was walking down the curved staircase with shiny wood steps, his stomach felt sick. He started to run down the steps. He knew he was going to throw up. His new black leather loafers with leather soles caused him to slip and fall down the rest of the stairs. His drink fell out of his hand. The glass smashed and there was vodka all over the place, and as he landed on the marble floor, he threw up.

It was a big mess. He found a bunch of towels in a kitchen drawer. As he started to clean everything up, the vomit smell made him vomit again. It took him a while to get the puke and glass and vodka all cleaned up. He had a little puke on his shoes but he didn't get any vodka or puke on his new clothes. He was a little bit sweaty by the time he put the towels in the trash can in the garage.

As he turned away from the trash can, to go back in the house, the garage door started to open. "Oh shit! They're home!" He ran over to the vomit spot to make sure he had gotten everything cleaned up. It looked okay so he ran into the family living room, turned on the TV and sat on the couch real fast so they would think he was just watching TV.

Mrs. G. called his name real loud from the garage. He thought she found the puke towels in the trash. He knew he was going to be in big trouble. He went to the garage and Mrs. G. told him, that her husband had too much to drink and for Clint to help him in the house, up the stairs and put him in his bed. Mr. G. didn't seem to be too drunk to not be able to walk by himself to the bedroom. He didn't even smell bad, like his dad used to.

As he was helping Mr. G. up the stairs, Mrs. G. hollered to him that his bedroom was at the far end of the hall and to make sure that he got undressed, and for him to put the covers over him. It came to him quickly, how Mrs. G. dared to leave him that note on the bathroom counter that called him baby and said "I love you" with a kiss mark on it. They each had their own bedrooms with their very own bathrooms! "Man, this is a really big house!" He felt a lot better knowing that Mr. G. didn't have to use her bathroom, so he could not have seen the note and he wasn't afraid of the big silver gun on his nightstand. But he knew he had to be careful with his wife. Clint helped Mr. G. take off his tuxedo jacket as Mr. G. untied his bow tie. Mr. G. sat down hard on the bed and told him to get his billfold out of the inside pocket of his coat. Clint took it out and handed it to him. He never saw a wallet that looked like that before.

It wasn't the fold up kind, like everyone carried in their back pocket. It looked like a fancy checkbook but a lot better. Mr. G. opened up his wallet, took out and handed Clint, a fifty-dollar bill. He had kind of a funny smile when he said "This is a special gift for being so nice to my wife." Clint gulped as he figured out what was going on with Mr. and Ms. G. He glanced at the gun to make sure it was still on the nightstand.

Mr. G. told him to please come to his house and help his wife any time she needed him to. He fell back on the bed and passed out. Clint tried to wake him up to take his clothes off, but he would not wake up. Clint wasn't about to help him undress, that was for sure! As he was leaving Mr. G.'s bedroom, he took one last glance at the silver gun on the nightstand, as he turned off the light switch. He was pretty sure now, that Mr. G. wasn't going to shoot him as he closed his bedroom door.

Clint looked in Ms. G.'s bedroom but she was not there. He went down the long curvy stairs to find Mrs. G. so she could call a taxi for him. There was a door a little bit open with light shining through, into the dark hallway. When he opened the door, Mrs. G. was laying on top of a red felt pool table, she was wearing shiny, yellow underwear. She was kind of like a snake, all slithering around. She was like crazy as she told him to undress, all the while talking through her clenched teeth. All the other times she was soft and purred like a kitten. But not this time. This time she grunted a lot and kept saying filthy words. She was like another person now, and he didn't like her. She seemed mean.

Clint got dressed and went out to sit on the shoe bench to wait for the taxi. Mrs. G. came out of the pool table room fully dressed. She handed him two twenty-dollar bills. Clint told her that her husband had already paid him. She said "The money he gave you, was because he likes how you take such good care of me."

And, as all of the other times, he was sternly warned to not tell anyone about what they did or the special money he was given.

Mrs. G. took his hand and he stood up. She put her hand in the middle of his shoulders, opened the front door and gave him a light shove as she said "You need to wait for the taxi out there," and closed the door hard, he heard the lock latch and the porch light went out.

Clint's mind raced and raced, more than ever before, as he sat in the back seat of the taxi. He laid awake that whole night through to put everything together in his mind. He was like a police guy trying to solve a crime. He knew all the facts. He just had to make sense of it all. First off, the lady was mean and crazy. She only had sex with him so she could screw up his young mind. Getting in the car at the bus stop, she was like the boss. In the bedroom she had to prove her powers. She faked being nice to disarm him and let him think he was safe and loved. It was all a set-up so she could tell him to wait outside in the dark cold winter night. She hated him and she wanted to ruin him. She wanted to make boys and men feel like shit. And the sooner she could get to afflict a young man the longer his life was to suffer. That is why she wanted a young boy like him. She paid him a lot of money to shovel snow. But the money really said "I own you and I am going to destroy you."

Secondly, he had heard that old men were not very good at sex. Mr. G. had to have known about their sex and he must have thought it was okay. Those two had a deal. He would let her have sex with boys, as long as she did not leave him. He needed her to make him look good. They wanted young boys so she couldn't run off with them, like she might with a grown up man. He wondered about how many other young boys they were doing this to. However, he really didn't much care. He was getting what he wanted. Mostly he wanted the money and the, vodka-7's. The vodka-7's the very most.

Clint hated her and felt sorry for him. As a man in the bedroom, he was a failure, so he had to buy his wife. She was a gold digger and they both thought he was a stupid little boy. He had to be smart about this deal. He had to pretend that he didn't hate her so he could get what he wanted.

Clint knew that he wasn't very smart in school. He never listened, he never studied and he got mostly F's and a few D's.

But in life, he was really smart. He could easily figure people out. He was smarter than big people and he was just a little kid. It was like he was a spy and tricking everyone. Clint smiled and laughed a lot for several days. It was going to be fun acting like a dumb little kid. He would fool them both, and get paid for it!

When Clint got in the car that next Saturday, he could see

the lady was mad. She said he was never to go into her husband's office, ever again. She said there was a water ring stain on his desk and he had left his vodka bottle and 7-Up bottle on the bar. She just kept bitching and said the maid had found the broken glass and puke clean up towels in the trash. "It made the whole garage stink!" She just kept bitching, and he loved it!

It had snowed the night before and as they pulled into the driveway she told him to get out of the car and get busy shoveling the driveway and sidewalk.

Clint decided he was going to play a card that he wasn't totally sure he had been dealt, but he was going to try it.

He got out of her car, didn't say a word and started to walk down the driveway toward the road. She shouted "Where are you going?" He didn't turn, he just kept walking and said over his shoulder "I am going home. Shovel your own fucking snow."

She ran up to him saying "Please don't go. Please don't go." She was crying and kept kissing his hands.

Clint knew he had just hit a grand-slam! She begged him to come into the house. He told her that he wasn't going to shovel snow or do anything else. He told her he would give her sex, but he wanted vodka and $30.00 each time. He also wanted two packs of Camel straights (non-filters cigarettes) and two pints of vodka to take home, every time he came there. His final demand was that she was not to ever again, call him Clint. She could only call him Flanagan. Not Mr. Flanagan, just Flanagan. She eagerly said yes to everything.

Now that he knew that she didn't love him and was just trying to push him around, the shower towels didn't feel so soft, the bed clothes no longer smelled fresh or felt like they once did. He didn't care about how pretty she was. He didn't care about her perfume, her dress, her underwear or about her dancing. He did care a little bit about the sex (not for her, just for him). He sat in the bed propped up with all those pillows and a vodka 7-Up and he just smiled at her. She thought he was having fun and really liked her. All he wanted was the Vodka, the cigarettes, and the money.

66

He wasn't screwing her for fun. He was now, on the job!

The early summer of 1960 Clint turned 12 years old. He had been doing the Saturday, 'chores' and periodic Friday night dog sitting thing for a year and a half. He was disgusted with himself and with them. The whole thing made him feel dirty. He just wanted to be a little kid again. He would miss all of the bedroom stuff and mostly he would miss the way she made him feel, even for just a few hours a week. It wasn't about feeling empowered or in charge. He would miss feeling loved, even knowing that it was fake. He would miss the security he felt in that warm bed with her warm and soft skin that made all the bad things in his life, go away. When he was with her or even thought about being with her, he was no longer a poor, dumb little kid that always felt unwanted and scared. Those times took his sadness away. He thought maybe he wouldn't ever have to hide out anymore. Maybe he could be someone different.

Clint's Mom had the new baby, his name was Stevie but Clint didn't talk to him. He didn't want to like Stevie, because if he did, he would have to take care of him. He pretended the new baby didn't live there.

Clint had saved most of the money he earned. He decided that he was going to trout fish for the whole summer and try to forget about Mr. and Mrs. G. and the rest of the entire world.

Clint bought a new 'Harnell' fly fishing rod, a 'Garcia' automatic fly reel and a fishing vest with a lot of pockets. He bought a woven reed fishing creel and hip waders. The guy at the fishing and hunting store had a fishing TV show on Sunday nights, and he was famous! The TV fishing show guy, helped him buy all the stuff to fill all the pockets of his new fishing vest. He rode the city bus to the Baker River to fish. Sometimes he hitched a ride further up the South Shore to fish on other rivers. For a little kid, he was a pretty good fisherman. He almost always got his limit of trout that was 10 trout a day.

He spent as much time fishing as he could except for the times his Mom made him babysit Petey. He spent the entire summer trying to forget about Mrs. G., the sex and the vodka. It was hard not to miss her, he was lonely at first, just like before. But, at least he finally had an idea of how good, being loved felt like.

Chapter 8 "FINDING A NEW LIFE"

Clint's Dad was sober for a while. He brought home several big white paper bags of chocolate candy from the candy store. He said it helped him not to drink beer and stuff. Dad brought home a lot of drunk guys. He would make the drunk guys eat a bunch of sandwiches, drink orange juice and drink a lot of coffee. Then he made them sit in the "stinky chair" and go to sleep. The boys' called it the "stinky chair" because those drunk guys would mess their pants and throw up on the chair. When the boys' got in real trouble, instead of standing in the corner, like they were used to, they now were made to sit in the 'stinky chair,' for a long time. They had lots of food to eat, now that Dad didn't spend all his money on getting drunk.

Dad would take Donnie and Clint to the AA club on Saturday mornings to get them out of Mom's hair. Dad played, "Hearts" with a bunch of other AA guys. The boys' got to play bumper pool and Ping-Pong. It was a lot of fun. When the men came out of the card room to use the bathroom they would go to the candy machine across the hall from the men's room. The boys could hear them put the coins in the candy machine and pull the knobs. The men would walk by the boys' and toss a candy bar on the table for each of them and say "Don't tell your old man." Each one of those card guys bought them candy bars. It was fun. They were really nice men.

During the late summer, big semi-trucks would come to the truck stop across the street from the boy's house. A lot of those trucks didn't have tops on them. They were full of corn-on-the-cob, tomatoes, potatoes, watermelons, and cantaloupes. The truck drivers would go into the restaurant and the Flanagan boy's would climb up in the truck and toss the stuff down to a couple of neighbor boys who had several gunnysacks that the boy's hid in some bushes, just for those occasions. First, they went to the old, poor people's houses in the neighborhood and gave them some food. They were grateful. They, of course, didn't know where they got all that food, but they surely knew that the boys weren't farmers. Everyone loved those old people in the neighborhood. The kids shoveled the snow from their walks and mowed their lawns for free and didn't let anyone mess with them. The leftover stuff they took home. They told their Mom that "We helped the truckers wash their trucks and they paid us in food." Mom would grab their hands and see the ground in dirt on their palms and would just shake her head, and say thank you.

Clint liked being a nice boy and helping people out, but at almost the same time he hated people. The first time he hit a kid for no reason was a turning point in his life. He was walking down Central Avenue. Just as he was walking under the railroad trestle there was a boy walking towards him. Clint never saw him before. He was bigger than Clint and was wearing much nicer clothes than him. He doesn't know what made him do it, but as they were about to pass, he hit him on the chin. The kid went down fast and was out cold. Clint's first instinct was to kneel down to help him. Then as he stood over him, he wanted to kick him in the head and make him bleed. Instead, he just turned and walked away. He felt the wolfish grin on his face and he really liked what he just did. It made him feel good, to hit people. From that day forward he loved to hit people. He fought several times each week. Most of the boys wouldn't fight back. Donnie said he had a crazy look on his face and had like sparks coming out of his eyes. The kids were scared that he would kill them if they tried to fight him back. Clint liked that, a lot!

Clint liked seeing the fear on their faces. He liked to see the older boys run away from him. He felt like he was somebody. He joined a gang called the "Venice Street Vipers." There were about 40 kids in the gang and 10 of them were big, tough guys, and even some had cars. They would go downtown every night and rumble. Clint and 'Little Stevie' were two of the smallest guys in the gang, but they were fearless. The big guys carried bats, chains, knives, and one guy even carried a gun. They let Clint and Little Stevie walk up front. They punched every kid they saw on the street. If a kid was really big they both hit him. Then the big guys took over. That was a good time. Clint got his ass kicked a few times, but always went back to even the score later. At the same time, he wanted to be a good kid. He never knew who would come out of him at any given time.

Clint, Donnie and a few other guys from the neighborhood, liked to go to the West Park, Y.M.C.A. You could swim, play pool, and Ping-Pong for 15 cents for the whole day. The manager's name was Bill. He was a really nice guy. A big, big man that you knew you dared, not to piss him off. One day Clint was putting his arm up the front chute of the candy machine, as he oftentimes did, to pull out candy bars and chips for free. But this time he got his arm stuck in the machine and could not get it out. 'Big Bill' put the key in the machine to open the door to get his arm out, but he still could not get his arm out. Big Bill, called the Fire Department. Clint knew he was in some deep shit now! The Cops and the Fire Dept. guys showed up. They were cracking jokes, but his arm hurt and he knew he was never going to be allowed back to the "Y" and the cops were going to lock him up. They had to saw and hammer the machine apart. It took a long time. More cops came and handcuffed Donnie, Little Stevie, his brother Bobbie, and the minute the fire guys got his arm out of the candy machine, the cops handcuffed him too. Big Bill, took them in his office and made them give him their phone numbers. Big Bill, called everyone's parents. Big bill told them they had to come there right now!

The cops made the boys' sit in the lobby until their parents got there. When Clint's Dad got there, he looked really pissed. The cops knew Dad and they all shook hands. Then Big Bill, came out of his office and he knew Dad too! They shook hands and Dad asked "What have my two darling little knuckleheads done this time?" Big Bill, took Dad and two of the cops into his office. They were laughing real loud. It didn't look good for the boys. One cop came out of Big Bill's office and stood in front of them, took out his night stick, and started to twirl it on a string. The other cop that was watching them took out his night stick and kept slapping the palm of his other hand. The boys' figured they were in for a beating and their Dads' were going to let the cops beat the crap out of them. It seemed like a long time that those cops stood there with big smiles and didn't say anything. They just kept smiling, twirling and slapping. Finally, they looked at each other and nodded. They put their nightsticks in their belt rings with a loud pop! The cops grabbed the boys by the front of their shirts, lifted them out of their chairs and shouted "On your feet!"

The cops took them to the wall next to Big Bill's office. The door was open and he saw his Dad, Big Bill and a cop, all were smoking cigars. The cops made the boys' put their foreheads on the wall and made them step back so their body weight was supported by their necks. First the cop took off Clint's handcuffs and grabbed his arm and shoved him into Big Bill's office. They did the same to Donnie. Big Bill's office was full of cigar smoke and it really stunk. Big Bill said they had to sell salt water taffy for the Y.M.C.A. to pay for a new machine. He then gave them free, one year passes to the 'Y.' Donnie and he sold more salt water taffy than any other kids in the whole city! Big Bill gave them free passes for a Y.M.C.A summer camp. It was a nice place; they were there for a week.

In Clint's neighborhood there was a drug store, a dentist that had his office in his house, the 'Corner Dairy Bar' (soda fountain with lots of pinball machines), a Grocery Store, a Laundromat, an 'A&W', a junk store (that sold used auto parts too) and a 'Watkins' store and, of course, the truck stop.

Clint's Mom sent him to the drug store a lot, to get her and Donnie's pills. The neighborhood dentist had an office on the enclosed front porch of his house. Clint had a lot of cavities and holes in his teeth. He got a lot of abscesses and most of the time, the dentist would pull the tooth out. His face hurt a lot from the swelling and the puss tasted really bad. Mom would give him eight dollars. He walked the seven blocks to the dentist, to get the tooth pulled out, and walked back home.

The Corner Dairy Bar was a bad-ass hangout. If you didn't want to fight you didn't go, there. Clint hung out there a lot. The place was full of pinball machines. You had to buy a coke or a burger or ice cream, to stay there. At 12 years old, he was the youngest kid there and they all knew, he would fight anyone. He carried two weapons: a 'church key' and a telescoping car antenna. The 'church key' was pointed and curved and was used to open beer and pop cans. He used it to put it into the corner of a boy's mouth, once he had him down and rip his face open. The car antenna was good for slashing a guy's face or anywhere else. You could whip a guy in the leg and it would tear his jeans open, and still put a gash in his leg. He was still a quiet kid but got a lot of respect. But Clint knew those bigger boys didn't respect him, they feared him, and that was just fine with him. He liked looking the bigger and older guys square in the eyes and not say anything. Their faces said "Yeah, I know you can kick my ass and hurt me" and they would turn away. He loved that power. He loved making them feel his pain and his fear that he had as a little kid. He wanted to beat the shit out of the whole world.

Cal Thompson had a corner grocery store five blocks from their house. He gave everyone credit. Each neighbor had their own credit book with their name on it. The whole back wall behind the counter was stacked with credit books. Clint's Mom would give him a note for cigarettes (23 cents a pack) and usually bread and stuff. A few times Cal said "No more credit." Cal was really a nice guy. Clint told Cal that Mom was out of cigarettes and she was real crabby. Clint promised he would bring him 23 cents later that day. Cal would always smile at him and say "I know you will." That always made Clint feel good. He was glad when they were out of credit and Cal would trust him to bring him his 23 cents, and he always did. He would bring Mom home her cigarettes and walk to another, better, neighborhood and steal hubcaps and sell them to the guy who had the junk store and sold used auto parts. The junk man would give him a dollar a hub cap. He always stole all four.

As soon as Clint got the four dollars for the hubcaps he would go back to Cal Thompsons's corner store, pay Cal the 23 cents and say "Oh yeah, my Dad wants a pack of Camel straights (non-filters)." Clint also paid $2.00 on their bill. He would walk out of Cal's store, open the pack, light one of the cigarettes with his Zippo chrome lighter, and roll that pack in the left sleeve of his white t-shirt. The "American Graffiti" guys had nothing on him. He would go to the Corner Dairy Bar and blow the rest of the four dollars that he got from the parts guy on pinball and sodas.

Clint and Donnie hated the Laundromat that was four blocks away. Mom used the community washing machine in the basement of their apartment building. But there was no dryer. So the boy's had to carry giant, cardboard box's full of wet clothes all the way to the Laundromat, sit there for hours and carry them back home. Winter time was the worst, they would have to walk thru snow drifts and icy streets with the heavy wet laundry.

The Watkins Store guy's name was Tom. He sold all kinds of hair stuff, cleaning supplies and brushes. Tom's store was small and only open a few hours a day because he spent the rest of the day selling door-to-door with his catalogues and he would bring people the stuff they bought the next day. Clint asked Tom if he could help him sell stuff. Tom gave him a bottle of hair shampoo and a bottle of conditioner. The shampoo was 65 cents and the conditioner was 75 cents. Tom promised to pay him 10 cents commission on each bottle he sold. Clint was back to Tom's store to get more bottles in the first half-hour since he had left the store. Tom started laughing at him and told him the bottles were just to show people. He said he would wear his shoes out if he had to walk back and forth after each sale. Tom gave him an "order book" and showed him how to fill it out. Clint collected the money for the stuff he sold, give the customer a receipt and Tom would deliver the goods the following day. In one month, Clint made thirty dollars. That's three hundred bottles of shampoo and conditioner!

Tom was proud of him, and Clint was proud of himself. Then, he hit the jackpot!

Fall was coming and the Watkins Company was selling, 'Currier & Ives' boxes of Christmas cards. Tom said the boxes of fifty cards sold for two dollars. Tom said if he could carry the cards in an old newspaper-boy sack, he would pay him 15 cents for each box he sold, if he didn't have to deliver them. The old paperboy bag carried 20 boxes of cards and Clint carried 3 boxes in his hands. He was back to the Watkins Store in less than two hours, his hands and his bag were empty. Tom couldn't stop shaking his hand. Tom said he was going to order a lot more Christmas cards and he would pay him an extra dollar for each case of 24 boxes he sold. Clint sold 400 boxes of Christmas cards. Tom shook his hand a lot and paid him all his money. Tom got sick with cancer and was closing the store. One day, Tom told him to take one of everything he had in the store and to put them in boxes. There was a lot of stuff. Tom and he put all those boxes in his car. Tom told him to get in his car and asked him where he lived.

Tom drove to Clint's house and said all the stuff was for his Mom. They made a lot of trips carrying that stuff up the stairs. Tom told his Mom that Clint was the greatest kid he had ever known. Tom told Mom that he was "gifted" and a natural salesman. Mom cried and smiled a lot and thanked Tom a lot. Clint went to see Tom at his store a few days later. The store was closed. He could see that everything in the store was gone. Clint never saw Tom again. Tom was a nice man. Tom made him feel like a good kid. Clint sold so much stuff, so that Tom would like him and so that he could show Tom that he liked him too.

Clint bought some real nice stuff for Christmas for his family with the money Tom paid him. He was proud to buy his Dad a new hunting knife. He always felt ashamed for taking his Dad's good hunting knife to kill those boys with. He bought his Mom a real nice scarf and matching gloves and some fancy handkerchiefs. He bought his brothers some candy. It was a nice

Christmas. He can only remember that they went to the woods and cut down a real Christmas tree. They had to put a lot of tinsel on the tree because it was kind of skinny, and there were a lot more lights on it that year and some of them even flashed on and off. The blue Ford Salvation Army station wagon didn't have to come.

Clint's Mom, had a Dad, a Mom, one Sister and two Brothers. Clint didn't like his Grandpa. He looked like a weasel, he was so small and short that he had to wear boy size clothes and shoes. He used a loud voice to sound tough, but Clint thought he was a sissy. His Grandpa didn't like kids. They didn't see him any time of year but during deer hunting season. Grandpa was afraid of getting lost in the woods so he sat on the side of a road all day and waited for a deer to cross the road. Everyone made fun of him. He was married to a real nice woman. Her name was Ellen, but Clint called her "E". E was real pretty, real clean and wore nice clothes and had a soft voice. E, always brought the boys' birthday presents (always shirts) and Christmas presents (always pajamas). The gifts were always wrapped with real nice paper. In the summertime, E took them all, to the end of Pine Point where there was an amusement park. They spent the whole day there. They rode all the rides and ate hot dogs, popcorn, and cotton candy. E always bought them all cowboy hats and those pinwheel guys. Grandpa and E moved seven blocks straight up the hill from them.

When it snowed Clint would walk up those seven blocks (12 degrees' steep) and shovel out the sidewalks and driveway and street. It took most of the day and the wind off the lake made it snot-running cold. E, would call him in for hot chocolate and cookies so he could warm up. E, gave him a pack of cigarettes and tried to pay him $15.00 for shoveling. Each time Clint would always refuse the money, telling E "You buy us Christmas presents and Birthday presents and take us to the carnival and amusement park all the time. I cannot take your money." E said he couldn't tell anyone that she let him smoke at the kitchen table as they drank their hot chocolate. It was a fun secret. They were buddies.

When Clint was 13 years old, E got bone cancer. She was in the hospital and in a lot of pain. He visited E every day for three weeks. Each visit, E would ask "How is my special young man?" Their visits were usually brief as E was in a lot of pain and needed rest. As he left after each visit he would kiss E on the forehead and say, "Take care of my special girl." E would say, "You're a fine young man." He was sad when E died. No one told him. He went to her hospital room and her bed was empty. He asked a nurse where E was. The nurse said "She is gone." As he started to ask where she went, the nurse started to cry and put her arms around him.

To this very day, Clint uses E as a true measure as to what a true friend and a real woman should be. He still carries the mantra: "If she isn't like E - she isn't for me." As they drank hot chocolate and smoked cigarettes at the kitchen table, E talked to him as a friend, not as a dumb little kid. He could ask and tell her anything. E, was the only adult that he ever trusted. To this day, he is grateful that he visited E, every day. He had to show her that she was special to him. She had to know that they were Pal's.

Clint's Dad had no parents. The truth of that comes later. Dad had two sisters and a younger brother, named Billy. One summer day, Dad was going to cut Clint's hair. Dad had electric barber clippers. They had an old high chair and Dad would put the kitchen table extender across the arms of the high chair and make them sit on it so he could cut their hair. He hated Dad cutting his hair. Dad was about to cut his hair when a man knocked on their door. Clint opened the door and there was a man standing there that looked just like his Dad! It was his younger brother, Billy. Dad and Billy had not seen each other since they were little kids. Clint was pretty sure that he was going to get a pass on the haircut that day. After they talked for a while, Billy asked "What the hell is that for?" As he pointed to the baby high chair with the table leaf on it. Dad said he was about to give Clint a haircut. Billy said he could give him a better haircut than Dad could. They decided to each take one side of Clint's head to see who could give the best haircut. Clint didn't like that. When they finished they got into

77

Billy's car and they took Clint to a barber. Billy looked a lot like Dad but Billy smiled a lot more. Billy was pretty rich. He owned a bunch of fast food restaurants in California. Billy took Donnie and him downtown to goof off.

They went to Woolworths 5 and 10 cent store. They had a big long soda fountain. They ate a lot of ice cream. Billy got them squirt guns and they squirted each other the rest of the day. Billy took them to a lot of different places for the next two days. Billy talked to everyone they saw. Billy was like a TV game show guy. He made talking to strangers seem really easy for him. Everyone Billy said hello to, said hi back. Billy made everyone smile. Clint decided that he would be just like Billy when he got bigger. He wanted everyone he saw, to like him too!

Dad's sister's name was Doris. She lived in California, just a few miles from Billy. Doris was real pretty and people liked her a lot, just like Billy. Doris and her husband Victor and their kids were rich, just like Billy. They came to see them that same summer and for the next several summers. Every year they came in a brand new, big Lincoln. Clint felt bad because, although they had lots of food now, they were still pretty poor. The Mom and Dad and the kids stayed in a real nice hotel when they came to visit. They had four kids. The three younger kids were a lot of fun and they all really liked each other and their Mom and Dad. They were always joking with each other. They never got mad at anyone. The oldest was a girl. She was smart, sweet and beautiful. She was Clint's age. The first time he ever saw her, she made his knees weak and he was ashamed of himself. Not that they were cousins and he thought she was pretty, but that he was dumb and poor.

Her family had been on trips all over the world, gone to all the rock-n-roll concerts, and Disneyland. They were real nice and never acted like they were better than him, but Clint knew, that they were better than him. The only time he ever left town was to go hunting or fishing, and not more than 30 miles away. He hated his life. He hated always feeling that people were better than him.

Chapter 9 "LEADING THE VIPERS"

Clint had very little memory from age 12 to 13. He hated school. He went to Barkers Jr. High School. Barkers Park was right next to the school. He walked the eight blocks to Barkers Park. They (the gang) always met at the pavilion before school to smoke. The 'Venice Street Vipers', hung out at the back of the Pavilion. They all wore red jackets. The 'Heights' was a gang from Brooklyn Heights. They smoked at the front of the Pavilion. They all wore black jackets. The Pavilion was a big stone (like castles were made of) building. The front of the Pavilion had a big stage for bands to play on in the summer. All the fights were on the stage. If you wanted to fight a guy you said "Meet me in the Pavilion after school." A lot of kids came to see the fights. If the guy didn't show up for the fight, you kicked his ass in the hallway the next day. In junior high school you had to cover your books with oil cloth. The poor kids got to use paper bags. Of course, Clint had to use paper bags. Everyone in school could see that he was poor, he hated that. The kids were from several different neighborhoods. Some kids wore real nice clothes and their parents would drive them to school in brand new cars. Those were the guys Clint always wanted to fight. All the girls liked to see him fight but he could tell they were afraid of him. He always said hi to the pretty rich girls but they mostly just said, 'hi' back, but never smiled at him. He knew he was too hard and mean for them. There were a lot of house parties that he heard about but no one ever invited him. They must have been afraid he would start a fight and break up their houses or start a fight with their Dad's. He acted like he didn't care but it made him feel like an outcast. So he fought even more. He made the rich, pansies give him their lunch money so he could buy cigarettes. He liked taking their money away from them, not so much so as he could buy cigarettes but to see the fear on the sissy's faces. After they gave him their money he would still slap them hard in the face and knock their books out of their hands. He liked being a bully. He got to show these rich pricks that they weren't better than him.

Clint never talked in school. Most times he put his head down on his desk for the whole period. The teachers never bothered him. They were afraid of him. One day a teacher caught him in the study hall (in the auditorium) smoking a cigarette behind the curtains of the stage. The teacher grabbed him and took his cigarettes out of his shirt pocket. He started to pull Clint by the arm to take him to the school detention office. Clint punched the teacher in the face, twice. His nose started to bleed and as the teacher started to run down the hallway, Clint tore the teacher's shirt pocket off to take his cigarettes back as the teacher ran down the hallway hollering for help. There were a lot of blood spots on the floor. Clint was laughing. The detention counselor was a huge guy, the kids all called him, 'Lurch,' like the guy from the 'Adams Family' (TV show). Lurch came running out of his office and grabbed Clint and twisted his arm behind his back. Lurch, took him to his office and he threw him in a chair and said he was going to call the Cops. Clint told him that his gang was a lot bigger than all the teachers at the school and if he called the Cops that they would burn down every teacher's house that night, starting with his. Lurch said he was suspended for one week. Clint stood up and said "Fuck you, see you tomorrow." He turned and punched a hole in the wall, turned back toward Lurch and smiled. He lit a cigarette in his office, walked out and blew smoke rings as he walked down the hall and laughed again when he saw the blood drops on the floor.

The next day he went to school and he went up and down the halls looking for teachers, to dare them to start some shit with him. Every teacher he saw looked at him and turned their heads away, real fast. He went to all his classes and none of his teachers would look at him. In every class he would tap his pencil on his desk real loud but the teachers didn't say anything. They all got his message. Nobody, teachers or students, ever screwed with him, ever again. He got really bored with seeing kids avoiding him. He felt more and more alone. He started hating himself. He quit making the sissies give him their lunch money. He even quit swearing at everyone. But everyone still seemed afraid of him.

One day, he heard a couple of the Heights' guys say they were going to beat the shit out of a couple of Jock guys and rape their bitch, girlfriends. The Jocks had called the cops on one of their 'Heights' buddies for stealing a car and now their buddy was in jail. The girls were both cheerleaders and the 'Heights' were going to get them after school in the girl's locker room. Clint hid in the janitor's closet across the hall from the girl's locker room. The janitor's closet door had wooden vents on it so he could see the door to the girl's locker room. Two 'Heights' guys (he could tell by their black jackets) ran into the girl's locker room. Clint ran out of the closet and could hear girls screaming for help. The 'Heights' had the two girls by the hair and had already torn their blouses open. He grabbed one guy and slammed him into a wall face first. His face exploded in blood. He slid down the wall leaving a big smear of blood. He was knocked out. Clint kicked the other guy in the face and he went down fast. He kept saying, "No more, no more." A bunch of teachers came in, saw the girls and thought Clint had torn off their blouses and beat them up. He just stood there and didn't say anything. The cheerleaders told everyone that he helped them. The teachers looked at him as if to say "I can't believe that you would help anyone." The cops came and took those guys to jail. They asked Clint a few questions and told him to go home. The school principle, Lurch, and a lady teacher walked him down the hall to the doors. Lurch put his hand out to shake hands and said "Thank you, Mister Flanagan." The school principle and the lady teacher told him he was a hero, and both said "Thank you."

As Clint walked home that day, he felt really sad for all the people he scared and beat up. He was sick of it and sick of himself. He vowed to never beat anyone up ever again. No more hateful looks, no more threats... He was done with it all. No more! He just had one more thing to do.

Clint went to the, 'Corner Dairy Bar' and it was full of

81

kids. He walked over to the juke box, pulled it away from the wall, and unplugged it. Everyone stopped what they were doing and it got real quiet. He told everyone to bring chains, bats and blades to the Pavilion in the morning; "We are going to wipe out the 'Heights.' He told them what happened at school. The kids were really pissed off, they went into a frenzy and started to chant "Kill those fucking Heights."

The next morning every guy in the gang was there at the Pavilion, with their weapons. There were a lot of other guys from school not in the gang and they had bats and chains too. He told everyone to stay real quiet and they did. There were at least 50 guys there. He put 20 guys on each side of the pavilion. He told the guys that when he walked around to the front of the Pavilion with the rest of the guys he was going to push through the crowd of 'Heights' and he and the guys were going to get up on the stage. The guys on each side of the Pavilion would walk out and surround the 'Heights' and jiggle their chains real loud.

The 'Heights' were scared shitless. Clint held his hand up and told everyone to shut up. It got as quiet as the, 'Corner Dairy Bar' was, when he unplugged the juke box. Clint told the 'Heights,' that they could never fight anyone anymore and if they ever wore a black jacket again or ever came to the Pavilion again that, 'The Vipers' were going to cut them all, like a fish. It was winter and he made them all take off their jackets and throw them on the ground in the snow. He told them they had 10 seconds to get into the school or we would kill them where they stood. Those kids ran their asses off toward the school. 'The Vipers', sliced up all their jackets, put them in a big pile and they all pissed on them.

That day in school was the weirdest day in his life. Word was getting around fast of what he did the day before and what, 'The Vipers' did to the 'Heights' that morning. By lunch time a whole bunch of kids came to the pavilion to hang out with, 'The Vipers.' There were a lot of kids that they had never seen at the park before. Some of the guys told a bunch of kids about their slicing up the 'Heights' jackets and pissing on them. The 'Vipers' were all standing around the pile of pissed-on jackets, smoking laughing and making jokes. It was like a big party. A few teachers even came to see the pile of black pissed-on jackets. Lurch came to the Pavilion too. Lurch said "Well done boys, well done." and walked away laughing.

A real nice and pretty girl walked up to Clint, (who he always thought was too good to ever talk to him) and said she wished she was a boy so she could pee on these jackets too! She asked him if he wanted to come to her house after school and have a coke and he could meet her Mom. Clint got real embarrassed and said thank you but he had to get back home, right after school.

After school, Clint went to the 'Corner Dairy Bar.' There were more kids there that day, than ever before. It was a big place but he could hardly get in the door. All these kids were slapping him on the back, telling him he was, and 'neat' and 'keen'. 'Pat', the owner of the Corner Dairy Bar, came around the counter with a big smile on his face. Pat never smiled, at anyone. Pat handed him a glass of coke and a plate with a burger and fries. He made some kids get out of a booth and said "This booth is reserved for Clint." Pat said, this was now his booth and he could have a free coke, burger and fries every day after school.

The next day at school was weird too. Now the whole school knew about the 'Heights' and the cheerleaders, the 'The Vipers' and the 'Heights' and the pile of pissed-on jackets. Everyone he saw in the hallways smiled and said, hi. A few dorky, dreamy-eyed girls' kind of just stood in front of him and hovered. It gave him the creeps. He knew that all those kids still didn't like him, they just pretended to because now they knew how tough he was and they thought he was the new leader of, 'The Vipers.' Joey, was their leader, but he had been in jail for the last month.

Lurch came to his art class (Clint was sleeping) and said he had to go to the principal's office with him. Well, he was sure that he was going to get kicked out of school.

He almost told, Lurch, to go fuck himself and just walk out the door. He knew the school would say his fight with the

'Heights' was his fault. The parents of the kids he beat up would say he was just a hoodlum and he would have to pay for their medical bills. He knew the cheerleaders would say that they were just goofing around and the two 'Heights', guys were really their boyfriends, and it would just be some bullshit, after more bullshit, after more bullshit. They all wanted him gone. He was also sure the Cops were going to be in the principal's office to arrest him for assault and he was going to jail. Just before he and Lurch got to the principal's office, Clint thought "Fuck it, I'll tell Lurch to go fuck himself, punch him in the face, and just go home. Fuck it, fuck them, and fuck it all! I will lie about my age, sneak into the Marine Corps, go to Vietnam, kill those fuckin gooks and hope I will get killed too, so just fuck-em!"

The principal's office was a big room with a lot of chairs in it. The principal's desk was huge. The principal was sitting behind his desk. He was a big fat guy. He looked real stupid but Clint know he must be smart because he was the boss of the school. He didn't think he ever knew his name. They all just called him, 'Bozo'. He looked like, 'Bozo the Clown'. The top of his head was shiny but the sides of his head had a lot of hair sticking out everywhere. Clint thought he looked dumb. He also had short, pink pudgy fingers, and he had a big bunch of fat under his chin that wiggled when he talked. He looked like a grown-up sissy.

Well, in Bozo's office, were the two cheerleaders and each of their parents. He thought "Oh shit, I should have punched Lurch in the face." Bozo introduced him to the girls and their Mom's and Dads. One of the girls said that she didn't know he was so nice, the other girl said "Thank you." One of the Dads said his daughter was having a big house party on Friday night and he and his wife would like for him to come. Then the Dad gave him his business card and said their address was on the back. He told him to bring a few friends. Then he said with a low voice "But not the whole gang!" They all shook hands and Lurch said "Now Clinton, I need to see you in my office." Clint thought "Now what the fuck is this, I can't take any more of this shit."

84

Lurch told him to sit down. He told Clint that he was a better man than he thought he was. He said he could tell that he had a hard time in life. He knew he had gone through a lot. Lurch said that he had earned a break and he was going to give him one. He said that he knew that he thought no one liked him. He said he knew that he was lonely. He said that when he was a kid, that he was just like him! And <u>that's</u> how he knew!

Clint started to cry. But it was Lurch's fault, he started to cry first. He told him about a real mean Sergeant in the Army that used to beat the crap out of him because the Army Sgt. said "You're a better man than you think you are, and I'm going to kick your ass until you believe it." Lurch said he grew up poor, got into a lot of trouble at school, everyone hated him, the cops always slapped him around, and so did his Dad.

Lurch said he admired his courage in protecting those girls. Lurch said he was a born leader of men in the way he rallied the, Vipers to handle the Heights, but he said that he most of all, was proud of the way he fought back and didn't take shit from no one, not even him. Lurch told Clint, that he was the kind of guy that could be the President. He said he has been looking for a boy like him all of his career. He said "You are a fine, fine man." Then he sat up real straight and got all official-like and said "This is the only break that you will ever get from me, don't fuck this up. And keep your fucking mouth shut, tell no one, not even your parents!" Then he leaned forward from behind his desk, and said real hard "Do you read me?" Clint about shit his pants and answered "Yes Sir." It was one of the very few times Clint ever called anyone "Sir"!

Lurch said that his teachers wanted to hold him back in the 7th grade for next year and he would have to go to summer school too. Lurch said "I have changed your grades, you have earned B's since the start of the school year, and you will get B's for the 8th and 9th grades too." He said "You have to go to college." Lurch said if he had one fight, talked back to one teacher, or put his head down or slept in just one class, the deal was over.

Clint knew he meant it and he also knew he wanted to be just like Lurch, when he got older. Then Lurch said "Did you read the front of that girl's Dad's business card?" Clint said "No." Lurch said "Read it now." So he did. He didn't remember the man's name but it said in big letters "Sheriff, Cook County, Wisconsin." So he asked Lurch if that meant that the guy worked for the Sheriff. Lurch said no, "That guy is the Sheriff!"

Clint invited some of the guys but Little Stevie, was the only one that had the guts to go to the party with him at the Sheriff's house. Clint didn't remember anything about the party. He didn't remember much of anything about the next two years. He had a lot of girlfriends, a lot of sex, but the sex part started years before (he was 9, she was 26). He didn't have any more fights at school. He didn't talk back to any teachers and he got all B's on his report cards.

****

Well readers, here is where you must stop for a moment. As you can see there were a lot of good people in Clinton's young life. Starting with the "Christmas Tree Cops" to getting all the B's on his Jr. High school report cards. The author just wrote 16 pages in long hand on an 8 1/2 x 11 notepad describing just three short days, in Clint's life. His reason is this: most people would think that all those nice people and their kind deeds would negate or at least neutralize young Clinton's first 14 years of this crummy life. Yeah, I guess you would think that. We would all, want to think that. But it just wasn't so.

Clint deeply regrets that he never knew those police officers' names, the tree owner, the witness who gave them each a five-dollar bill. How do you thank them? Mac the shoe shop guy, Tom the Fuller brush guy, Bozo the principal, and mostly Lurch, the guidance/detention counselor. Clint doesn't believe that any kid at his age, got that much attention, that much validation. And yet, it wasn't enough. None of it was enough. The damage was already done. All the fear, the hitting, the hollering, the cold, the constant hunger, the lonely nights, all had their way with him. He was convinced that his Mom should have never had him and as she, he too, wish he were dead.

At his current age of 66 years old, he fondly recalls those wonderful people who tried to make a difference in his young life. He carries them all in his heart every day and has for the last 23 years of his sober and blessed life. He honors them by extending his hand to the down-trodden and less fortunate. Today, because of them, he is a man with a kind heart and a loving soul. The man, he always wanted to be.

Chapter 10 "HOTEL TRICKS"

At age 14, Clint got a job as a busboy at a high class hotel. A real fancy hotel with several ballrooms, a big bar and a dinner-dance lounge. They always had good bands and the people dressed real nice. He liked being around people like them. The food was real fancy and expensive. The chefs came to every table to ask how the food was. The waitresses wore real pretty dresses that all matched, and the hostesses wore a ladies' tuxedo. The women all looked like movie stars. The customers drank fancy drinks, a lot of them were different colored liquors and ice cream drinks, and all kinds of beer, wine and whiskey. There were three busboys for the lounge. One kid was a lazy dork, but Clint's pal, Tommy and he worked their guts out. And for a really good reason. Clint and Tommy looked a lot alike, except Tommy was Italian and Clint was Irish. They were both dark-skinned with black hair and green eyes. And, they were both drunks. When the customers finished with their dinners and started to dance and drink in earnest, Clint and Tommy would steal their drinks off their tables. If a customer noticed their drink missing, they did not know which busboy took it. The waitresses, hostesses and bartenders all knew what they were doing but they didn't care, because the customer got a new drink and the customer had to pay for it. When the customer paid their bill they were charged a 15% tip. They all made more money and Clint and Tommy got to stay drunk all night, every night. The bus boys used silver, serving trays that they had to carry with one hand, and at ear level. When they got the tray to the kitchen they had to sort the plates and silverware into different bins, the drink glasses and beer bottles were their prize. They had a monster size jar (the kind used for olives and pickles in restaurants) that they poured all the leftover liquids into. At the end of the night they would use a big strainer to pour the stuff through to get out the cigarette butts, toothpicks, cherries, nuts and those plastic swords. Every night the stuff was a different color, thickness, and smell, but they didn't care. They took the service elevator to the roof and sat on the ledge with their feet dangling over the side looking 16 stories down at the people and traffic. A lot of summer nights they got too drunk to make it off the roof. They would wake up, or come-to, mid-day with the sun beating down on them and the hot tar burning their skin. But they sure did get some good tans!

Clint loved working at that hotel for a number of reasons. The first reason and most importantly, he changed his name. Clint hated his abbreviated name. He decided that Clinton sounded like a phony or a made up name. Clinton Flanagan, was now; "Flanagan!" Flanagan would be the only name he would answer to, for the rest of his life.

The local people who came for dinner, drinks and dance got pretty drunk. Oftentimes, the wives and girlfriends would give him a piece of paper with their phone number on it when the guys went to the men's room. He got these phone numbers and hotel guest room numbers, almost every night. For a 14-year old, he was a real, real busy kid. The lounge was closed on Sunday and Monday each week. The liquor stores were closed on Sundays and were only open until 6:00 at night during the week. Flanagan hung out after 6:00 at night at the room service desk. When a hotel guest called down for a bottle of booze or a bucket of ice, he would tell them that the liquor stores were all closed but he would try to find them a bottle from a guy he knows, but he charges fifteen-dollars cash per bottle for bar liquor and twenty-five dollars, for top shelf. The guest would always say OK. Flanagan would go to one of his three lockers in the men's employee locker room, pull out a four to six-dollar bottle of booze, take it to their room, charge them fifteen dollars per bottle, two dollars for a bucket of ice (which was supposed to be free) and walk away with at least twenty dollars. Life was good. Where else could a kid go to work, get paid, collect tips, have free booze, and women?

Those hotel workers were like a big family. Most everyone in beverage and food service had a scam. They all knew it, and they all kept their mouths shut. When he got too drunk to work they would hide him in the elevator control room. They all

89

covered for each other. When there were large banquets or wedding receptions (which was often), he would hide and sell the leftover plates of food through room service, as a nightly special, for five bucks. Flanagan had a constant smile on his face, he was pretty sure that there were times, he made more money than the hotel manager. He had that job for three years. He spent some of his money on new clothes. It was the 'Beatles' era. The fashions mostly came from England. He bought all he could find but he spent most of his money on dental work. The years of poor hygiene and malnutrition left him with weak, rotting teeth.

Flanagan had to leave home due to his heavy drinking. He was a stow-away at the hotel. He slept in the hotel elevator control house on the roof. The maintenance guys moved some lockers into it, put in new insulation and fixed the roof. Flanagan was pretty comfortable with the set-up, other than the racket of the big roller drums and the snapping of the elevator cables. There was also the smell of hot grease from the drive motors which reminded him of the winter shed and the burnt motor oil that saturated the dirt floor. The chefs always fixed him good and free meals. He was happy, everyone liked and respected him. He finally had a real family!

Flanagan had a childhood friend named Dickey. He and Dickey heard about the bigger guys breaking into small businesses and looked in desk drawers for money or anything they could easily carry to sell to the junk shop guy. Dickey and he talked about doing that too, but he was too scared that they would get caught.

One day, Dickey asked him if he wanted to do a "big job" break-in with him and his older cousin. Flanagan didn't like Dickie's cousin. He was always drunk and a loud mouth. He told Dickey that he didn't trust his cousin and he wanted no part of him. Clint tried to talk Dickey out of it because he knew he would get caught.

A few days later he couldn't find Dickey, either at the, Corner Dairy Bar or at his house. Nobody was home at his house, but his Mom was always home. But not that day. Flanagan got a sick feeling in his belly. He knew Dickey got caught. The next day Flanagan's Mom showed him the morning newspaper. There was a big picture of a Stanford police car, the headlines read, "Stanford Police Sergeant Shot to Death." He knew in his gut that it was Dickey and his cousin, who did it. A few days after, there was Dickey's and his cousin's picture's in the paper. They had done it! Flanagan felt responsible for not being able to talk Dickey out of it. That, and he felt grateful that he trusted his own instincts. It was to be a simple burglary for big money, not shooting a Police Officer.

This was his first of four premonitions, to this point, in Flanagan's young life. He somehow knew that the "big job" would go down bad, really bad. He was sure of prison, even worse maybe, but not a murder! Something told him that this was not over. In the distant future, he somehow knew he would get to revisit this story on a much more personal level.

Chapter 11 "DREAMS COMING TRUE"

When Flanagan was 16 years old and in high school he met a girl named Paula, at the, 'Coney Island,' a burger joint just down the avenue from school. The first time he saw her he thought she was Ann Margaret. Incredible beauty, confident walk, a shape of absolute, perfect proportions. What a babe! She was a year older than him and she had a boyfriend. He didn't care about the boyfriend. She was the gal for him. They snuck around for a while, then she broke up with the guy and they were steady. He quit drinking and playing around with other girls. Paula was smart and had a lot of street savvy and would tell you to go to hell if she didn't like you. Yet, at the same time, she was sweet and tender-hearted.

They were crazy about each other. Her Dad was very well-to-do. Her Dad was quiet but engaging. He was nice to Flanagan. Paula's Mom always said he should be a movie star. She was nice to him too and always offered him snacks. Her Mom and Dad gave them the T.V. room and plenty of privacy. They lived in a modest house at the east end of the city. He would ride the city bus 12 miles to see her and catch the last bus of the night to go back home. Sometimes they would fall asleep on the couch in the T.V. room and he would miss the last bus. When her older brother came home from his date, he would give him a ride home. He was a cool guy. His name was Tommy.

Flanagan's parents really liked Paula but his Mother would always say "Women that beautiful, rarely stay with a man for very long." Flanagan hated that! "It is different! I am different! We are in love with each other!"

Paula got sick for two weeks and she missed a lot of school. She said she was too sick to see him, but they did talk for several hours each night on the phone. Paula's parents took her to the doctor. The next day Paula called him and said she was pregnant. They had sex a lot. He thought rubbers were dumb. He didn't know what to do. He couldn't tell his Mom or Dad.

He stayed away from Paula's house. He thought her Dad and big brother were going to kill him. He saw Paula in school and they had cokes after school, but neither of them could, for some reason, talk about her pregnancy. Those many years of his only dreaming of being a Daddy had just come true. He never considered before, what kind of woman he wanted for a wife or even what kind of Mother she should be. But he knew they were too young to get married and have a baby.

It was about a week after they found out she was pregnant, that her big brother was waiting for him outside of school. He walked up to Flanagan and smiled. He said "I'll buy you a coke." Tommy was a good guy, Flanagan liked him a lot. They were pals, they even went fishing and duck hunting together. Tommy had the most perfect teeth he ever saw, always with a big smile. But that day Tommy's big smile with perfect teeth scared the hell out of him. They got into Tommy's custom 1956 Chevy 327 with lake pipes and they went to the A&W. Tommy told him that he and his parents were not mad at him. He said that his Mom and Dad wanted to have him over for dinner tonight. Flanagan thought "Oh shit! Tonight? Oh shit, oh shit, oh shit!" Tommy saw the panic in Flanagan's eyes and smoothly said they just wanted to talk with Paula and him. Tommy said his parents really liked him and there would be no trouble. Flanagan said "Yeah, ok." Tommy honked the horn for the carhop to come and get their tray. Flanagan only had one sip of his root beer. Tommy started the car, they drove out of the A&W real slow. Tommy looked at him with a big grin and said, "Don't worry, I will drive real slow on the way to the house. So if you need to jump out to run, or vomit you won't get hurt too bad." Flanagan called him a fucker and they both laughed till there were tears in their eyes. Tommy was a great guy.

When they got to the house her Dad came out to the driveway and shook his hand and put his arm around his shoulder and walked him into the house. Paula's Mom gave him a big smile and patted him on the back, she said dinner was ready but told him to "Take a few minutes and say hello to Paula, she is in her bedroom." He gulped and went to her bedroom. Paula was crying. He sat on the bed with her and they held each other. She said she didn't think he would come for dinner. She thought he would not talk to her anymore.

They had Mallard ducks with wild rice for dinner that Tommy and he had shot a few weeks before. It was a good meal. No one talked much. Paula's Mom cleared the table and sat back down. Paula's Dad said that he and her Mom and Paula have a few different plans. He first said that they did not believe in abortion. Then he said, "You kids can get married, and we will help you with all the costs of the baby." He went on to say Paula and he must stay in school and he could stay at their house on weekends and Paula and he could sleep in her bedroom with the baby. "Or, if you didn't want to marry Paula it would be ok, but I will have to ask you, never to see Paula again." Flanagan loved her, she was wonderful, and of course he will marry her! The problem was, they were underage. He was 16, Paula was 17. Her Dad said they could get married in Wisconsin, with parental consent. He told Paula's Dad that he would tell his Dad and ask him for his permission. Paula's Mom started to cry and hugged him real hard and kept kissing his cheeks, as Dad kept shaking his hand and slapping him on the shoulder. Paula kept wiping her eyes then said she had to go and lay down. She gave him a kiss on the cheek and went to her bedroom. Tommy appeared out of nowhere (with that same shit-eating grin he had when he said he would drive real-slow so he could jump out) and said, "Hi brother, welcome to the family" and gave him a big ole bear hug. By the time he got home that night it was too late to talk to Dad. He was glad for that, he thought "Yeah, one more day to live!"

The next day as his Dad came into the house after work, Flanagan almost ran him over, to tell him he needed to talk to him without Mom hearing. His Dad said he could talk with him and Mom after he said hello to her and had a cup of coffee. After a while Dad called him into the kitchen. Mom was sitting there too. Flanagan mumbled that he just had to talk to Dad. Dad said that there was nothing he couldn't discuss in front of Mother. He said, "Dad, please, just you and me." Dad looked at Mom and she nodded (as if to say ok) and Dad said "OK, come upstairs and you can talk." Dad opened their bedroom door and said "Come in here and close the door." Flanagan about shit himself. This was Mom and Dad's room. This was their second apartment and he had never been in this bedroom.

Mom and Dad's bedroom was off limits. They never said that, but he just knew that. Now, Flanagan freaked out with being in their bedroom and he had to tell Dad that Paula was pregnant and they wanted to get married. He wanted to throw up. It took him several tries to say a full sentence. He finally blurted out "Paula is in trouble, she's pregnant." His Dad stood there for a few minutes without any kind of expression on his face, then he took a breath and said "No Clint, Paula is not in trouble, you are." Flanagan could taste the vomit in his mouth. Dad said that he and Mom already knew. He said Mom and he would do all they can to help them. Dad said "Let's go talk to your Mother." When they walked down the stairs Mom was waiting at the bottom. She had tears in her eyes but with a big smile. Mom said she loved Paula and she wanted them to be happy. The only condition was Flanagan had to move back home and he could not drink while living there. Flanagan and Paula got married in Stanford, Wisconsin by a judge. Donnie was his best man; Tommy was his groomsman. He was the happiest he ever had been in his life.

They had a big dinner at a supper club and Tommy drove them to their hotel for a 2-day honeymoon. They both had to go to school on Monday. On Saturday afternoon (the first day of their honeymoon) there was a knock at the motel door. It was his dumb-shit brother Donnie. He had a bottle of Jim Beam and a bottle of Old Grand-Dad and a book. The cover said, '101 Ways to Have Sex.' The three of them just sat in that little motel room, Donnie and he drank, Paula did not. Suddenly he didn't see Paula, and Donnie and he were snot-slinging drunk. They were laying back on the bed watching "The Wizard of Oz", passing the last bottle back and forth. He kept wondering where Paula was. Donnie went to the bathroom and hollered "Hey Flanagan, I found your wife." There was his beautiful Paula, laying in the bathtub asleep, with a pillow and blanket. Donnie left, Flanagan tried to wake Paula to come to bed. She said several unkind words. He left her alone, he laid on the bed and threw up all over the place. He didn't remember the next day.

The school board found out that a high school senior and a junior were married and pregnant. The school board had a special meeting to decide if they could stay in school. They never before had married kids in high school, in the entire school district. Paula's Dad hired a big deal lawyer; they got to stay in school. He almost got kicked out of school a few weeks later. Flanagan and Paula were holding hands, walking down the stairs from the fourth floor. Some dumb-assed kid, came running down the stairs and bumped into Paula hard, almost knocking her down. Flanagan got so pissed-off that he threw the kid over the banister and he landed below, on the next flight of stairs. None of his bones were broken but he was told not to do that again.

Flanagan had a lot of fun with being the only married student in high school. He was sick for a few days and missed school. When he came back to school his homeroom teacher told him he needed to bring a note from one of his parents to excuse his absence. The next day he brought a note explaining his absence, signed by his wife! His bitch homeroom teacher about shit herself. He told her that he was an emancipated adult and she would just have to deal with it. She hated his guts. She was also his English teacher. She failed him in English Literature so he would have to go to summer school. The day he was told that he would have to go to summer school the strangest thing happened. The English Lit bitch had four flat tires, a broken windshield and the head and taillights on her new Plymouth Fury were busted out. She cost him a full-time summer job, and he made her pay.

Flanagan's summer school English Lit teacher's name was Rick Thirst. He seemed ok, kind of relaxed and he told some corny jokes. The start of the third week, Mr. Thirst told him to stay after class. Flanagan thought he was going to tell him that he was flunking out of summer school. His mind went right back to the, "Go fuck yourself" and then punch him in the face, mode. He was going to drop that big goofy son-of-a-bitch right where he stood and he was going to put the boots to him just like he did the Nun. Flanagan wasn't going to let him even finish the first sentence. He was going to take that fat prick apart.

When the bell rang it was just him and the teacher. He sat in his desk. Mr. Thirst walked up to him, turned the desk in front of him around to face him, and sat down. He looked different. He looked scared but calm, at the same time. He told Flanagan that he knew he was a bad ass, but he wanted him to listen to him before he tried to do something. He said he had been watching him and his work. He said he didn't understand how one of the brightest kids in school got such lousy grades and had to go to summer school. Then, he said he had figured it out. He leaned forward, put his hand on his arm and said "Flanagan, you don't know how to read." He wanted to hit him so fucking hard that his dog would bleed! Then he started to cry.

Rick Thirst, "Mr. Rick Thirst", had only known him (he was from another school) for two weeks and cared enough about him, to tell him the truth. Finally, someone knew that he wasn't just stupid. He could read and pronounce most any word, but he couldn't put a sentence together where it made any sense. He couldn't comprehend what a paragraph said no matter how many times he read it. Mr. Thirst said he had a plan. He told him that he could teach him to read as good as he could in just four weeks. He showed him how to use the S.R.A. reading lab system. He told him to ignore the class and what he was teaching. He told him to only do the reading labs, and as soon as he finished a section to go to the next one, right away. His classmates couldn't figure out what he was doing. He should have done two sections in a 4-hour day. After the first week he was doing five sections a day. Flanagan had never felt so good about himself in all his life.

97

Before Mr. Thirst came into his life, he secretly thought that maybe he was a dummy. Maybe he did belong in the, 'Oppy Class'. Mr. Thirst, had changed his life forever. He is gone now, but he has been and will forever, be in his heart.

It was mid-August; Paula was getting really big now. She was even prettier than before. Her hair was even thicker and was the color of a well-groomed Irish-Setter. He could never take his eyes off of her. She was wonderful. She had quit smoking and swearing shortly after she got pregnant. She wanted to be a good Mom with a healthy baby. She smiled a lot, showing her perfect white teeth, (like her brother Tommy) and her bright green eyes sparkled. She was the most beautiful woman in the word.

The phone call came just after dark, on August 22, 1967. It was her Dad, he said that they were at the hospital with Paula. It was time for the baby to come, he told him to hurry. Flanagan had named his little girl several months before, her name was Saundra Leeann. He walked the 10 blocks to the hospital, smoked as much as he possibly could, repeatedly saying "I love you Paula, I love you Saundra." When he got to the hospital, he didn't see her parents, he found a nurse and asked where his wife was. The nurse told him he had a baby girl but she was real sick and he couldn't see her right now. She also told him that his wife was also very sick and he couldn't see her either. He wanted to kill that fucking bitch and tear the walls down of that Goddamn hospital. He sat alone in the 'Father's Room', no one came by. He kept going to the nurse's station to check on his wife and little baby girl. They said they would let him know when something changed. After several hours of sitting there alone, that same fucking nurse came in and told him to go home and sleep and come back the next day.

Flanagan walked in the dark. He went downtown and just aimlessly walked from one end of the shopping district to the other.

As day broke and before the sun came up he went back to the hospital. There was that same nurse. She said he couldn't see his wife, because, her seeing him, might upset her. She said his baby was dead.

The only dream he ever had, the dream that had carried him through as a damaged child, was gone...gone forever. He left the hospital and ran and ran, he didn't know how far or for how long. He just ran, and cried. He vowed that early morning in the false dawn that he would never allow himself to dream, ever again.

The day of Saundra's funeral was like watching a slow motion movie. Nothing seemed real, even people were talking in slow motion. Paula looked real tired and old. Her hair and eyes were now dull. She was weak and shaky. He hadn't seen her since before she had the baby. Paula and her parents were at the mortuary before he got there. Paula was sitting in an over-stuffed chair next to a coffee table with the same kind of chair on the other side of it. He walked up to Paula, put his hand on her hand and tried to kiss her cheek. She turned her head away.
She was crying. He knelt down in front of her and waited for her to look at him. He asked her where their baby was. She glanced at the coffee table next to her and nodded her head, where there was kind of a fancy-looking marble box. It took him a few seconds to realize, that was not a fancy marble box. It, was his baby girl's coffin. All he remembered of that day was putting his head in Paula's lap, and crying, as she stroked his hair.

At some point Flanagan and Paula found themselves in an apartment together. They didn't talk much. He could only remember, her putting her makeup on and her saying she was going to her friend's house for dinner. It was almost every night. He would just sit there and wait for her to come home, some nights she didn't. One night, after several months of Paula's late nights (and about six months after losing Saundra), he lost it. Paula came home the next day after being out all night and he didn't say a word. He walked over to her and slapped her several times, his hands were covered with her blood. He called her Dad to come and get her. It was winter. He told her Dad he could pick her up on the front porch. He walked her down the stairs, he opened the door, she walked out and he closed and locked the door behind her.

He only saw her once after that, in divorce court. A high school senior in divorce court, what a heartbreaking mess.

Paula was a wonderful girl with a broken heart. He was a young man with a shattered dream. They were just kids. They didn't know how to talk to each other. They were both full of shame and guilt. They had betrayed each other. It was each of their faults that their baby was dead. Paula was adopted and there was no medical history other than her having Rheumatic Fever as a child, so the doctor said because of Paula's Rheumatic fever, their baby died. Flanagan thought it was his fault because of his family's blood disease that Donnie had as a child. They both secretly blamed themselves for 'killing', each other's baby. Their individual, shame, self-loathing, heartaches, and loneliness (which they never spoke of), destroyed their love. In those days there was no such thing as grief counseling. Their parents just said "Oh, you kids are young, you can have more children."

The day he stood in Divorce court he looked over at Paula, she never looked at him. She looked straight ahead. She was composed and looked happy. There were no outward signs of her sorrow. Flanagan, was crushed, he felt like he was going to have a heart attack. He found himself, wishing he would have a heart attack and die. He knew this was just the beginning of a lifetime of loss, sorrow and loneliness. He sensed that each time it would be worse than the time before. It would get much worse and it would come often.

Paula, his beautiful Paula died from cancer last year. It had been 32 years that he last saw her. He still loved Paula, there will always be a special place in his heart for her. At times, he still dreams of how it could have been, and he cries. Every time he goes back to Stanford, he goes to the cemetery to visit his Saundra. He stands at her headstone and looks at her name and the engraved baby booties.

He visualizes Paula, Saundra, and him, holding hands. He had a ring made with three tiny diamond chips laid in a row. The center chip, is Saundra laying between Mommy and Daddy, to keep her safe. He still wears that ring today.

Flanagan's sorrow and heartache led him to a lifetime of alcoholism and depression. As you read on you will see how a man bent on self-destruction, does not only injure himself.

There is a time frame of three years that Flanagan has omitted from his memories. His friends who know of his life story, all but demand he include these three years and a few other incidents that they believe are crucial to this story. He disagrees. In his mind and his heart, he knows the mold of his life had already been cast. He doesn't believe those three years, to be germane to his story.

There are many, many things he doesn't remember, and the order of events and time periods are of question. Flanagan believed it is his brain's way to protect him from being overwhelmed.

It was booze and sex. But the booze was more important. He tried to drink the pain away but it just numbed it. Loneliness was his constant companion, and it was a secret that he closely guarded. His best kept secret; God had extracted his pound of flesh. He was now, finally, being punished for his wicked ways as a youth. He truly was damned, and he knew he deserved it.

Chapter 12 "REDEMPTION"

One early spring day, in 1972, Flanagan was driving down the street and a guy and girl were on a motorcycle in front of him. The kid did a wheelie and lost control. The bike went down and they were both stuck by an oncoming car. They were both pretty well messed up. She had the entire car go over her. She had a lot of deep cuts and compound fractures. She was conscious, the boy was not. His face was bloody and the blood was coming from his ears and the back of his head, blood started to pool on the ground around him. Flanagan had a small, first aid kit in his car. He held pressure on the boy's head wound as best he could. The boy did a lot of thrashing while Flanagan held his head in his lap, to try to protect him from further injury, while waiting for the ambulance to arrive. As he helped load those two kids into the ambulance, the driver told him he did a good job and asked him where he got his training. Flanagan told him he had none. The ambulance driver said that they were adding a new crew to the central station and gave him his name for a reference. Flanagan thought it over for a few days and went to apply for the job. The man who gave him his name turned out to be the owner's son. He got the job.

Little did Flanagan know, that the new job, would change the entire course of his life. In those days, all you needed was a Basic, Advanced First Aid, and a CPR card to work on an ambulance. There was no such thing as EMT or Paramedic training. The company bought cases of Kotex, cut off the 'wings' and used them for trauma dressings. It was mostly load-and-go like hell, to the hospital. They had nice rigs and uniforms.

There were four news stations in the city, and they were always trying to 'out-scoop' each other. They all showed up at car crashes and fires and Flanagan was usually on the news, several times a week.

He, was a standout, handsome guy. With the looks of a movie actor, and the physique of a body-builder, he didn't have much trouble meeting women.

A few years later, when Flanagan was a Paramedic, he joined the, 'National Ski Patrol' and who do you think one of the ski patrolmen was? Yup. Standing in front of him, was Mr. Rick Thirst. They became good friends. Mr. Thirst, told him one day to drop the "Mr. Thirst." Rick was bald with a few hairs on top of his head, and because Mr. Thirst was Scottish, Flanagan dubbed him; "Fuzzy Mc Thirst." Rick laughed his ass off, he said he liked that name. It stuck. Everyone on the ski patrol and the ski hill called him Fuzzy, or Mc Thirst. For Flanagan it was always "Fuzzy Mc Thirst." Rick and he were always kidding each other. When Flanagan got the best of him, Rick would say "Hey hoodlum, go read a book." They would both laugh their asses off. Flanagan skied with Rick's kids, they went camping together in the summer and he always went to his kids' birthday parties. As time went on, they lost touch with each other. He wished he wouldn't have.

Flanagan worked 24 hours on and 24 hours off. Every other weekend he worked 72 hours straight. The main headquarters station had a bunk room, TV room, kitchen, and a bumper pool and ping pong table. The crews rarely slept. On the summer nights and between calls they opened all the overhead doors and sat in the driveway in lawn chairs. The headquarters station was on the main drag in the center of the Downtown area. During the course of those nights, girls (a lot of girls) would walk up to the crews with cokes, malts, pizzas, or something they had baked. Flanagan was the only single guy on the entire crew. They kept their station spotless, they had a wash bay and the rigs all gleamed. The girls were drawn to all the lights and chrome. Flanagan was the tour master. He would show the girls their quarters and rigs and gear. The married guys got fat on all the treats. He got a lot of dates.

He would be at a night club and rarely had to ask a girl to dance. The girls would come to him and would say they saw him on TV and would tell him he was even more handsome in person. Flanagan's life was jammed with, babes, booze, blood and death. There was an awful, awful lot of death.

Flanagan, then met this second wife, Liz. It of course, was at a bar, the Saturday after New Year's Eve. He had to work New Year's Eve, so he was making up for it, that night. She was exquisite, thick dark brown hair, green sparkling eyes, a dark tan, and with perfectly white gleaming teeth. That night, he was obnoxiously drunk and he had to have her. He introduced himself to her. She seemed very sweet as she told him she knew who he was, as she had seen him on the T.V. and in the newspapers a lot, and in bars with a lot of different women. She acted unimpressed. They danced a few times but she acted bored. He thought "Screw you." He left the bar and went to a house party. An hour later, that same girl showed up at the house party. She walked over to him with two beers and handed him one as she said "I know you're a nice guy. A lot of people like you. You are a local hero, the most handsome man anyone has ever seen and you have screwed most of the girls in this entire city. I don't want to be just another notch in your bedpost." He told her that he was too drunk to talk with her right then, but he would like to get to know her better "But right now, I have to go home." She asked to see his car keys and without thinking, he pulled them out of his pocket and she snatched them from his hand in a blur. After a brief lecture on his obvious state of drunkenness, he relented to allow her to drive him home. She drove his car and one of her friends followed in her car. She parked his car in the driveway and said "Don't even think about inviting me in." She handed him his car keys with a firm admonishment not to go anywhere, but to bed. As she was getting out of his car she handed him her business card and said "My home number is on the back, call me when you're sober."

He laid in bed that night and couldn't get her out of his mind. He knew she was different, different than most women, different than any woman he had met for sure, and it wasn't just her beauty. Beautiful she was, but there was more, much, much, more. Then his mind flashed back on her last words, "Call me when your sober" …you bitch! Then he came back to the thoughts that she was caring, honest and mature, and a nice girl. That "sober" statement bothered him. It could be a deal breaker.

They dated just a few times a month for six months, there was no sex. She was beyond cautious and he knew she had reason to be. She had nice parents, and one brother, and as his first wife she and her brother were also adopted. Her brother, Tommy (yes, the same name as his former brother-in-law) and he became pals. They hunted and fished and drank together, a lot. Tommy and he both had a high degree of martial arts training. On days off and a few evenings they worked out together, often times using full contact, without pads. They beat the hell out of each other and each time they were done they would sit for a few beers, laughing as they were wiping away blood and massaging sore muscles and bones.

Flanagan and Liz were married in the early spring, a year and a half after they had met. They were married in a Catholic church. It was a big wedding and there are no words to describe how lovely Liz looked.

Flanagan enrolled in a Federal training program that was designed to teach alcoholics (yes, he came to terms with his drinking and attended AA meetings on a regular basis) to become counselors for chemically dependent people. It was a two-year program. He still worked a few nights a week and some weekends on the ambulance, just to keep current and for a few extra bucks. Liz was a lot of fun, always affectionate, always sweet, but he didn't know her very well. They both had monster size abandonment issues. Neither of them spoke of true affairs of the heart. They just wanted to have fun. He guessed they both knew that they would not last.

The first sign of their marriage being in trouble came on their first Christmas Eve together. They had just finished some last minute Christmas shopping, late that afternoon and it was near dark. They had to get home and clean up as they were expected at be at her parents' house for dinner and the gift exchange. He hated that kind of shit and didn't much care for her folks once he got to know them. Flanagan was driving down a side street when in his

105

headlights, he saw two little kids pulling an old snow sled with a Christmas tree on it. The sled runners were sparking as they hit bare pavement and then the tree would fall off the sled. The kids' struggled to get the tree back on the sled. He instantly knew what he was seeing, and his past blew up in his guts (he told Liz very little of his childhood).

Christmas tree lots gave away their left over trees on Christmas Eve, so poor people could have a Christmas tree. He said to Liz "Do you see that?" She responded with "Yes, cute kids." His heart sunk and he was crushed. He felt every bit alone as when he was a child. Liz didn't see it. It meant nothing to her, to see those children struggling with that tree and the fact that it was Christmas Eve. He knew that they were about to have their first fight and it was going to be huge. Flanagan pulled up to the little kids and asked them how far away their house was? They breathlessly said they didn't know for sure. The girl was nine and her brother was seven. They told him their address, which was still three blocks away. He put their tree and sled in his trunk and drove them home. They told him "Mommy was hurt bad and has a broken arm, and we don't have a Daddy."

The kids lived in an old, run down, three story wood frame apartment building. Liz sat in the car as he dragged the scrawny tree and sled up to the third floor. Mom cautiously opened the door, her face was bruised and her arm was in a cast. They didn't have a tree stand and only had two strings of lights. The bulbs were faded and had a lot of paint chips on them, the wires were badly frayed. He told Mom that he had some extra strings of lights and ornaments at home and would be back within an hour and he would help them with their tree. Mom had a weak smile and moist eyes, like his own Mother did, several years ago. When he got back to the car Liz was about to burst into flames. He thought "If you're pissed now, you're going to be a whole lot more pissed in the next few minutes." She said thru clinched teeth "You are going to make us late to dinner." He drove in silence for a few minutes before he told her that she needed to drive her own car to her parents, and he would catch up to them a bit later for the gift exchange. She snidely asked him if he was going to see his girlfriend, as she slapped his face.

He dropped her off in front of the house without his saying a word. He went to (of all places) JC Penny and bought Christmas tree lights, ornaments, tinsel, a tree stand and a few stuffed animals and two snow sleds. He vowed (to himself) to buy them some groceries when the stores re-opened, the day after Christmas. He put up their tree and strung the lights. Mommy and the kids just stood there, not believing their eyes. He was on his way to the parent's house within forty-five minutes from dropping Liz off. He did what he had to do and was not about to apologize for that, to anyone!

Flanagan walked into Liz's folk's house and got a cold reception. They were starting desert. Her Dad said "So, you're playing social worker tonight was more important than having dinner with us?"

Without a word, Flanagan went to the fridge and pulled out a beer, then to the liquor cabinet and pulled out a bottle of Vodka. He drank the Vodka straight from the bottle. He was drunk and full of seething rage before they had the table cleared.

He hated them all. He hated their arrogance of having it all. Mother, in her wool plaid holiday skirt, angora holiday sweater and wearing enough gold and diamonds to buy a new car. Dad, in his asshole matching cardigan sweater, his phony 'prop pipe' and velvet house shoes. Looking at Liz, he realized that she was every bit, a part of it. He walked out of the house with the Vodka bottle, without saying a word to anyone. He drank as he drove home, wiping the tears as best as he could. He took an oath that he would accept the truth of his marriage and just try to be nice to her, enjoy the sex, and try not to hate her, until he could find a real woman. Secretly, he hoped she would want to understand him, be in love with him and they would live happily ever after. He was lying to himself about wanting a real woman. He did not want another woman, any woman, he just wanted his Liz.

Flanagan completed the federal training program early and took a job in Florida as a program director of a large therapeutic community. The treatment program was designed after "Day-top" and "Syn-anon" programs for drug addicts. It was an intensive, two year live in treatment program. He managed a large staff and they had forty-five clients. On behalf of the treatment center, he spoke on addictions to small and large industries, colleges, professional and civic groups and did a twice a week radio call-in, talk show. He liked the job, he liked the admiration and respect shown to him and the money was very good. Liz and he loved the beach. They spent the weekends in the sun and strolled the beach together several evenings each week. It was fun to be with her as long as he blocked out his needs and used caution to avoid having expectations of Liz showing compassion, consideration, or any level of personal disclosure. There would be no truths here. It hurt him. He loved her, she only liked him. He couldn't live with the lies any longer. He got burnt out from the job and tired of carrying around an empty heart. He started to hit the beach bars, looking for booze and women. He found plenty of both. Neither his wife nor his employer liked what he was doing. He lost his job and they returned to Wisconsin.

Liz didn't like him much for cheating on her but he promised her that he would never cheat again and he didn't. Flanagan went back to work on the ambulance. It was as if he had never left. He worked 24 hours on 24 hours off, and every other weekend for 72 hours. He also worked a lot of his days off (he was trying to stay out of the bars). He took a lot of road trips to Minneapolis/St. Paul and Rochester, MN (Mayo Clinic). Patients who had serious head injuries or brain bleeds could not take an air ambulance due to their conditions. Many others who needed constant care couldn't afford the cost of an air ambulance.

On one such trip from a Stanford hospital to St. Paul, MN for a brain scan (at that time, there was only one brain scanner in the three state area), they had an elderly gentleman with a suspected brain bleed. Scotty drove and Flanagan attended the patient. The old timer was a very nice fellow. They joked a lot and he was quick witted. His name was Ivan. Ivan had been a lumberjack all of his life. Shortly after they started the 160-mile trip Flanagan noticed nicotine stains on Ivan's right hand. He asked Ivan if he was a smoker. He said yes, but he had been in the hospital for 11 days and they would not let him smoke. Flanagan asked him if he was pretty much done with people telling him what to do and having to listen to them, tell him, what was best for him. Ivan said he was 83 years old and all he wanted was a few packs of cigarettes, a jug of whiskey-or two and he would then be happy to meet his maker. Ivan was on a re-breather mask with 4 liters of oxygen. Flanagan told him he couldn't help him with the whiskey but he had something, he might like. He turned off the oxygen lead, removed his mask, rolled down the side window, reached into his shirt pocket and pulled a cigarette out, lit it and handed it to Ivan. Ivan's eyes welled up, as he swore to tell St. Peter of his blessed angel with the pack of Camels. Ivan finished his smoke and Flanagan put his mask back on and kicked Ivan's oxygen up 2 liters to make up for the cigarette.

They were beyond the half-way mark to St. Paul, when they received a state wide emergency radio call from a Minnesota State Trooper who was pulled over with a women and her infant child. The baby was vomiting with a high fever and had a bright red face and was unresponsive. The trooper was just ten miles ahead of them. Scotty (the driver) launched the rig with lights and sirens. Flanagan looked thru the sliding window port and the speedometer read 155 mph. They pulled in behind the trooper to exam the infant. This little girl was in a lot more trouble than Mom or the Trooper realized. This kid's organs were shutting down and her brain was burning up. Without fluids and ice packs they were going to lose her in just a matter of minutes. The infant was lethargic and not responding to stimulation. It took Scotty and him both, to get IV's in both of the tiny baby's arms. They wrapped her in several layers of ice packs.

Since they didn't know the area or the location of the

109

nearest hospital, the Trooper escorted them, 'Code 3.' Scotty damn near ran over the top of that state patrol car. Flanagan didn't even want to look at the speedometer. The infant responded remarkably quickly. He told Scotty to radio the trooper that they could slow down as the baby was stable. Ivan was watching everything he was doing, as he was removing the ice packs (he didn't want the baby to go into shock from the cold). Ivan pulled his mask up and said he had not seen a baby that small in over 50 years. Flanagan rearranged a few things on Ivan's gurney and laid the baby against his ribs and put Ivan's left arm around the baby. Ivan said "This is even better than the cigarette, you gave me." Ivan grinned and spoke to the baby in a shockingly soft and tender voice.

They got the baby to a hospital where the Emergency Room Doctor, declared the baby to be stable but guarded. They went on to St. Paul for Ivan's brain scan.

Ivan was sleepy on the way back to Stanford. He woke up and asked, (in a weak voice) if Flanagan could possibly find another, extra, Camel in his shirt pocket. Flanagan turned off the oxygen, lit the cigarette and gave it to him. Ivan took a deep drag and blew out several perfect smoke rings. He grinned and said, "This is the last smoke I will ever need." Flanagan sat quietly for a few seconds and let it sink in. He asked Ivan if it was time for him. Ivan said "Yup." Flanagan took the cigarette as Ivan closed his eyes. Flanagan watched Ivan's chest rise and fall as his breathing became shallow. Ivan coughed, opened his eyes and whispered "You are a sweet man."

As they were reaching the city lights of Stanford, his pal Ivan, went to meet the Lord. Flanagan radioed the hospital that they were returning with Ivan and that he had expired. He had Scotty radio dispatch with the same information. Dispatch ordered them to fuel up, bring Ivan to the hospital and pick up another patient at the same hospital to make the same trip back to St. Paul.

This patient, was only thirty years old with a similar problem as Ivan but was critical, they would have to run 'Code 3', both ways. Flanagan told Scotty he needed to drive, to clear his mind. Running with lights and sirens at night, on the freeway at 90 mph and in heavy Saturday night traffic, was mind numbing. The Ivan-infant situation had affected him greatly. Flanagan was a pretty good guy already, but from now on, he promised himself that he would go out of his way to treat the elderly with more respect and compassion. Seeing that sweet old man, holding that tiny child, both helpless, both trusting, both in his care and in God's hands, was life changing. He felt as though he was finally, a part of something bigger. Something much bigger than himself!

Seconds later, the worm turned. He so much wished that when he got home from this trip, he could sit down with Liz and tell her about Ivan and the Infant. Flanagan wished she would be there to hold him. But she would not be home. Liz had become a happy-hour diva. On weekends, she and a few of her pals went night clubbing to the Playboy Club in Lake Geneva, WI. He was pretty sure that she had a serious boyfriend. Their deal was over; his heart was sad that she didn't want him anymore. He was lost and alone, and he knew it was of his own making.

Flanagan was both physically and emotionally exhausted. He needed sleep and found himself, obsessing about getting drunk and staying that way. He didn't remember the trip, he just drove. As he pulled up to the clinic with the EMI brain scan unit, his ass was as numb as his mind. He pushed the after-hour buzzer. A female voice said "Welcome to St. Paul, Rampart Rescue Ambulance, we will be right up." She had an unbelievable, soft, angelic and soothing voice that pulled him from his funk.

When the doors slid open, out stepped two stunning women. The first was a cute buxom brunette with the soft voice and a sweet smile to match. (He was most certain that she sang in the church choir every Sunday). The other woman was a very buxom, attractive blonde with a direct look about her. Without question, this gal knew who she was. Just in her posture, she exuded confidence with a level of humility that was refreshing.

They rode down the elevator with them as they took over the care of their patient. They were all set up for them and the

transfer went smooth, those gals were real pros. The blonde leaned over to him and whispered "Handsome, you look like hell." He felt like hell and wished they could have met when he was rested with a fresh shower and shave. She smiled and said "I like my men fresh from the fight, and you, Sir, look like you have been in one hell of a battle."
God, he liked her!

"Blonde" said it would take a full hour or more for the exam. She said she would take them back up the elevator so they could go get something to eat. Scotty was kind of a medical geek and said he wanted to stay and observe the exam. Flanagan wasn't hungry but needed coffee and several smokes. As the elevator door closed, Blondie turned to face him and said "You look like you need a poor baby." Before he could ask what the hell a poor baby was, she pinned him to the elevator wall. She brought him back to life, for sure.

Flanagan smiled for the full hour that he sat in that restaurant, he couldn't remember ever enjoying drinking coffee and smoking as much as he did that night. When he drove back to the clinic he saw the two girls and Scotty standing outside talking. His first thought was "Oh shit, we lost another one." Blondie said the patient was failing so they sent him to the nearest hospital via another ambulance. They all said good night and he hoped he would get to see her again. In part he wanted to kick his own ass for not getting Blondie's phone number, on the other hand he was glad that he didn't. He gave his word to Liz that he wouldn't screw around anymore, so until they had a talk when she got home, he was going to stand true to his word.

Scotty told him on the way home that, Blondie had asked him a million questions about him. Blondie said she had never had a man give her the "Vapors" before. Scotty handed him a note from Blondie and he said her phone number was on there. Flanagan didn't reach for it. He told Scotty to put it in his locker and if he didn't ask for it in a month or so, to throw it away.

112

Liz came home on Sunday afternoon, rushed in the door and said she was going to pack some things and spend a few days at her friend's house. As she was packing she said she was going to file for a divorce in the morning. After she left he just sat on the couch and without much effort, found peace within himself. They had a cordial divorce.

Chapter 13 "THEIR TRUTHS, HIS LIES"

- To the casual reader of this book, it may all sound like a cheap reason to be a drunk. And perhaps so, opinions vary. But he did become a drunk. Maybe it was just meant to be.

Rampart Rescue Ambulance Company had a city and county contract to provide emergency medical services. A new ambulance company came to town. They jumped (stole) their calls' all the time. This new company played patty-cake and romanced the city and county administrators. The following year this new company was awarded both the city and county contracts.

Rampart Rescue Ambulance Service went out of business and he was out of a job. The new company offered Flanagan a job. He told them to go fuck themselves. He hated slimy people and corruption. Most of the Rampart guys felt the same. He took a job with a major steel company and worked in an open pit, Iron Ore mine. He worked pit labor but was issued a company truck and radio, to respond to any medical emergencies. Half of his shift was treating injured workers. This mine was the size of a small city. It had paved highways, a railroad, its' own fire and police departments. He liked the job and the people. The 70 mile drive each way, was the downside.

The new ambulance company had lied to the city and county about their rate structures, the number of certified personal and the number of ambulances in their fleet. The level of care was far below par and the two hospitals emergency departments complained, but to no avail. The police and fire departments complained about poor response times, and again, to no avail.

The public and end users flipped out, over their bills for services. The owner of this new company was a thief and the council members all, had their palms well-greased.

One of the former longtime employees of Rampart Rescue Ambulance was a smart guy and a good friend. He called Flanagan to say that all the boys were going to meet at the 'Lumberjack Bar' for beers, and he had a plan to propose to bring back the company and their jobs. They had themselves a real 'Puker,' that night. Some of the men vowed to return but most had other, much better paying jobs, with families to support.

Jack re-opened "Rampart Emergency Rescue Services." After a year apart, the old gang was once again. They used the same old headquarters, bought used rigs and had small, but efficient crews. The ER staffs were thrilled to have them back. Their level of care was far superior to the competitions, and their patients were in much better shape when they arrived at the hospitals. Flanagan took a straight day shift, and pulled a few over-night shifts each week for drinking money. He got a new partner, he was a good guy and he learned fast.

To this very day, Flanagan still has nightmares on a weekly basis. He can still see their faces; he hears their screams. Children whimpering, and adults gasping for their final breaths. The cars were made of steel, no air bags, and there were no shoulder belts. The injuries were much more severe. In a head-on crash the front seat passenger was usually dead.

Flanagan's nightmares are always of the same five calls: "My Blue Baby"; "Daddy's Little Buddy"; "The Road Builder"; "The Train Man"; and "The Station Wagon." Every dream ends the same. He asks himself what more could he have done? The guilt is life-lasting. He has never talked of it, to anyone. It hurts too much.

*** *If you are squeamish or have lost someone in a tragic accident, it is strongly suggested you skip the next two chapters. It will break your heart. He only tells of this to honor them and tell of the life's lessons learned. How to value all of those you care for, each day and every day. And maybe, just maybe, find peace for himself.* ***

Chapter 14 "MY BLUE BABY"

It was a bit before 5:00 am on a frigid, Wisconsin winter morning. Everyone was in quarters, sleeping. His crew was next up. The four beep tone alarm came over the loud speaker system. Flanagan's feet hit the deck, and he was dressing, as the Police Dispatcher announced: "Rampart Rescue Ambulance Unit #164, Engine #2, Truck #12, Ladder #3, Rescue #6 and Police Squads 24, 18 and 33. Respond to a natural gas leak in a residence, infant not breathing. Possible 10:72 (D.O.A.). All Units respond Code 3."

Flanagan, damn near drove through the garage door waiting for it to open. He had the lights and sirens on before he left the garage. He could hear the tires screaming on the polished concrete floor, over both the 'Federal-Q' and 'Electronic' sirens.

When any emergency worker hears a call to a "Child Down" they drive faster and harder to that call, than any other. When you hear a call for an infant not breathing you drive as though the devil himself was after you. The streets were hard packed with snow and ice. The temperature was greater than 20 degrees below zero. There has not yet been a NASCAR driver born, who would not have grabbed a sissy bar and cried out to Jesus. Flanagan's partner, Kenny, kept hollering at him to slow down. He didn't. Flanagan was thinking "Not this time, you son-of-a-bitch! ... NO! ... God Damn you! ... Not this time!" (Flanagan was talking to God).

As they drove into the neighborhood there was the heavy, putrid odor of natural gas. Flanagan radioed for a second alarm, fearing an explosion and knowing that they would have to do a house to house search through the entire neighborhood, looking for additional victims.

They were the first Unit on the scene. Flanagan all but tore the front storm door off of the house. As he opened the door, the Father opened the main door and thrust the tiny baby into his arms. The little boy had only a diaper on, his entire body was limp and

117

he was a deep splotchy purple color. He could smell natural gas coming from the house. Flanagan ordered the Father and anyone in the house to leave immediately. He could hear the sirens of the responding fire trucks.

He looked down at the baby, and saw he was void of all life. As he looked at him he saw his own baby, Saundra. He had a chance to get his baby back or maybe just a small part of his heart back. All of his thoughts came in Nano seconds. Thoughts that he had held in his heart but never spoke of.

As he spun from the father, Kenny was almost to the house, Flanagan hollered to him to "Get back to the rig, open the front door for me, you are driving, turn off the heater and put down all the windows."

Protocol, insurance, and good sense says you never transport a patient in the front seat of an ambulance. "Fuck that! We have a dead baby to revive." Kenny would be the first to admit that he wasn't much behind the wheel of his own car, now he is wheeling a Cadillac ambulance, 19 feet long, 9,800 hundred pounds with 500+horsepower, through narrow, snow and ice packed streets with cars parked on each side. Kenny did just fine. Flanagan held the baby's head on his right shoulder trying to get his head as much, fresh, cold air to him as he could, to revive him. He gave him firm two-finger chest compressions and strong puffs of air with his mouth covering the tiny baby's nose and mouth.

Kenny was on the radio as Flanagan worked on the baby. He could feel the rig sliding and fishtailing. It didn't bother him in the least. There was his pal Kenny, wheeling that monster land yacht with one hand, driving his guts out and calmly talking to the emergency room doctor, requesting a full neonatal team and any pediatric specialist on hand. The emergency room doctor advised that a full staff would meet them at the door upon arrival.

At one point, Flanagan glanced over at Kenny and saw sweat running down his forehead. He was proud of him; he would march into hell with this man. All of Flanagan's breaths and chest compressions were mechanical and precise. Suddenly there was a strange acidic taste in his mouth. The baby was throwing up! Usually that happens when you fill the stomach with air from mouth-to-mouth. But this somehow felt and tasted different. He sucked as hard as he dared on the infants' mouth to clear his airway. He got a mouthful. The baby started to choke. He sucked a little lighter, got half of a mouthful, and the baby started to cry.

Then, he started to wail. Kenny grabbed the radio mic and told the emergency room doctor that the baby was conscious and breathing on his own. They could hear the waiting team in the emergency room erupt in shouts of joy. They knew the doctor intentionally left his radio mic keyed so they could hear the celebration. They heard a nurse say "God Bless Rampart 164!"

The baby's color was starting to come back and he was as loud as the sirens. Flanagan reached over and turned off the sirens and keyed the radio mic so they could hear the baby. He let go of the radio mic key, and turned the sirens back on. Kenny shifted in his seat and sat as though he was sitting at a traffic light. He slowed down a bit, they both took a deep breath, as they quietly savored that moment. Minutes later they pulled up to the emergency room, both of their faces were wet with sweat and tears. The medical team, all had set jaws and determined looks on their faces. But those professional, non-descript faces all had brilliant twinkles in their eyes. They took the baby from him.

Flanagan and Kenny, hung around for a while to see how the little guy was doing. All three of the Main station crews and one West Unit came to the hospital to congratulate them. Fire crews, came in from all over the city. There was a mob of Cops. Flanagan slipped outside for a cigarette. As Flanagan lit his cigarette he tasted the baby's vomit that he had swallowed. It made him smile.

The streets were jammed with fire trucks, police cars, and ambulances. All with their emergency lights on. It's extremely rare that you get to bring an infant back from death. They all knew that. Those emergency lights were all left on intentionally, as a tribute to all the ones that they had lost.

119

Today was truly a glorious day. As daybreak came, Flanagan looked into the sky and whispered "Saundra, Daddy did this for you."

Flanagan walked back into the hospital. The emergency room was a sea of uniforms. It was very quiet, the uniforms formed two lines. Kenny came over to stand next to him. The Cops, Paramedics, and Firefighters filed by with a handshake, a slap on the shoulder and a nod. They all went to their vehicles and quietly drove away. One more check on their new little friend and they too, walked in silence to their rig, and returned to quarters.

There was a throng of TV and newspaper crews that blinded him with their cameras bright lights as he backed into the station. The other crews stood with their backs to the cameras to block them from getting pictures of them. 'This was a private moment for all of them. The warriors had returned victoriously from the battle.' As they drove in, the dispatcher saluted them, and pushed the button to close the overhead door.

Not another word was spoken by anyone in the station, about that call. The relief shift arrived at 7:00 am. Flanagan spent a half hour in the shower, dressed and found Kenny in the TV room reading a newspaper. Kenny looked as calm as ever. Flanagan said "Come on, I'll buy you a beer." The dispatcher was standing in the doorway of the TV room. His name was Clark.

Clark said "You ain't buying him nothin!" Clark and Kenny both had shit-eating grins on their faces. Kenny said "While you were out for a smoke at the E.R., all those uniforms filled a suction machine canister with money to buy us a beer." As they walked out of headquarters the media was gone. Flanagan guessed even they, figured out that some of the greatest victory celebrations, are done in silence. Flanagan and Kenny walked the block and a half to the "Lumberjack Bar and Grill." Kenny kept patting the bulging front pockets of his jeans saying "Yup, we're gonna have us some beers."

Stanford was an industrial town, with a lot of shift workers. The Lumberjack Bar was open at 7:00 am for the night shift workers. When they walked into the bar, there was a lot of cheering and clapping. The joint was full of off-duty hospital and emergency room workers from all three hospitals. The guys from their station and even some crew guys on days off. Off-shift firefighters and Cops were everywhere and with just a handful of blue collar, shift workers.

Bennie the bartender, rang the "Buy the bar a round" bell, several times. The crowd quieted down as he said "Nobody is to reach into their pockets to pay for a drink. Dr. Long is paying for all your drinks, all day!" Dr. Long, was the Director of Emergency Services and the head emergency room doctor for the "Level 1 Trauma Center." He always wore sandals long before they were fashionable. Dr. Long was also their EMT/Paramedic Certification sponsor. He was currently giving them their I.V. Therapy classes. Dr. Long was a very calm guy, with a great sense of humor.

Nobody in the bar spoke of 'The Call.' They talked of hunting, fishing, the Green Bay Packers, and cars. But not 'The Call.' Flanagan was well into his fourth or fifth beer when Dr. Long came up to him and said "Follow me." They walked to the back of the bar and sat in an empty booth. Doc said "I want you to listen to me. What happened with that infant today was a miracle. There is no medical reason why that baby is alive, let alone him having no obvious signs of brain damage." Doc told him that Kenny and he should be proud of their efforts, as he knew they were. Doc said he was proud of them too. Doc got a real serious look on his face and said "Now, God damn it, you listen to me! You can't take 'credit' for saving that baby today. If you do, you will have to take the 'blame' for the one you may lose tomorrow, and you couldn't live with that." Doc said "Bucko, you had a good day, that's the end of it, and you damn well better know, that a cup of coffee is still fifty cents."
Doc stood up, punched him in the shoulder and walked out of the bar.

Flanagan went to the bar and asked Benny for three beers, he took them back to the furthest and darkest corner of the bar. He

121

sat in the booth with his back to the room. Flanagan heard a distant voice ask Kenny where he was. Kenny responded "He's in the back, we are going to leave him alone for a while." Flanagan couldn't help but smile, to know that his pal Kenny was guarding over him. Kenny knew his heart.

Flanagan sat in that dingy corner and drank to quiet himself. He could not shut off his thoughts. He knew he had to let go of "The Call." He knew that saving that baby would not mend his broken heart. He knew he had to accept the fact that he would always be a broken man.

He thought about leaving the bar, going to his car (parked in front of the headquarters station) reaching under his seat, grabbing his gun and blowing his brains out. He laughed to himself at what a site it would be and the irony of having those same news crews who were standing in the same place a few hours ago, capturing a celebration, now reporting and photographing the body of a dead hero. "Fuck-em! I won't give those sick fucks the pleasure of rummaging thru my past and exploring the darkness of a deeply disturbed young man. They are just a bunch of morbid bastards making a living off of exploiting other people's suffering and failings. Yah, report this, you piece of shit!"

As he sat in that booth he became more and more depressed. He thought about his second wife, Liz, and their empty marriage. They were nothing more than an attractive young couple who always lit up any room they entered. Neither of them had the emotional depth of a Petri Dish. He wondered what she would say when he told her of 'The Call.' He sadly knew that she would not see him as a hero. She would say "That's nice, you're drunk." He knew she would not want to hear about it. He knew he had to somehow come to terms with loosing Saundra and Paula, as well as accepting the cruel fact that his current marriage was doomed......and so was he.

Flanagan didn't know how he got home that afternoon, he didn't remember if he told Liz about 'The Call' or not. He didn't remember any part of that day after leaving the bar. Liz woke him early the next morning, telling him that her parents were there and wanted to see him. As he walked into the kitchen they were both smiling as they pointed to the morning newspaper laid out on the table. The entire front page was one big picture of a silhouette of him outside of the ER. You could see the cherry of his cigarette as he was taking a drag, the entire background was a blur of red lights. The next few pages had several close-up pictures of him and Kenny. His Mother-in-law pointed out that it looked like he had tears running down his face in several pictures. He told her, and them, that he was sweating and not crying. Flanagan, went back to bed.

Chapter 15 "DADDY'S LITTLE BUDDY"

Flanagan and Kenny were on duty. It was early summer, on a Saturday. They had just been served their lunch at their favorite Mom & Pop, greasy spoon restaurant. The place was packed. They had to sit in the far rear of the restaurant. It had been a quiet day, they had only three calls since 7:00 am. There were eight crews on shift and all were in quarters. They were sixth up and felt pretty good about having a relaxing and undisturbed meal. For a change.

Before Flanagan could pour the ketchup for his fries, a four tone alert came over their portable radio from police dispatch: (4 tone alerts are always emergencies. Medical, fire and police all respond Code 3, lights and sirens). "Rampart Rescue Ambulance Unit #158, respond to an industrial accident, reference; party has his arm caught in a meat grinder."

Flanagan and Kenny looked at each other, both full well knowing that, that man would be dead long before they got his arm out of the meat grinder. There were three meat packing plants in town and the meat grinders don't know the difference between human and animal flesh. They had been on several meat grinder calls. All of the victims bleed to death. With Unit #158 being dispatched, they lost their comfort of a relaxed meal. They started to eat with earnest.

Within two minutes of Unit #158 going out, another four tone alert was broadcast; "Rampart Rescue Ambulance Units #159, #160, and #161, respond to a signal 10-52, State Highway #34 and County Road #13, head-on traffic accident. Semi-truck VS. Church bus, unknown injury's. All area medical Units clear your calls ASAP and standby. All emergency teams are now on full alert; mutual-aid is rolling."

They wolfed down their meal. Within a few minutes, a State Trooper on the scene of the head-on traffic accident requested four additional ambulance Units respond Code 3, reporting several serious injuries with signal 10:54, (multiple fatality's). Ambulances from the adjoining county were dispatched to fill the troopers' request. Flanagan and Kenny pushed their plates away and reached into their pockets to get out their money to pay for their unfinished meals. They were next up. Before they could stand up to walk to the cashier, there came another, four tone alert broadcast from police dispatch; "Rampart Rescue Ambulance Unit #164, respond to a child with head injuries, possible 10:72 (D.O.A.)"

Before dispatch could air the address, they were sprinting thru the restaurant. Flanagan and Kenny both knew that parents often times panicked and over reported the seriousness of their child's injuries. The kid could have fallen out of a tree or off his bike, but most injuries were minor. That, of course, did not slow them down. Flanagan drove hard, risking life and limb. An 'on scene' police officer radioed to them "Rampart Unit #164, step it up, blood and gray matter is oozing from the side of this kids head, he looks dead." Flanagan was already sliding thru corners and driving into oncoming traffic, but then, he drove even harder. They were on the ragged edge of crashing. As they arrived at the scene, there was a rescue squad, a pumper truck and a couple of police cars and a large crowd of onlookers. At a glance, he saw the dejected look on the faces of the fire fighters and he knew, the child was dead.

When you arrive on scene, you are trained to scan the entire area in Nano seconds. He saw a woman sitting on the steps of the front porch of the house, with a police officer and two firefighters talking with her. While they were talking, he could see the lady was mentally and emotionally checked-out. He radioed dispatch for another Unit for Mom and sent Kenny to tend to her. He found Daddy, sitting on the lawn, rocking from side to side, holding his little boy. He checked the child and he, was indeed, dead.

Flanagan saw a kid's play lawn mower with a clear plastic dome with several colored small plastic balls. Next to it was a gas lawn mower. A cop came up to him and whispered that the Dad was mowing the lawn with the three-year-old boy walking alongside his Daddy, with his play lawn mower. Daddy's lawn mower kicked up a rock and it struck the child in the left temple.

Flanagan went back to the rig, radioed for a coroner and deemed the area a crime scene. All accidental deaths are looked at, as a homicide, until a coroner arrives to make a determination as to, cause of death. Wisconsin state law requires the lead police officer to secure the scene and the lead paramedic to take charge of the body until the Coroner arrives to make the determination. From radio chatter on the way to this call they heard that the head-on crash had several fatalities. He knew the Coroner would be some time out. He brought a blanket from the rig and draped it over Daddy's shoulder to give him some comfort and privacy. Flanagan was not about to remove that child, from his father's arms. He stood next to Daddy with his hand on his shoulder, again to comfort, but more importantly to keep Daddy seated. He had seen parents' panic and run with their injured children in the past.

The back-up crew arrived to transport the Mother. Kenny had already started an IV, pushed a sedative, and had her on oxygen. Mom was catatonic and in respiratory distress. As the second Unit was loading Mom, Daddy started to wail and kept sobbing "My baby, my baby, my baby." The Coroner radioed that he would be another half hour or so at the head-on crash.

Flanagan had no choice, as he could see that Daddy was about to lose it. In his fresh cleaned and well pressed uniform, he sat behind Daddy on the grass and scooted up to him like two little kids would do on a snow sled. He held Daddy and they rocked back and forth with the baby in Daddy's arms. The Coroner arrived and asked Flanagan if everything looked right. He nodded and asked "Permission to transport?" The Coroner ruled the death, as accidental and ordered him to take physical control of the body, (until the autopsy is complete the body is treated as evidence and the rules of evidence must be followed) and transport the body to the morgue. The Coroner said he had to leave and go across town for a suicide. As he started to leave, he brushed his hand thru Daddy's hair and kissed Daddy on the head. The Coroner told Flanagan "Don't leave this man alone."

126

In cases like this, the surviving family member would ride in the front of the ambulance with the driver. The attending paramedic rides in the back with the body. Flanagan waited until he heard a car door slam and a car drive away. He looked up at a firefighter standing in front of them and asked "Is he gone?" The firefighter nodded his head. Flanagan said "Slowly, help us up." Several hands gently lifted them to their feet. He walked Daddy to the side door of the rig and sat him (with his son in his arms) on the paramedic's jump seat and strapped them in. As he closed the door, he looked at the firefighters and cops in front of him and said "Not a word." They all nodded, (they all knew that what he was doing was against the law and the rules of evidence). As Flanagan walked around the front of the rig to get behind the wheel, a man stepped out of the crowd of onlookers and told him he lived across the street and was Daddy's best friend. The friend asked him if there was anything he could do. Flanagan looked at the lawn mower and told him "Finish mowing the lawn. When you're done, put the lawn mower along with the toy mower in your garage and cover them with a tarp. Hire a lawn service for them, for the rest of the summer."

Flanagan and Kenny rode in silence on the way to the morgue. When they arrived, he opened the side door to let Daddy out. Daddy stepped out with a slight smile on his face and extended his arms and laid his son into Flanagan's arms as he said, "Thank you for giving me this time with my boy."

Kenny stayed with Daddy as Flanagan carried the little guy into the morgue. He checked him into the morgue with the attendant. When the paper work was completed and signed, Flanagan kissed "Daddy's Little Buddy" on the forehead and stepped out the back door for a smoke, and a few tears of his own.

They took Daddy to the hospital and signed him into the Emergency Room for an evaluation. Flanagan wished him well and they shook hands. Daddy pulled out a $10 bill from his shirt pocket and said "When you were walking my son into the morgue, I noticed your pants were full of grass stains, I want to pay for your dry cleaning." Flanagan took the $10 bill as a sign of honor and respect and thanked him. Little did Daddy know that he would change uniforms three times, before shift change. The grass stains were of little concern. That $10 bill would put him and Kenny into their fourth beers, shortly after their end of watch.

A few weeks later, Flanagan ran into one of the Cops who was at the scene that day and he told him that he was at that same house last night, to take a missing person's report. Daddy said his wife didn't come home from work. The Officer said he searched the wife's bedroom closet and dresser drawers. They were all empty. Mom was not missing; she had left him.

The day following Flanagan's conversation with the Cop, they were dispatched to Daddy's house for a stand-by, for a suicidal person with a gun. It took several hours for the Police and a Catholic Priest to convince Daddy to put the gun down and come outside. Daddy was every bit as catatonic as Mommy was a few weeks ago, sitting on the stairs of their front porch.

S.O.P. calls for suicidal patients to be handcuffed and put into four-point leather restraints prior to transport. It broke his heart to do that but it was his responsibility to protect his patient. Flanagan held Daddy's hand and wiped his tears during the ride to the hospital. Daddy was admitted to a locked physic unit.

That November, during the Wisconsin, White-Tail, Deer hunting season a hunter found a dead human body. The dead man died from a self- inflicted gunshot wound. It was Daddy.

Flanagan felt a kinship with Daddy, a kind of shared soulfulness. He carried Daddy's suffering quietly in his own heart. He tried to book off his shift for Daddy's funeral but all the guys on days off, were deer hunting. He had to attend Daddy's funeral on duty and in uniform.

Kenny stayed out front of the church leaning on a fender of the rig. Kenny was Native American and found churches to be creepy. Flanagan knelt at Daddy's casket. He told Daddy that he understood his reasons, his pain, his sorrow and his shame. He told Daddy that he, had had the same thoughts of ending it all. He told him he understood that the pain of loving someone you can't have, must be far greater than the pain of dying. He told Daddy that they would meet-up on the other-side, someday. They will drink a beer together as they watch their kid's playing and laughing together.

As Flanagan stood to leave the church, the 'across the street neighbor and best buddy,' of Daddy, blocked his path. He and his wife threw their arms around him and kissed his cheeks. The neighbor told him that Daddy and all the other neighbors who were in the crowd on that tragic day, spoke of him often and of his tenderness and compassion. The neighbor's wife buried her face in his chest and said several kind words that caused him to blush. She did say, if he were to run for Mayor the entire neighborhood would see to it that he would be elected. Flanagan thanked them both and wished them well.

As he started to walk down that seemingly never ending isle, several people stood and reached out to touch him and shake his hand. They nodded their heads and smiled thru their swollen, tear filled eyes. Flanagan's feet would not carry him as fast as his own tears came. As he walked to the rig, he told Kenny to "Put us back in service." Kenny said "Nope, were going to have a smoke together first." Kenny smoked a cigarette about once a month and he had to be drunk to do it. They leaned against the rig and smoked in silence.

Flanagan climbed behind the wheel, picked up the mic to radio dispatch and said "Rampart Rescue Ambulance Unit #164 is 10:8, (clear from this call), back in service, returning to quarters." But he was not "Back in Service." He knew, he would never again, be… "Back in Service."

That day, and all the other day's and months and years had taken their toll. Having to witness all the carnage, the screams, the suffering, the fear of the afflicted, the sorrow and tears of family whose lives would change forever, put a hole in his belly. There was no peace for him, no comfort, and no joy. He had nowhere to go to get away from it. It all lived inside of him and he had been gutted by it. He couldn't quit the job however, he still had the burning desire to save lives. He just didn't know how to save his own.

That night, he laid in his bunk in the darkness of the squad room. He felt like a self-absorbed, phony ass-hole. He was comparing the loss of his little baby girl to Daddy's loss of his son. He knew he had no right to do that. He never got to hold his baby, or to hear her make a sound, he just got to look at a fancy marble box on an end table and know that she was inside of it. Daddy had a son who he raised, he taught him how to eat, how to crawl, how to walk and how to talk. Daddy lost his reason and his will to live. He killed his baby and he had lost his soul. Flanagan only had a dream and nothing else. Yes, he still had not found the ability to mourn the loss of Saundra, the loss of his wife and the loss of his lifelong friend. The lifelong friend who carried him thru the fear, the hunger, the cold, the many, childhood beatings. His lifelong friend that he clung to, and gave him the only reason to live when he had no other. His lifelong best friend: was his dream. His dream, to someday, be a good Daddy.

Chapter 16 "BECOMING A SON AND FINALLY A MAN"

When Donnie was 27 years old, he died. It was sudden. Flanagan went to pick Donnie up early one morning to go trout fishing. When his brother answered the door his eyes were jaundice, his skin a pale yellow. Flanagan took him to his doctor and then, on to the hospital. Donnie died three weeks later. Donnie was a drunk but had been sober for two years. The day he died he told Flanagan "I didn't care if I lived or died, most all of my life, now I want to live, and I can't."

Flanagan's Dad took it real hard. Dad had been sober for the last twelve years. Flanagan thought Donnie's death would send Dad back to the bottle and he told him so. Dad, very calmly but firmly, said "I will not dishonor your brother's sobriety and his passing, by drinking. It would not serve me." Mom and Dad were heartbroken. Donnie was a hard case, full of hate and contempt, he spent half of his young adult life in jail. He was finally trying to make something of his life. Mom, Dad and he started to trust Donnie again, he was becoming a good guy, and then, they lost him. That fall, Flanagan and his Dad went deer hunting. It was strange not to have Donnie there with them. They both felt the void but they only said "Yeah, I miss him too" and they let it go. It was too fresh. It would hurt too much to talk about him.

Flanagan's Dad worked on the railroad as a brakeman. He was always in ore dust and smoked two packs of cigarettes a day along with five cigars. His Dad coughed a lot. On this hunting trip, his Dad was coughing more than usual. They agreed on a time and place to meet in the woods so they could walk out together, before nightfall. Flanagan could not find him at the designated meeting place. He found his Dad a half mile away, sitting on a windfall. He was having extreme trouble breathing. His Dad had a good 60 pounds on him. Flanagan carried his dad out of the woods. He can't explain how. His Dad had the same family cancer that Donnie had. Dad suffered a lot with weakness, pain, nausea, but he mostly suffered from the loss of his dignity.

Dad was well respected in the AA group community, and was known as the go-to guy when you're troubled, he was a rock for all. He would drag, push, pull or carry you through the hard times. From who his Dad was when Flanagan was a child, to who he became were worlds apart. But now the, 'rock,' his rock, was crumbling. His Dad was dying. His Dad was a proud but humble man. He always did for himself. Suddenly it would take him twenty minutes to get dressed. He would break out in a sweat just trying to button his shirt. His Dad hurt most of all, when he lost his voice and his ability to walk. Oh, but not for himself. It hurt him not to be able to attend AA meetings, not to take phone calls and give council to those desperate to find sobriety. The pain of his cancer was minor, compared to the pain in his heart. Dad had dedicated his entire being and life to AA.

While his Dad still had his voice he called Flanagan to have lunch with him and Phil (one of the guys his Dad sponsored and one of the Hearts card players who gave them candy bars on Saturdays when they were kids.) Dad had sponsored Phil for ten years. The entire family liked Phil. At lunch that day, his Dad told Phil that he wasn't going to last much longer. His Dad asked Phil to take care of Mom and the two boys still at home (Petey, 16 years old, and Stevie, 11 years old). Mother didn't know how to drive, pay a bill, not even how to read a bill, let alone how to write out a check. No, Mom wasn't stupid, Dad just always did it all. Dad asked Phil to take care of the "mob." Phil said he would. And he did.

As his Dad was at his very end of life, his Mom had read about Laetrile treatments in Mexico. His Dad had all the standard cancer treatments of the era. They even opened him up to remove a lung but he was too far gone. They just closed him back up and gave him a month to live. At that time, his Dad could not stand to his full height, could not keep any food down, couldn't walk without help and could not speak. He was just a shell of the man he once was. His Mom decided to take his Dad to Tijuana, Mexico, for the Laetrile treatments.

Flanagan took his Dad to his final doctor appointment and told the doctor that this was his Dad's last visit, as they were going to take Dad to Mexico. The doctor was upset and said "You don't know the side effects of Laetrile." Flanagan told the doctor that the side effects of all of his treatments were death. Flanagan couldn't remember if he called the doctor a fucking quack, or if he just wanted to.

So here is his little Mother, four-foot four inches, ninety pounds, hadn't been on an airplane in all her life, never been out of the state, didn't know Spanish or the Mexican culture or ways. His Mom cashed in his Dad's hundred dollar U.S. savings bonds that he bought through payroll deductions. There were a lot of them, but none had matured to full value. So, get this, this was 1976. No computers, no web, no cell phones, yet 'never been anywhere,' Mom, set up a flight, set up a hospital and doctor in Tijuana for Dad, and rented an apartment on the U.S. side of the border, all by herself. Mom would walk across the bridge each morning to spend the day with Dad and take a bus to her rented room at night and stayed by herself. Flanagan had yet to meet anyone with that level of courage, conviction and love.

After Dad was in the Tijuana hospital for two weeks he was a different man. After the U.S. doctors gave up on him and were ready to deliver him to death's door, Dad came back. Well, of sorts he did. The pain that dulled his eyes and put a constant grimace on his face was gone. Dad could talk again and walked without assistance and stood at his full height. Flanagan had gotten along ok with his Dad and secretly admired him for who he had become, but he never let on. He couldn't forgive him for his childhood. He was distant, he guessed he was still trying to punish him. Oh, they fished together, hunted, played cards (family stuff), but he still kept him at bay. Clinton and his wife went to their AA monthly club dinners, the turkey Bingos, and the annual AA roundups where his Dad was oftentimes the keynote speaker. When his Dad spoke, Flanagan would sit in amazement. Here stood a man with profound command of the English language, who spoke from his heart, his eyes glistened with sorrows of the past and extreme gratitude and joy for the present and future. He could make you cry and laugh in the same breath. He told the truth. His Dad's message of hope inspired thousands of hopelessly lost souls. So many times Flanagan heard people tell his Dad and others of how his Dad's words had changed their lives, forever.

But no, not him, he couldn't let go of it. When Dad told his 'story,' of what it was like, what happened, and what it is like now, he moved mountains. But not him. His Dad told of his wrongs and shortcomings but they were just words. He felt it, he was there! It was like yesterday. Flanagan still felt the fear, the pain, and tasted the blood in his mouth and the hunger in his belly. He would sit in an arena auditorium with five to eight thousand people in recovery, with his Dad at the podium on a huge stage with the audience hanging on every one of his words, and Flanagan secretly was thinking "No fucker, I'm not going to let you off that easy, I was fucking there!" After each one of his Dad's talks the applause was deafening, you could see thousands of smiling faces with moist eyes and hope in their hearts. Flanagan's Dad was magical.

Flanagan hated his dad for not being that way when he was a little boy. That's how he wanted his Daddy to be. And again, he would say in his head "Yeah, you're some kind of fucking hero now, aren't you? Go fuck yourself."

His heart told him a whole other thing. His heart said "Get in the receiving line with the rest of these glad handing phonies and when you work your way up to your Dad, in about an hour's time, shake his hand and say quietly, Dad, I forgive you. I love you." Flanagan had many chances to do that. He never did. In 1976 Flanagan was twenty-eight years old, living in the pain of a long-time passed. Full of sorrow, full of hate, and yet he couldn't admit to his Father or himself that he loved him. He quit saying that twenty years ago.

Flanagan spoke to his Mom every night on the phone while Dad was in the hospital in Mexico. He could hear the fear in her voice, but her bravery spoke louder as she talked of the days events and Dad's condition. One night, as he hung up the phone from speaking with his Mother, it struck him "You, Clinton Flanagan, are a coward. You are a fucking phony!" And he knew it was time.

The next morning, he bought a new suit, tie, shirt, argyle socks and shoes. He got a haircut, and a flight to Los Angeles. Liz (his second wife) was pissed off that he spent their money that way and she didn't see the urgency and necessity for the trip, he knew she wouldn't. Flanagan's Uncle Billy, picked him up at the airport. The following day he put on his new suit to show his Dad his respect for him. It humbled him. It felt good. Billy and he drove to Tijuana to see Dad. He didn't tell his Mom he was coming.

When Billy and he walked into Dad's hospital room that morning Dad was asleep. Mother was startled and began to cry. She leapt into his arms and sobbed, saying "I've been so lonely, so scared." Billy, all but pushed them out of Dad's hospital room, saying "We don't want to wake up that handsome old bastard." Billy was grinning as Mom and Flanagan held each other. Billy got it, he got every bit of it. He somehow knew.

They all went to lunch. As they ate he could see his Mom's loneliness. It broke his heart. "How could I be so selfish to let poor little Mom be here all alone? Why didn't I step up and be a man and take charge of this from the very beginning? I'm a self-centered prick." Flanagan had only planned to see Dad for that day and had a reservation to fly back home that night. He had his suitcase in Billy's trunk. Billy was going to drop him off at the LAX airport on his way back home, to Anaheim.

Watching Mom eat her sandwich and trying to dab her eyes dry, he found himself saying to his Mother that he was going to stay with her, until it was time to take Dad back home. Then he thought "Holy shit, I got to be back to work tomorrow! Liz is going to lose her mind."

He found himself thinking the strangest thought of his life. "This is family, everyone else, can wait." He felt a peace wash over him, like he had never known. He knew he had finally become a man, a real man.

They left the hospital cafeteria and as they were walking to the elevator Billy nudged him, winked and said "You two go ahead. I'm going to go and buy Claudia, (his wife) a little gift and I'll catch up with you guys a little later." Flanagan and his Mother held hands as they got into the elevator and as they walked down the hall to Dad's room. Mom told him to wait in the hall as she peeked in on him. She came out of his room smiling. Mom said she told Dad that he was there, so as not to startle him, and Dad wanted a few minutes to put on a shirt and comb his hair. When Flanagan walked into Dad's room, he was sitting on the side of his bed. Dad looked him up and down, grinning, and gave a low whistle and said "I knew you were here. I overheard the nurses giggling about a movie star on the floor, wearing an expensive three-piece suit." Dad said "I think I can get you a date and you could probably be married before breakfast tomorrow."

That was his Dad! That's the way he kidded with his friends. It meant they were friends! Mom tried to excuse herself, to let "you boys talk." Flanagan said "No, I don't have anything to say to Dad, that you can't hear." Flanagan told his Dad that he was sorry for treating him so poorly, for his trying to punish him by withholding his forgiveness.

As weak as he was, Dad stood on his feet and said "Thank you, Son. I have been wanting and praying to hear those words from you, ever since I've been sober." They hugged. Dad kissed his cheek and said "I love you." Flanagan said the same. They both cried. His Dad said he was always proud of him but didn't feel worthy of telling him so. Again, Flanagan said the same.

Flanagan finally got to have his Dad, and he got to be his Son, but he knew not to trust it. Dad looked better than he had in the last three months. But he knew in his heart that he would die soon. Flanagan knew he had to cherish these moments.

Mom had the brightest eyes and biggest smile he had ever seen. The three of them hugged and felt God's presence. They said the Lord's Prayer together. He didn't ever remember praying with his parents before. It felt honest.

Several hours later, Uncle Billy came into the room with that, 'Flanagan boys' patented, shit-eating grin, sparkling green eyes, and a wink that was faster than the speed of sound. Billy had a big cardboard box in his hands and Flanagan could smell steak! "Billy was only gone a few hours. Where did he get this kind of food in Tijuana?" In the box were four, vary large T-bone steaks, (still hot), mashed potatoes, gravy, dinner rolls, green beans, and corn. They had a feast. His Dad ate less than half of his meal. Mom (who he could see had lost weight) ate all of hers. After dinner, his Dad suggested that they head back across the border before nightfall. Flanagan kissed his Dad's forehead and told him he would see him in the morning.

Billy drove them to Mom's apartment, but it wasn't an apartment – it was an eight-by-ten foot, cinder block room, with a little kids' bed and an unfinished cement floor. No bathroom, no T.V., no phone. Mom was using a pay phone at the apartment office, which was also the location of the community bathroom and bathtub. He was disgusted with himself for allowing his Mother to have to live like that. If only he had known. But then again, his selfish bullshit didn't allow for that. Mom went to the office to use the bathroom. He was about to tell Billy to drive them the hell out of there to a decent motel. Billy beat him to it. Billy told him he had rented them two adjoining rooms at a much better hotel just a few miles away. Billy pulled an envelope from his pocket and said "Here, use this for meals and cab fare. Don't walk anywhere and don't ride the bus, it's too dangerous." He also said that the hotel rooms were paid for as long as they needed them. In the envelope was five thousand dollars. Flanagan said, "Billy, it's too much. We don't need all of this." Billy then told him of the plan. When Dad got out of the hospital he would still need his medications for two months, and that medication was illegal in the United States. Billy and Claudia (his wife and a registered nurse) had set up a room for Dad at their house to take care of him. Billy had been paying the doctor for the drugs and the

137

doctor had a 'mule' smuggle the drugs across the border to treat Dad with when he got to the States, in another week or so.

Mom came back from the office after using the bathroom. He could see she was repulsed and humiliated from the experience but she did not complain. Billy told Mom to pack her bags, as he had found a better hotel for her to stay in. Mom's face said it all. She was back out of that room in less than five minutes (a lot less). Mom was broke; she had spent all her money, every bit, just trying to keep Dad alive. Flanagan had very little money himself. Billy's kindness and generosity saved them all. Mom stood next to Billy, reached down and grasped Billy's hand as she trembled with tears streaming down her face with her head bowed. They all had tears, as they stood in that rutted dirt parking lot of that shit-hole motel. On the way to the new hotel Mother kept asking "Clint, are you really going to stay with me?" He kept saying "Yes Mom, I planned for it all along." He knew God should punish him for this lie.

Billy had them all checked into the hotel and as they were unloading Mom's bags from the back seat of the car, Billy opened the trunk so Flanagan could get his bag out. Flanagan grabbed his bag and noticed a second piece of luggage in the trunk. Billy whispered "I got this one for you." Flanagan glanced at him and Billy gave him quick headshake as to say "shut-up" and he shut-up.

That was a nice hotel, nice rooms, with an upscale restaurant and bar. Mom and he had adjoining rooms. Billy and he let Mom into her room. She said she wanted to wash up. He put his two bags in his room and walked Billy to his car for his trip home, to Anaheim, California. He asked Billy about the second bag. Billy grinned and said "Just a few things you may need for the next week. Besides, your Mom, would have caught on. It will be our secret." In thanking Billy for all he had done and given, Billy said "Keep in mind that your Dad is also my brother." Enough said!

Here Billy and he stood; 1976, two men hugging in the

138

parking lot of an upscale hotel. Strange, even in California. Flanagan went to his room and opened the 'second suitcase,' and there he found a few packs of underwear, socks, casual shoes, two pairs of jeans, two pairs of slacks, six shirts and toiletries. It brought back the memories of the Stanford Police Department Christmas stockings with his name in glitter on it. The memories of Billy and Dad each cutting a side of his hair, the subsequent barber shop visit, the squirt gun fights, the ice cream, Billy's quick smile, his polished, kind voice. How even strangers smiled at him. What a quality guy! So kind, so generous, so honorable. He sat down looking at all those new expensive, quality clothes, the envelope of money, the room itself, and he thanked God.

Flanagan went to his Mom's room and asked her if she wanted to go downstairs to the restaurant for a cup of tea (Mom loved tea, she only drank a common brand but she liked it). He saw on the dresser a partial loaf of bread and a small jar of peanut butter and on top of the jar of peanut butter was an old, used, soggy, 'Lipton' tea bag wrapped in cellophane. He got it. He knew what he was looking at; Mom losing weight, going hungry to save money to take care of Dad. He sat down next to his Mom on the bed. He held her hand and said that he would take care of her. He told his Mom about the five thousand dollars that Billy gave them, as they left the room to go have tea. He collected the bread, the peanut butter, and the tired-out tea bag as they left the room, and dropped them in the trash can next to the elevator. At tea, his Mom kept raving about how wonderful and delicious the T-bone dinner was that Billy brought. He told Mom that he had never seen her eat a whole stake with all the fixings before. Mom said she was hungry. He asked her what she had been eating for the last ten days. She lowered her head and whispered "Half of a peanut butter sandwich for breakfast and the other half for dinner." She sheepishly then said, she stole the tea bag from the hospital cafeteria four days ago. She looked shameful. He ordered his Mom a piece of pie. They talked for a bit longer and he took her to her room. Mom held him tightly and cried and thanked him

139

profusely for coming. He kissed her on the cheek and said good night. After Mom closed her door he stood there for a moment. With gut punching shame washing over him, he turned and sprinted down the hallway to the elevator. He needed a drink.

It was the slowest elevator ride of his life! As he was riding down his mind raced. Here he was, two years sober, on his way to get drunk. "Oh, screw it, I'm in deep Southern California, next to the Mexican border, no one will know. And if they do find out, fuck-em." Flanagan got stupid drunk, sitting at the bar, and hating himself. He was a lousy bastard. What kind of man, what kind of son, is he, to allow his Mother to suffer like this? She standing in a hotel hallway thanking her own son profusely for doing what any other son would have done without a second thought. His final thought, as he wallowed in self-disgust, was as he was leaving the bar; "Donnie should have lived, I should have died."

The following morning, he shaved off all the hair on his body. His Mother and he met for breakfast. He told his Mom "We're not going to pay the $275 a day for the pharmacy mule to smuggle the drugs for Dad across the border. I am going to do it myself." His Mom looked horrified but she knew, that's what had to be done. Each day they had breakfast and rode a taxi to the hospital. Flanagan had bought an over-sized shirt and pair of pants. He would visit with his Dad for an hour, go to the pharmacy, buy the drugs and tape them to his body (everywhere), and walk across the border and go to their hotel. He made the trip twice a day. In the evening, he would visit with his Dad for an hour and Mom and he would take a taxi back to the hotel, have dinner and go to bed. All that walking made him want to sleep and not drink. And for the 100th plus times, he swore off booze, forever.

Flanagan's Dad was to be released from the Tijuana hospital the next day. As Flanagan made his final trip across the border that afternoon, he got caught. The drugs were not narcotics but illegal in the U.S. The Mexican border agents took all of the drugs he had taped to his body and told him the fine was exactly sixty-two dollars for smuggling. Sixty-two dollars was the exact amount of money they took from his pockets. He wanted to kill those fucking thieves. He was most certain that those pricks sold his drugs back to the pharmacy long before dinner time. He wasn't allowed back across the border. He called the hospital and told his Mom that she would have to ride the taxi back to the hotel alone that night. He was wore out but walked back to the hotel. Flanagan got their money from the guest safe, went to the bar, and got drunk. He had left his Mom a note at the hotel desk, he told her he was sick and he was going to bed. He put $50.00 in the envelope so she could call room service for dinner.

He sat at the bar in another pool of self-loathing, disgust. Flanagan's Mom and Billy picked up his Dad from the hospital and then him and his bags the next morning. Billy dropped him off at the airport on his way back to Anaheim with Mom and Dad.

Flanagan went to the airport ticket counter and got a flight that was leaving in three hours. He went to the bar and got drunk. But this time it wasn't over his dying Dad, his lost, helpless Mother, or any other of the thousands of excuses he has used. This time it was having to face a wife, that didn't love him. He had to face his own broken heart, again. The airline wouldn't let him on the flight, he was too drunk. It was the last flight to Minneapolis that night. He was too embarrassed to go back to the bar. He sat in a chair at the gate all night and flew out the next morning. He called his wife, Liz from the Stanford Airport to pick him up. She said she was busy. He took a taxi home.

Flanagan's Dad got pneumonia the next week. His Mom called him and asked him to "Talk some sense into your father, he needs to go back to Tijuana to be treated for pneumonia as he can't get the drugs he needs in a U.S. hospital." Mom put Dad on the phone. Dad told Mom to leave the room. Dad said "I am tired, and I am done. I just want to die right where I am laying." Flanagan told him he understood. His father told him that he loved him and to take care of Mom and Peter and Stevie. Flanagan told

141

his father that he would, and told him he loved him. Flanagan's Dad, died two days later, on February 20, 1976.

Flanagan knew he had to ask his wife, Liz for a divorce as he didn't like her lifestyle. But in truth, it was her lack of heart. She never saw or felt the sadness for the two little kids pulling that piece of shit sled in the street on Christmas Eve. She didn't understand his breaking heart of losing his Dad, the lousy Son he was, and his lifelong loneliness. It wasn't her fault, she was not a heartless bitch, she just never knew…because he never told her.

One of the many and perhaps, greater commonalities of being a drunk is that "They (we or I) just simply expect people to understand us and to somehow make us feel better. When our loved ones don't meet those expectations of healing us, to our entire satisfaction. We retaliate, we punish them, and we run away. If not physically, we most certainly do emotionally. Our loved ones, don't have a chance. They never did."

The Flanagan luck (or lack thereof) once again reared its ugly head. The Los Angeles County Coroner's office lost his Dad's body – for three days! Billy couldn't tell Mom as they were sure, that would be the end of her sanity. Flanagan didn't have the money to fly back to L.A. to escort his Mom and his Dad's body back home.

Here he was, twenty-seven years old, the oldest surviving Son, such a pathetic drunk that he can't even take care of his own Mother in her greatest time of need. What does a drunk do when he is so full of shame and self-loathing? He drinks, and he did.

Flanagan was overwhelmed on the day of his Dad's funeral. The service was at a Catholic Cathedral, jammed full of sober alcoholics. Flanagan stopped drinking that day, he stopped drinking forever, but it only lasted for nine months. He did his best to help Mom settle in. The boys, Petey and Stevie, were inconsolable.

Petey, was two years old when Dad got sober. He knew Dad was a mean drunk but Dad never hurt him. Petey had forgiven him and they were pals. Stevie had yet to be born when Dad sobered up and had no, first-hand knowledge of Dad as a drinker. Stevie idolized Dad. Stevie was 11 years old when Dad died and he was crushed. You could see his deep depression. Flanagan worried more about Stevie than he did his Mom. He tried to take Stevie to several different places to cheer him up but Stevie would have none of it. Stevie would not leave Mother's side. When Stevie was 15 years old, he earned a full-ride scholarship in music, to Boston College. Stevie turned the scholarship in, to stay home and take care of Mom. From that day to this, Stevie had never complained about passing on the coveted once-in-a-lifetime, 'Hunt Scholarship.'

Phil also stepped up, just as Dad had asked and as Phil promised. Phil did all he could to help Mom and the boys. He would stop in to see them a few times a week. Phil took Mom to all of her many Doctors' appointments, grocery shopping and anywhere else she needed to go.

Mom had been as involved in Al-anon as Dad was in AA. They were both highly-regarded, special event speakers. Mom lost her passion for Al-anon, and stopped attending AA events, and Al-anon meetings, she let go of her responsibilities to the groups and her sponsees'. Mom had just shut and locked the door on the world. On more than one occasion, Flanagan had thought he smelled beer on her breath. On one visit, Mom had a welt on her cheek. When he asked her what happened, she said she tripped while carrying a laundry basket up the basement stairs. Stevie was at the kitchen table when he asked the question. He saw Stevie roll his eyes. Flanagan finished his coffee with Mom and invited Stevie out to the driveway to shoot some hoops. He asked him about his kitchen table 'eye roll.' Stevie said Mom was drunk and fell in the kitchen. Stevie went on to tell him how Mom was drinking a six-pack of beer every night. Falling down, passing out with lit cigarettes and constantly crying. Petey later supported that, and added that for him to use Dad's car, Mom first made him drive her to the liquor store each afternoon before she would hand over the car keys to him for the night.

Flanagan started to call his Mom each morning, and on his days off, he would ask her what she wanted for dinner that night. He would pick up the groceries and fix them dinner, then would hang around all night until Mom got sleepy, thinking that she would go to bed and not drink. She out-foxed him. She would start drinking in the early morning as soon as the boys left for school. This went on for several months.

One evening at work, Flanagan was dispatched to a car accident with multiple injuries. As Rampart Unit #164 was rolling out from headquarters, another crew was dispatched to an "Unconscious woman down, bleeding from the head." It was Flanagan's Mother's home address. Flanagan radioed the second-out crew and told them that they were trading calls.

When Flanagan arrived at his Mothers' house his Mom was sitting up, Petey was holding a towel to the back of Mom's head to stop the blood flow. Mom had a two-inch gash on the back of her head and she reeked of beer. Mom didn't want to go to the hospital. Flanagan went out to the rig and radioed for a police squad.

Cops and paramedics work together all the time. Everyone knows everyone and they all get along. He asked the cop to, "Baker Act" his Mom and take her into protective custody and order him to transport her to the hospital. Mother, who he hadn't even heard her say, 'poop', in the last 10 years, told the cop to go fuck himself. So here he was, wrestling his own Mother on the floor with his partner and two cops. Mom used some hard language as blood was spurting from her head. Flanagan had to handcuff his own Mother. As he strapped her to the gurney she was trying to kick his partner, and she spit in his face several times. Flanagan's Mother called him every bad word there was, and kept saying the very same things he heard as a small child. "I wish I had never had you, I wish you were dead." Flanagan was choking back his tears as he was trying to settle his Mother down and trying to think of what he was going to do, to help her.

Flanagan took his Mom to the hospital where he knew his old pal Dr. Long, was on duty in the E.R. He told Dr. Long of Mom's heavy drinking, hard times and heartaches. He asked him to order a, 'seventy-two-hour mental health hold,' to give him time to get a court order for a thirty-day in-patient alcohol treatment program. Dr. Long honored his request. In part, Dr. Long wanted to help him and his family, and his Mom had called him some harsh names with very, unladylike language.

Before Flanagan's shift was over the next morning, Petey called him and said "Mom is at the house, sitting at the kitchen table in a hospital gown, drinking beer." Flanagan told Petey not to go to school and to watch Mom, and that he would be there in the late afternoon. Flanagan dashed through the many County Social Services offices. By 2:00 pm that same day, he stood before a judge and swore an oath and attested that all of his statements were true and correct. The judge signed the court order for a thirty-day in-patient, locked, alcohol recovery treatment center. When Flanagan got to the house to serve his Mother the warrant, she was drunk and passed out. He had brought Liz with him to help keep Mom calm (his Mother adored Liz). He carried Mom to the car and put her in the back seat. Liz sat with her in case Mom started to act up. Mom never came-to. As Flanagan lifted his Mother out of the car to put her on a gurney, he knew it was the last time he would ever get to touch or see his Mother. She would hate him forever. But at least, she would be alive. He would just have to deal with it.

Four days later, on August 10, 1977 Flanagan's Mother called him and said "Clinton, thank you. I never knew you loved me, this much." Mom and he became great pals, and she lived out her life as an active and respected member of Alcoholics Anonymous. Mother died with 34 years of continuous sobriety.

Chapter 17 "ANOTHER FRESH START"

After Flanagan's divorce was final. Flanagan did ask Scotty for Blondie's note. He called her a week later and she invited him to her home to spend the next weekend. Blondie's name was Sandy. He drove 170 miles to see her. When he arrived at Sandy's apartment building, she walked out pouring a cold Michelob beer into a frosted mug. She thrust the mug at him and just stood back with her arms folded and a huge smile. He drank the beer, they hugged and it felt like the elevator crush all over again. She broke the hug and took his hand and said "Come with me, Mister. We have some talking to do." They entered her apartment and she pointed to a chair and said "Sit there, I'm going to get us a beer." She came back in the room, handed him the beer and pulled a chair directly in front of him. She looked serious, yet, still sweet. She was shockingly direct. She said that she had been looking for him all of her life and she was not ever going to let him go. She told him of her past, her failings and her faults and he was pretty sure she didn't leave anything out. She spilled her guts in less than an hour and another two beers. She leaned forward in her chair, put both her hands on his knees, looked him directly in the eyes and said "I told you all these things to clear the deck, I will keep no secrets from you, because I want to marry you." She cried for a few moments than wiped her eyes, stood up, took his hand and said, "Now, come make love to me."

Flanagan called his boss that evening and told him he was taking a week off. His boss laughed and said "I am not surprised, see you next week and come in on time for a change."

That week was like spending every moment in Disneyland. Every morning she would wake him with a fresh cup of coffee and asked "What can I do to make you happy today?" Flanagan's response was always the same "I would like you to make time stand still." And he meant it.

Sandy was the first woman that he loved who he could also

146

be friends with. He was able to tell her of his truths without fear of being judged or viewed as weak. Well, at least some of his truths.

It was hard for them to live so far away from each other. On her days off she would drive up to visit and he would do the same. If they had the same night off, they would meet half way and spend the night together. They oftentimes spoke of one of them moving so they could be together.

Sandy wanted him to meet her family who lived in Cheyenne, Wyoming. He couldn't afford the time off of work or the cost of the airfare. Sandy called him one evening and told him there was a package on its way and he should look for an overnight envelope the following day. Sandy would not tell him of its contents. The next day he was called into the dispatch booth and handed the overnight envelope. Inside was a round trip airline ticket to Denver along with two, one hundred dollar bills. The ticket showed a December 24th departure from Mpls/St. Paul. When he spoke with Sandy that night, he thanked her for the ticket and told her he had booked off the time for the trip. When he asked her what the $200 was for, she just laughed and said "It's for anything you want." She was just that way. Sandy flew out a few days before him to spend some time with her family.

Flanagan's flight was delayed for several hours due to snow storms, both in Minneapolis and Denver. Flanagan's plane had to return to the gate twice for de-icing. The airline was giving free booze to keep the few passengers on the flight calm. He became very, very calm. They circled Denver, for quite some time.

As he came off the plane, he knew that he was so drunk that he couldn't find his ass with either hand. He was ashamed of himself for being so stupid, as he knew he was about to meet Sandy's sister Connie, for the first time. He didn't want to embarrass Sandy and make a bad impression on her sister. As he came out of the jet-way, he thanked God for smiling down upon him. For there stood, (or should he say, weaved), Sandy and her sister Connie. They had red swollen eyes, and they both had the same Cheshire-Cat grin and those girls were snott-slingin drunk!

Sandy almost knocked him off his feet when she threw herself into his arms. She sobbed as her entire body trembled. Connie was also crying.

When Sandy finally calmed down, she told him that the airlines told them that they had lost contact with his plane. They were given drink vouchers for the airport lounge and were told that an airline representative would brief them in the lounge as soon as they got word of the flight. Sandy was sure that his plane had crashed. As they were walking to the baggage claim Sandy spun in front of him and grabbed him by the collar with both hands, she shook him much harder than she had to, and said "Mister, I will never let you out of my sight, ever again. If one of us dies, we will die together!"

There was an ice storm in Denver and the 110 mile ride to Cheyanne was a slide job most all of the way. Sandy was babbling non-stop, (that was not like her to act that way) she said that she was going to quit her job, move to Stanford and flip burgers if she had to, but they would never be apart, ever again. He blew most of her rant off and chalked it up to whiskey talk. Yet, a part of him knew that she was locked in fear of losing him. He had those same fears of losing her, but he could never speak of it.

He didn't remember getting to her folks house of even going to bed, but he had this strange vision of cowboy boots and thought "Who the fuck wears cowboy boots, cowboys all died off in the early 1900's!"

At 7:30 the next morning (Sunday) he was awoken by a booming voice that belonged to the guy leaning on the doorjamb. He recognized him from some pictures Sandy had shown him, as Dad. Dad announced "We are going to service in twenty minutes, get up and get dressed, we can't be late."

Sandy was not in bed. He thought, "Oh shit.... church...with this hangover? Not without a shower and what the hell am I supposed to wear?" Sandy flounced into the bedroom with a smirk on her face and said, "I see you met Dad" and started laughing. She was wearing a robe. He asked her why she wasn't dressed for church, she again laughed at him and reached into his suitcase and threw a pair of jeans at him. She went to his garment bag and tossed a shirt from it, onto the bed, as she said "Put these on, just you and Dad are going to service this morning." As he was buttoning his shirt he asked, "What the hell" for the dozenth time in as many minutes. He washed his face, brushed his teeth and stumbled into the kitchen.

There sat Mom and Dad. Mom stood up and gave him a warm hug. Dad said "Sit down, no time for coffee, we are going to be late." Flanagan could see and smell fresh coffee all around. Sandy was grinning at him over her coffee cup, as she slurped loudly and smacked her lips saying "This is sure some mighty fine coffee." She and Mom were giggling. Dad thrust a big box in front of Flanagan's face and said "Put these on, I'll be damned if I'm going to take you to service wearing those stupid, `flat-lander` shoes." In the box were a pair of light tan, suede, 'Tony Lama', rough-out cowboy boots. Even he, had to admit that they were beautiful. He put them on, stood up and almost fell over with his first step. Now the whole kitchen was giggling, Dad pushed him out of the kitchen as Mom reached into the hall closet and pulled out a navy blue poplin, down jacket that had front and back yokes that were inlaid with rough-out suede, the very same light tan color as his new boots. Mom held the jacket so he could put it on. The jacket fit like a glove. Mom kissed him on the cheek and said, "Welcome to Wyoming, Son!"

As Dad and he walked to his truck he said under his breath "Guess I'm going to be a God damn cowboy!" So here he was, hung-over (if not still a bit drunk), trying to walk on an icy sidewalk, wearing pointed toed cowboy boots with two inch heels. Flanagan was thinking "Y'all can kiss my flat-lander ass. Cowboy clothes? Church? Bullshit! Where the hell is the airport?"

Dad pulled up to the front of a sleazy looking bar with a bright red door with a sign reading: Red Door Saloon. He looked to dad and said "So…. Sunday service is held in a bar?"

As Dad stepped out of the truck he said "Yup, and you better get ready to God-damn pray."

So it was, at 8:00 am in Cheyanne, Wyoming, on Christmas morning, wearing new cowboy stuff on his feet and back, Flanagan made a new best friend and they toasted all things good in the world. They toasted his new boots and jacket, they toasted any and everything they could come up with. Flanagan had a new drinking buddy and it was a perfect world. As they returned to the house with a fresh drunk on, Flanagan half carried-half dragged his 'new best friend' Dad, into the house. As he was 'helping' Dad thru the door, he noticed that the vast sea of cowboy boots he (kind of) saw the night before in the entry-way had grown. Substantially grown! There were several pairs of boots so big that he thought the girls were playing a joke on him. Like Paul Bunyan and Babe the Blue Ox, kind of stuff.

That is, until he looked up to see the kitchen doorway darken and saw the man that could wear those monster sized, 'joke boots.' No man should have to duck and turn sideways to get thru a standard size doorway, but he did have to! He was not fat, just damn big. It was big brother, who had flown in, with his wife and son from Texas to meet Sandy's almost husband. Big brother grinned as they shook hands. He had teeth the size of tombstones and hands the size of a catcher's mitt. Flanagan felt his power in his grip and took an oath to be very, very nice to him. 'Big tooth' brother was a good guy and they slid a few beers down their gullets in short order. Sandy was their beer chaser and gave them both kisses on the cheek each time she delivered the goods. After an hour or so, Sandy came into the den and announced to Tooth, that they were going to go and have a nap. She kissed Tooth on the cheek and said "He is mine and you can't keep him." As she reached for Flanagan's hand to lift him from his chair she said "I'm going to whisper naughty words to him all the way down the hall."

Sandy woke him around 2:00 pm. As he got off the bed she pulled a scarf from her back pocket. She said "Turn around so I can put this on you, you have to trust me, we are going outside." Flanagan didn't like anyone's hands near his face. He couldn't help but flinch, as she covered his eyes and tied the scarf.

It was icy, drizzling and overcast when Dad and he got home a few hours back, but as Sandy led him down the front steps he could feel the intense heat of the sun. She turned him and said "I'm going to take this off now (the scarf) but don't open your eyes and don't turn around until I tell you to." When she told him to turn around, Flanagan almost passed out. In front of him, right in front of his face, was the Colorado Rocky Mountains! She squeezed his hand and said "Baby, its 67 degrees and beautiful, want to move here?" She said the foothills were only 7 miles away and they were going to go to the top of the mountain the next day.

Flanagan marveled at what a lucky man he was. Sandy was the absolute, perfect woman. Any man would think the same. She had big city refinement, a lot of grace, and at the same time she could barrel race, cut cattle and rope a horse. Every now and then she was known to take a pinch and could spit with the best of them. Shortly after they returned to Wisconsin, Sandy took a hospital job in Stanford so they could be together. Her staff and associates called her, 'Wonder Woman.' Sandy worked tirelessly to teach them the latest stuff. They were married in August of that year. Sandy, was every bit as good a wife as she was a woman. He was as happy as he had ever been or ever dared to dream to be. His family loved her and she was good to them.

Chapter 18 "LOVING WHAT YOU HATE"

All and all, Flanagan enjoyed being a paramedic. The rush of blasting thru traffic, and the challenge of stealing one from God, was what made him smile. The special flirtations from the nurses and female staff at the hospitals and nursing homes was always entertaining. He got a big kick out of watching a nurse walking toward him and stumble or break stride when she saw his eyes as he smiled at her. The women would lower their eyes in embarrassment and as they passed, he would look back quickly and catch them looking back at him.

He enjoyed watching the news when they showed him climbing into a wrecked car to tend a patient, or doing a crazy and dangerous rescue. He liked it when he received letters from recovered patients and when they came into headquarters to personally thank him for taking care of them. He liked people stopping him on the street and giving thanks. The flirting waitresses that would say "You are even better looking in person than on T.V." The endless free drinks, from bartenders and bar patrons, the celebrity status itself, was intoxicating. He mostly enjoyed the respect from his peers and the other first responders. The reason that this attention was so enjoyable was that those simple distractions, took him from his demons, at least for a while.

Flanagan also hated that very same attention, he hated every bit of it. He was trapped by his own ego. Yes, he promoted it, he even postured for it . . . to stay alive. Remove the good looks, the swagger of confidence, the smooth words and quick smile with an even quicker wink and he was a nothing. A total nothing. He was still a little kid hiding from his haunting fears, he knew those fears and insecurities would never leave him. He questioned every call he ever responded to. In the dark stillness of the night he would lay in bed as the guilt washed over him. He would re-play each call of that day, over and over in his head. Asking himself each time, if he could have done better, if he screwed up and with that constant, ever present, nagging question "Did I allow someone to die today, did they die because of me?"

At times, he knew he was intentionally doing this to stave off sleep to avoid the nightmares that he knew would come. Every night he would be startled awake with terror and saturated sheets and pillow case. His chest and his hair were wet with sweat and he was gasping for air. So many times he wanted to tear off his uniform, throw it on his bunk and run out the door, saying nothing to no one, and get to the closest bar and drink himself, safe. Safe.... from his own mind.

Every day that he could, he would sit alone in a seedy bar and wonder if the guilt would ever leave him. Wondering if he would, if he could, ever be a man, or would he always be a weak, pathetic, self-absorbed ass-hole. He studied his beer bottles and tried to drink thru and around his self-loathing. When he left the bars and was driving home he would have to steel himself to avoid the tears and the rage. Sometimes he would have to drive past his house, for a few miles, to dry his eyes. Sandy always greeted him when he came thru the door. On those days he had to, 'put some miles on', she would ask him "What happened to your face? Your eyes are swollen and you have red tear streaks on your cheeks, you look like you have been crying?" He always gave her the same vague answer, that they had to fight with a violent drunk or a nut case and they had to mace them. Sandy never bought those stories, she knew that his heart hurt and she knew he had to work thru it alone. He hated to have to live in those lies and he hated the conditions that brought them on. He couldn't speak of his sorrows because he feared he would look weak, that he would lose his glossy finish and she would no longer want him. Sandy was not that shallow (far from it) she would and did understand, she never failed him. Flanagan, was simply, an emotional coward.

There was a dark and nasty side of the emergency rescue business, he saw it most every day and it greatly sickened him. His company had to have three stations, ten on-line units and twenty-six E.M.T./Paramedic personal. The company billed the patient's insurance company and private pay patients. Most often

153

times the insurance company's payments were three months out and the people without insurance were slow to pay, many never paid at all. The company was always broke. He could never plan to get a paycheck on payday and he never knew if the paycheck would clear the bank. When he did get a paycheck, he and his partner would jump in the rig and run, 'Code 3' (no joke) to the bank before the funds ran out from the other crew members cashing their checks. If he was on a call when paychecks were handed out at headquarters, there was less than a twenty-five percent chance that his check would clear. It was not uncommon to have the teller rubber stamp those three ugly red letters, N.S.F. and slide his check back to him. He would ask Jack (the company owner) when he could hope to receive his pay. Jack would roll his shoulders with a genuine look of childlike shame and say "We're broke, I'm sorry. Hopefully we will get some payments in the next few days." Jack would have him walk with him to his locker, open it and pull out two rolls of quarters and say "I am sorry, this is all the money I have." He knew Jack was telling the truth. Jack was so broke that he did not always have food. Flanagan and the other guys always brought extra food and cooked plenty extra for all.

Flanagan had nothing but the utmost respect for Jack, he was a great guy, and more honest than most any man. Jack went thru a painful divorce. His dedication to the company, its success and his constant drive to deliver a superior service kept him away from home. His wife simply said he worked too much. Jack sold his house and all of his personal property. Jack put every penny into the business. He lived at the headquarters station and never went out. He kept his few clothes in two lockers, he owned nothing else. Jack took his calls like everyone else, he never claimed executive privilege, if the weather was bad or because he was tired. Jack cleaned the station like all the other crew members, he was never too good to clean toilets or mop floors.

You would have never known that Jack owned the company. When Jack returned to quarters after a call, he would back into the wash rack and hand wash the entire rig himself. If it was a bloody and messy call, he would return, wash his rig and pull an on-line Unit, out of service and hand wax it. Jack would never let anyone help him, they all knew it was his therapy time. None of the crews ever talked to other crew members about their calls, it would be viewed as a sign of weakness. You may have just returned from the Morgue after dropping off an entire family from a house fire, hop out of your rig and act like you just returned from having a banana split. This business had no room for Sissies' and it was never, a place to discuss your feelings. You sucked it up and kept your mouth shut, because that, is what real men do. You had to force the last call out of your mind because the next call would demand, that you have your head in the game. Someone's life would depend upon it.

Many nights, the crews would stay up and play Ping-Pong or pool or cards or watch T.V., to avoid laying down in the dark with their thoughts and their fears. After 11:00 pm there were only 8 crew members and the dispatcher in quarters. Almost nightly, someone would cry out in their sleep. No one ever mentioned that they heard it the next morning. They were all too busy, chasing their own demons. Flanagan attended three crew members' funerals. They all died, at their own hands.

Flanagan hated people for more reasons than them just not paying their bills. He hated them for their comfort and their security as well. They knew that help was just a phone call away, regardless of the time of night, the weather or road conditions. He would drive by houses that were all dark inside, knowing that they were all safe in their warm beds, when he and his partner were out freezing their asses off. They knew no one gave a shit about them, nor did they know they even existed. That is until they needed help. Then they always took too long to arrive. Never mind the weather or that they were pushing snow over the hood of the rig and the defrosters couldn't keep up with howling winds. On more than one occasion they would arrive at a residence where the caller would not stop bitching about their response time as they were trying to work on the patient. With the caller threatening a law suit, threating to call the mayor, and of course, would go on and on with saying how they were not going to pay their bill. On more than one occasion, Flanagan or his partner, would stand up from the patient, take the stethoscope from his ears and say "We were having dinner at The Black Bear Lounge (a place none of them could afford) when your call came in. We weren't even half way thru the finest steaks we have ever had, and we would be damned, if we were going to walk away from a meal like that." Followed with "Besides, this Cats' been dead for more than an hour!" Yea, the calls came in from lawyers and the mayors' office. Jack would jump his ass for talking to people like that, Jack would always shake his head at him and call him a silly bastard, as they both would start to laugh and end with their normal response, 'fuck-em!'

Only about a third of the calls were for auto accidents or personal injuries. The bulk of the calls were for; difficulty breathing, chest pain and heart attacks. When they were already in the rig and received a, 'Hot Call' (emergency) they would grin at each other and say in unison "its show time", as they pushed the buttons on the master panel for the emergency lights and sirens. When they pulled up to an auto accident with a lot of onlookers and T.V. cameras, they would look at each other and say "You ready to get famous?" And yes, again in perfect unison. They used that kind of humor to relax and calm their nerves. There was also a certain level of showmanship thrown in just for fun. Flanagan liked bringing that gleaming, red and white, fire breathing, 9,800 pound Cadillac to a sliding stop with screeching tires, in a cloud of rubber smoke. It scared the shit out of people and got them out of their way so they could do their work.

One day, Flanagan and Scotty put together a plan to have some fun with the media and their boss, Jack. They waited for the perfect call, a simple fender bender with some asshole faking a neck injury for some quick insurance money. It didn't take long to get that call, they got them all the time. They pulled up to the traffic accident where some clown was staggering around, holding his neck. They both had their windows down as they did their patented slide job. There were two T.V. camera crews filming them arrive. Rather than jumping out of the rig to attend to the injured, they sat there and reached for their hair brushes and began brushing their hair as they loudly argued about the Minnesota Twins pitching staff. The news crews had their cameras right into each of their windows. The shock on the faces of the bystanders was exactly what they were going for.

All the crews were in quarters and in the T.V. room that evening along with Jack and Clark, the dispatcher. Just before the 10:00 pm news came on, Scotty said "Aw shit, I left the Meds-Kit at the hospital E.R.!" Flanagan and Scotty jumped in their rig and launched the hell out of there, while laughing their asses off. They parked a few blocks away and just sat and waited for all hell to break loose. Within 10 minutes of the start of the newscast, they received orders from dispatch to return to quarters, immediately. Flanagan radioed back to dispatch that they were breaking up and to please repeat their transmission. Clark (the dispatcher) was always a top notch professional on the radio. He wouldn't allow any monkey-business or profanity on the radios and always used the 10 code system (all radio talk was to be brief and only 'plain speak' was allowed when they were talking to the Emergency Room Physicians). Clark came back on the radio and said "You guys quit screwing around, God dammit! Jack is really pissed and you better get your asses back here right now!" Flanagan and Scotty could not quit giggling as they heard Clark break all his own rules. They both visualized everyone's faces as they watched and saw them brushing their hair on the 10:00 o'clock news and Jack's eruption and Clarks melt down. The other crews obviously thought it was funny too, as several of them keyed their mic's and radioed them to go to Walgreens to pick up some combs, curling irons, hair spray and they all needed new hair brushes, like the ones they just saw on T.V.

Flanagan and Scotty almost pissed themselves laughing. Suddenly, Jack's voice came over the dispatch radio and said,

"Rampart Rescue Unit #164 return to quarters immediately" (he had a hard edge in his voice). He then said "Bring back my God Damn Ambulance! You assholes have fucked with me for the last time." Flanagan and Scotty almost shit their pants. Flanagan had worked with and for Jack for more than six years and he had never known him to be so mad. They both took a deep breath, (the laughter left when they heard Jack's voice) and he radioed, "Rampart Rescue Unit #164 returning to quarters, E.T.A. 3 minutes."

There was always someone in the garage cleaning their equipment, restocking supplies or just hanging out. Not tonight however. As he backed into his stall, there was no one in sight. No one in sight.... other than Jack!

As Flanagan stepped from behind the wheel, Jack glared at him with a red face and the veins were about to burst in his neck. He stood with clinched teeth and fists. Flanagan didn't know what came over him when he said "We had to go out and we missed the news. Did we miss anything interesting?" In the dead silence that followed, you could have heard a mouse fart in the next block. Jack stood with a stone face, blinked his eyes a few times (like he just got punched in the nose) and a slow grin come over his face, then he started laughing. Jack was in hysterics, he dropped to his knees, his eyes welled up and he was laughing so hard that he couldn't talk. When he was finally able to breathe, he said thru ragged gasps "I have wanted to do something like that all my career, leave it up to you two clowns to pull it off." The other guys came out of their hiding places, all laughing and clapping their hands. Jack said he would take the heat for this one but the bullshit had to stop and he meant it. They all racked out around midnight. Just as everyone had settled down, someone said "How about them Minnesota Twins?" They laughed and giggled all night, no one got any sleep. For the next few days, everywhere they went, nurses, doctors, cops and firefighters burst out laughing when they saw them.

Flanagan and Scotty had just transferred a patient from their gurney to an exam bed in the E.R. when Dr. Long looked up from the patient he was working on, and shouted across the room "Hey, Hollywood, how you doing?" The entire room burst out laughing and that name took. In just a few weeks the entire city was calling Flanagan "Hollywood."

Those brief moments of laughter were rare, at best. Rampart Rescue Ambulance company received several complaints from traffic accident victims' for damaging their cars while in the process of effecting their rescue. Homeowners complained about the crews dragging mud and snow into their house from their boots or scratching the paint on their walls as they carried their loved ones out of their house. That kind of bullshit was never ending. The company was in small claims court all the time. They all worked their guts out and risked their lives to save the lives of total strangers and the ungrateful bastards would sue them! If the crews couldn't revive or save someone, the survivor family member would say "You didn't save him, so I'm not going to pay the bill!" Flanagan hated those assholes.

The best lawsuit (if ever there was such a thing), came from a call on a mid-summer evening.

The call came in for a man having difficulty breathing. Flanagan and Scotty were just clearing from a traffic accident, (the people had refused treatment) when they got the call. The accident scene had a lot of fluids on the ground. Motor oil, anti-freeze and gasoline were all over the ground. Rampart Rescue Unit #164 was only 6 blocks away from the medical call.

They arrived at a monster sized mansion in just a few minutes of dispatch. The woman of the house let them in and led them to a huge bedroom on the main level. Flanagan happened to glance back before entering the bedroom and saw that their gurney wheels had left black oil marks on their super plush, beige carpet. He thought "Here we go again, another fucking lawsuit."

159

The patient was in full cardiac arrest. They ran IV's, pushed drugs and did CPR. The ER Dr. ordered them to defibrillate, times 2. The strip showed a straight line. The Dr. ordered more drugs on board and to defibrillate at maximum power. The patient instantly showed heart activity, in a few minutes he showed a strong pulse and his respirations were becoming normal. Twenty minutes after their arrival, the patient was speaking as they wheeled him thru the living room. Flanagan looked down at their wheel tracks they had left on the carpet then told the patient's wife that he was sorry for soiling her carpet. He told her that his company would pay for cleaning it. She was beaming thru wet eyes and said "My husband was dead when you arrived, you guys just brought him back to me and saved his life! Don't worry about the damn carpet!"

When the crew arrived at the emergency room, every bed was full and all the staff was busy. Flanagan and Scotty stayed with, and monitored, their patient as his family members arrived at the hospital. The Doctor told the family that he reviewed the strips from their "Life-Pack 5" monitor and said "This man should not be alive, let alone sitting up and talking. You have these two men to thank" as he pointed to Flanagan and Scotty. The family repeatedly thanked them. As they cleared the hospital, Flanagan and Scotty marveled at the vastness of the mansion and its furnishings. They both wondered how the patient got all that wealth and whom he had to fuck to own all that shit.

In less than two weeks came the "Blue Back" notice of intent to file suit. The 'Dead Man' and his lovely, grateful wife were suing the company for the replacement costs of their carpet throughout all levels of the entire house. They were also going to file a suit, in a separate action, against Flanagan and Scotty for causing pain and suffering that was inflicted by their negligent and intentional actions to harm their property. And, of course, there was mention that they were not going to pay their bill. And who was the attorney of record? Of course, it was the 'Dead Man.'
Flanagan and Scotty's thoughts after reading that 'Blue Back' were

the same. "We should have let that fucker die!"

They dubbed The Dead Man as 'Ole' Ass Face' from that time forward. The lawsuit never made it to court and there was no settlement.

It was late at night, all crews were in quarters and they were all racked out. Flanagan and Scotty were second out. Police dispatched toned out Unit #166 (#164 would be next out) the call reference was "Male with a cardiac history, not breathing." As the police dispatcher aired the address, Jack sat up in bed and said "That's Ole' Ass Face's address; Unit #166, stand down. Unit #164 is taking this call. Flanagan and Scotty, this one is all yours!"

There was a lot of snickering in the squad room as they were dressing. As they pulled out of Headquarters, Scotty hit the master switches for the lights and sirens as Flanagan radioed police dispatch. "Attention all cars and stations, Rampart Rescue Ambulance Unit #164 is responding to a man not breathing in place of Rampart Rescue Unit #166. We are responding Code 3." There was a lot of giggling over the radio that came from several police and fire units.

There are no secrets in the emergency response business. Everybody knew about Ole' Ass Face's bullshit lawsuit. On the way to the call Flanagan took his foot of the gas pedal and turned off the master switch. Scotty looked over and grinned, as they both said in perfect unison "Fuck-em!" Flanagan mashed hard on the gas pedal and turned the master panel switches back on. Scotty said what he was thinking "Too bad we don't have an accident scene we could stop by and visit with our gurney. Let's hope we can find a wet flower bed to stomp thru!"

Common decency dictates that as soon as you turn off a major street and into a neighborhood, you should turn off your sirens so as not to draw a crowd or disturb peoples sleep at night. Flanagan ran their sirens right up to the front door of the mansion. As they got out of the rig and gathered their gear, they were both looking for mud but there was none to be found.

Mrs. Ass Face opened the door with a look of sheer terror

on her face. In part, of course, there was the fear of losing her husband but perhaps as great, was the shock of seeing the two guys she and her husband were trying to screw. She had to think that they would let him die, just out of spite. The Hippocratic Oath to "Do no harm," was always in the forefront of every paramedics' mind. They may be pissed off at times but they were always willing to risk their lives, several times a day, to save total strangers. No paramedic would ever do harm, regardless of who the patient was or what their personal opinions may be.

Ole' Ass Face, was ashen in color and his lips were blue. He was cold to the touch, his eyes were of a dull gloss, and with fixed pupils. He had no pulse or heart activity. Because of the lawsuit and the character of these fuckers, they both knew that they had to take extreme measures to show they made every attempt to revive him. Flanagan radioed the ER Doctor and sent a strip from their monitor, as Scotty started an IV and did chest compressions. The Doctor ordered him to defibrillate at full power. The results were negative, showing a flat line. After giving the Doctor the patients' medical history the Doctor ordered them to cease all efforts and gave T.O.D. (time of death) and signed off the radio. Flanagan radioed for a Coroner and went to advise the wife that he was dead and they would have to wait for a Coroner. She was in the kitchen crying. He informed her that her husband had passed and she went limp. He asked her for the phone numbers of her close family members who lived in the city. Flanagan called those people and advised them to come to the home to comfort her. He rummaged thru the kitchen cabinets, found the coffee and made an extra strong pot of coffee and sat with her at the kitchen table without any conversation. When the first person arrived, Flanagan informed her that her father had expired.

He poured 2 cups of coffee and took them into the bedroom and closed the door. Flanagan and Scotty sat in the bedroom with the body, drinking coffee while waiting for the Coroner. As they sat there on a plush couch, looking around the expansive Master Bedroom, they again wondered about all the poor bastards this prick had screwed to have all this shit.

They sat and picked dried mud and pebbles from the lugs of the souls of their boots with their ink pens. As family and friends arrived they could hear them sobbing and Flanagan and Scotty wondered how any of them could have loved this asshole or felt any true loss. They both agreed that there were some theatrics in play, in hopes that they were in the will. As they cleared the Morgue after dropping off Ole' Ass Face, Flanagan made his decision. The job had made him hard, he was sick of all the ungrateful people. He gave his two-week notice at shift change that morning.

There are many, many stories. He only spoke of the worst nightmares. He doesn't have the heart to tell of the rest. He will tell you this: in those three other haunting stories, 14 people died. Eight were children. All were alive when they got to them. All of the victims knew they were dying. They and he, knew that he was the last person they would ever see or talk to on earth. Those 14 and so many more asked him to tell their loved ones that they loved them; that they were sorry for their shortcomings. He always passed on those requests to their families, along with many deeply personal words from the dying. The look in their eyes, as they died, he can't describe. He hopes you will never have to see it.

Chapter 19 "THE HEALING MOVE?"

Once again the ghosts of his past came to visit. And this time, they stayed. Poor, sweet Sandy didn't have a chance. He drank even more. He became moody and reclusive. They moved to a major city, in a Western state, where Flanagan became a Police Officer. He very soon became disillusioned and deeply troubled with police work. He had never fully realized that when a cop pinned on a badge, they instantly became 'the enemy.' The enemy to all people. At least that was his experience. Family, friends, neighbors and the public in general, showed distrust and even contempt towards the uniform and the man wearing it. He understood that it was their fear of his power. They saw him as having absolute power over them. He could arrest them, deny them their freedoms and change their lives forever. He could even shoot them!

Flanagan's neighbors told him how they enjoyed seeing his marked police cruiser (his take home car) in his driveway and they felt safe having a cop nearby. They said how it gave them a sense of security. How it told the 'Bad Guys' to move on. He had a number of neighbors come to his door to report on other neighbors (parking, barking dogs, loud music and underage drinking parties) and they wanted him to straighten those people out. He even had a person come to his door on an early Sunday morning to report a street light that was burnt out, that was three blocks away, and wanted to know when he was going to have it fixed! He had a neighbor call the Police Dept. to complain that he was drinking a beer while doing yard work, on his day off. Flanagan lived in a major city and the neighbors treated him like he was "Andy of Mayberry!" His wife and he were never invited to neighborhood gatherings. He never got to be 'the guy down the block' or 'the friendly neighbor.' He was, "The Cop."

His family and friends were no different. They all wanted to hear about his taking a bad guy down, or of a grizzly death and nasty, bloody crime scenes.

Rarely did they ask how he was. He was never a person, he was .... 'the Cop.' At every gathering, they would hush-up when he entered a room. People would always bring up the same subjects; some story of police abuse, wrongful arrests, or a chicken-shit ticket a cop wrote to a friend or coworker. Poor Sandy got to hear that same bullshit at her work. People at parties would watch, and even comment, on his drinking a beer. When Sandy and he left those parties, he would make a big production of staggering to the car, open the driver's door and bow to his wife as she got behind the wheel of her car. He enthusiastically waved to the windows (where the party goers rushed to, to see if the drunken cop was going to drive) and he blew them several kisses as he muttered that they all needed to "Kiss my entire ass!" Most cops socialized with just other cops. They celebrated children's birthdays and family events together. Police work was never discussed. It was just a safe time and place to be with friends to relax and enjoy each other.

Uniformed patrol officers faced the greatest dangers but were looked down upon by the many levels of police command and support units. Often times, even some patrol Sergeants were bureaucrats. Their oath to "Serve and Protect" was secondary to their self-interests to achieve greater rank and protect their pensions. Their looking good was far more important than serving the public or supporting their officers. Traffic tickets and arrest reports involving people of influence seemed to disappear on a regular basis. Command officers took full credit for making arrests in sensational cases, when they had never left their desks. The grandstanding and political posturing sickened him.

Federal Agents and Police undercover officers were not to be trusted. They would roll-over the 'Bad Guys' and cut them loose, while turning a blind eye to their continuing criminal activities. He hated the games that the 'Spooks' (under-cover agents) played, that put the public at risk by releasing these dangerous criminals (to use as informants), back on the street to further their own cases. The 'Spooks' would burn a uniformed

165

officer with no regret. On more than one occasion, 'Bad Guys' were tipped off, prior to a raid. He knew it was the 'Spooks' that tipped them off. He could never prove it and nobody in command had the balls to confront them. The uniform officers and the 'Spooks' were not on the same team. When a 'Spook' called for immediate back-up, it seemed that the uniform officers were always busy. Each and every time!

The worst kinds of calls for him were the domestic abuse and child assaults. The chills that ran down his spine when he heard a woman screaming or a child crying out in pain made his blood boil. Every domestic call he went on, he saw his Mom with a bloody face and him cowering from the last slap or punch. He never waited for his back-up to arrive. He charged into the middle of it. Flanagan always told the male "We can do this the easy way or we can do this….. 'My way." He gave them his murderous 1000-mile stare if they didn't comply or resisted in the very least. Flanagan took them down; hard, fast and dirty! The ones who thought they could take him, got to visit the hospital emergency room before they got to go to jail. Those stupid bastards didn't know that the 5ft. 9in, 180 pound, well-muscled cop carried a lifetime of rage and that a Silverback Gorilla was now on the loose. Admittedly, Flanagan very much enjoyed hurting them.

Flanagan thought it would be fun to take a child beater into another room in their own house, where there would be no witnesses and beat them unconscious. Repeatedly stomping on their nuts, kicking them so many times in the ribs and kidneys that they would piss blood for weeks, and every breath they took would remind them not to hit a kid, ever again. He wanted to screw the barrel his gun up under their chin so hard that it would snap their heads back, as he told them thru clenched teeth "If I ever have to come back to this house, you will look back on these few moments like it was a night at the prom!"

Of course he never did such a thing, at least, not to the best of his recollections.

The constant pressure to use minimal force in effecting an

arrest caused a lot of cops to get hurt. The street cop feared Internal Affairs and police administration more than the Bad Guys. The street cop was expendable and they knew that they were all alone.

There was also another and even worse ugliness to Police work. The Courts, aptly named "The Criminal Justice System" because the victims rarely received justice. Bad Guys got all the attention and were allowed to walk or were given light sentences. Prosecutors and Judges were cowards and fearful of retribution from the Street Gangs. In his experience he had witnessed more corruption in a court room and in the law offices, than he ever had on the street. Prosecutors almost never filed the cases as presented to their offices. The 'Assault on a Police Officer' cases were dropped or amended to a simple disorderly conduct (it was the D.A.'s way to give the cops the finger for making them work). Most cases were pled down or dismissed.

The "Good Old Boys" with law degrees violated crime victims for a second time. Criminal Defense attorneys were allowed to discredit and debase police officers and suggest that incest and rape victims were somehow asking for it. The Judges did little to protect the crime victims, while defense attorneys badgered them and repeatedly challenged their character.

Many times Flanagan would find himself on the witness stand, being worked over by a defense attorney. He would think "I wish the drug dealer you're defending had sold to your kid and turned his life upside down" or "Too bad it wasn't your daughter or wife that was beaten and raped."

Flanagan thought about how much fun it would be to go to the lawyer's small daughter's school and show his daughter pictures of her Daddy's clients and their victims, as she sat in class in her pretty new dress and patent leather shoes. Better yet, to show up on their vacations with crime scene photos of victims that were beaten and murdered by Daddy's clients after Daddy got them off the charges, as they were enjoying tea with 'Snow White.' Their vacation was paid for with someone else's blood and horrors. He fucking hated those arrogant, asshole lawyers. They only wanted a win. They didn't care if the puke they were defending (who they knew was guilty) went back out on the street and harmed someone else. It was always, and only, about the win. Even more so, it was always, always, about the money.

So many times, he wanted to tell rape victims that they would never get their 'day in court' they would never be vindicated. They would never receive validation. They most assuredly would never receive or know any kind of closure. The 'Good Old Boys' could give a shit less about them. They all belonged to the same country club and, as the victim, you are just a necessary inconvenience to their lives.

There was another type of corruption in Law Enforcement. Fiscal irresponsibility. The cities' and counties' always claimed to be broke. As cost savings measures, patrol officers were ordered to release violent offenders on a summons because the jails were full. Officers were ordered to ignore arrest warrants. They were told not to patrol but to remain stationary. Only respond to 911 calls in order to save gas. If your patrol Unit had a miss in the motor, the City mechanics only changed the one bad spark plug or plug wire. Yet the Police Chief, Sheriff, Mayor and all Department heads, had well-appointed offices with top dollar, oversized Mahogany desks, overstuffed chairs, and only the finest silk rugs. They and their lap dogs attended several International and National conferences. Enjoyed free golf, free skiing, posh lodging, and the finest meals and booze, all on the taxpayer's dime. The DA's office had no money to fully prosecute criminals yet the assistant DA's were paid huge commissions each month based on the number of cases that they plea-bargained. Again, the self-serving administrators ate up the tax payer's money for their own pleasures. Service to the community was not of their concern.

- As a foot note; several years later Flanagan had the pleasure of becoming friends with a retired lawyer. He and Tom are dear friends; they have been close and trusting pals for the last twenty years.

Tom was a Prosecutor and a multi-level Judge. Tom is the all too rare exception.

In spite of those many afore mentioned frustrations, Flanagan did get to practice the second of his childhood dreams. And oh yes, he called stressed women "Ma'am." He gave drunks rides home and carried their groceries. Made pals with little kids in his district, comforted the sick and injured, and intently listened to those who wanted to tell their sides of, 'The Story.'

Flanagan un-arrested a large number of people that he put in cuffs. Most of the 'cuffed' were having the worst day of their lives. They were wracked with confusion, fear, sorrow and hatred. They were just folks trying to find their way, just like the rest of us. They didn't need jail. They needed compassion, understanding and most of all, they needed validation. Again, just like all of us. When he could, he bought some groceries for a few of the old folks. During Christmas time, he found a couple of families in need and left a few boxes at their door steps.

There were two distinct sides to Officer Clinton Flanagan. The "Cops-Cop" described above, vanished when it came to bullies and assholes. He absolutely loved to go, "Toe-to-toe" with them. He hunted them. It was his passion. He tried to settle his emotional scores.

Several years later, Flanagan was having lunch with his third wife Sandy and her Mother in a suburb of Denver, Colorado. Her Mother told him that she had a new girl at work from Stanford, Wisconsin. She went on to say that the girl's Father was a Stanford, Wisconsin Police Sergeant who was shot to death. Flanagan sucked in his breath as his heart and his burger dropped into his plate. He looked at the left side of his shirt, placed his right hand over his badge, and said he had to go back to work. When he got into his patrol car, he said a prayer for the Police Sergeant, his family, cops and their families everywhere.

Flanagan met this woman that his Mother-in-law told him about a few months later. She knew he was a cop and originally from Stanford, WI. They only exchanged a few pleasantries. He told her he was sorry for the loss of her Father. He guessed that's as close as he will ever get to closure with that. But he still somehow felt guilty. If he would have gone with them that night, maybe he could have stopped them. If he was there, maybe he could have saved the Sergeant's life. He knows that's a real strange way of thinking, but it's where his mind goes. Like most things in his life, he never told anyone about that fateful night, not until just now.

Sadly, Flanagan, like most all cops, could never speak of his fears or of his good deeds. It would make him look weak and vulnerable. The greatest fear for any first responder is losing face with, and the trust of your peers.

PTSD was not known of at the time. You just sucked it up and kept your mouth shut. Most every city offered family assistance programs to all employees. No cop who wanted to keep his job dared to ask for help. You could never admit to depression, loneliness or feeling lost. If you did, you would be instantly pulled from the duty roster and be assigned to the 'Rubber bullet' room. The 'Rubber bullet' room was any assignment that did not require the officer to be armed. Which meant "We no longer trust you, you need to find a new job." A lot of cops eat their guns, even after retirement. Unwarranted shame and silence kills.

At home, Flanagan was surly and brooding. He went to the bars at night and on his days off. Women were soon to follow. He hated himself for his actions. He deeply loved Sandy but he couldn't let her get too close to him. He had to keep his distance from her. What if she saw through all the good looks, the wit, the charm, and the tenderness? What if she found out that he was still a scared little boy, who didn't think anyone liked him? What if she found out that sometimes he cried?

Flanagan, actually had a 'Big Book' (the basic text of Alcoholics Anonymous) hidden in the rafters in his garage just like a drunk would hide a bottle. When he was absolutely sure Sandy wouldn't be home to catch him, he would read that book and try to find a way to stop drinking. He would even shower and change clothes after dinner, as though he was going out drinking for the night, but in truth, he would drive out of town to another city to attend an AA meeting, hoping once again, to find a way to stop drinking and to change his life. It was to no avail.

He couldn't find the courage to tell her that he knew he was a drunk and he wanted to change his life. If he declared himself as having a drinking problem, or worse yet, to him being an alcoholic, he would be expected to do something about it. He knew he would fail. She would then see him as a loser, and that, would break his heart.

Sandy did all she could for him. Flanagan had to leave police work after a number of years or go nuts. Not being allowed to be a cop was heart-breaking. He still missed the excitement, the challenges, the opportunity to be a good guy and help folks out. It was his only chance to show people (and secretly himself) that he had a kind heart. It's like mourning the loss of a dead family member or close friend. The loss never leaves you.

Sandy knew he was lost, lost in a dark place, maybe lost forever. She always had a smile, a kiss, always offered to make love with him, she always cooked his favorite meals. The house was spotless; he always had clean clothes; and yes, none of it was enough. She couldn't penetrate those demons that drove him. He was too severely broken. She finally left him. With tears streaming down her face, squeezing his hands, telling him she was sorry for not being enough for him. She only asked him for one thing that day. She said her greatest fear over the last seven years was that he would kill himself. She told him that if he could hold out, that someday the answers would come. She said that she has been, and would continue, to pray that someday he would become whole. "But please, don't quit on yourself. Don't think that the only answer will come from the barrel of your gun." They hugged and she kissed his lips repeatedly.

He tasted the salt from her tears as she drove away. With his shoulders set squarely back and chest out, he strolled calmly into the house. He stood in the center of the living room for a moment. Then his lower lip began to quiver and he tasted the salt of his own tears. They too had a cordial divorce and remained friends.

Chapter 20 "I KNOW WHAT I KNOW"

In 1981, Flanagan was flying to Wisconsin to visit his family. He put his off-duty badge and wallet in his rear pocket. It's a standard courtesy for Police Officers to show the greeting flight attendant their badge covered by their boarding pass. That way the attendants know what seat they are in and that they can count on a Cop if there was trouble. There is also a hand signal to let them know if the officer is armed. If you are unarmed, it's free drinks. As an after-thought, he put a suit and dress coat in his garment bag. Flanagan was not a coat and tie guy, he didn't eat at fancy restaurants, and the opera was out of the question. He didn't know what drove him to pack a suit and coat ... until a few days later.

Flanagan was at one of his old haunts, sitting at the bar and watching the overhead, corner T.V. set. The local station broke into the program with a breaking news story. The field reporter announced that a Stanford Police Detective Sergeant, had just been shot in the head by a barricaded suspect, who was wanted for a shooting he committed earlier in the day. The reporter did not identify the wounded officer. It came to Flanagan in an instant ... Terry Watson! He saw Terry several years ago when he was a rookie patrolman and he hadn't seen him since. Terry and he had worked at Rampart Rescue Ambulance several years ago. They were never on the same crew but worked on a lot of second Unit calls; usually a car accident where there were more injuries that the first crew could handle.

Terry's Dad was part owner and the manager of Rampart Rescue Ambulance Service. His Dad was known as 'High Pockets.' Flanagan and High Pockets were pals. Flanagan called him "Uncle Pockets." A neat guy and funny as hell. High Pockets was also the Town Constable of Rainy Lake Township. High Pockets hired Terry part-time and High Pockets paid for Terry to go to the state police academy. Terry was solid, you could trust him to do the job. He never panicked or overreached.

On the morning T.V. news, the following day, the Stanford Chief of Police announced that "Detective Sergeant Terry Watson, lost his life in the line of duty."

Yes, Flanagan was shocked but not surprised. He knew what he knew but he didn't know where it came from.

So ... the suit and dress coat was for Terry's funeral. His off-duty badge wallet can be reversed to hang the exposed badge from a pocket or belt. The day of Terry's funeral, Flanagan's badge hung from the front of his suit coat. He once again had to set his jaws and deny his sorrow.

After the service, he went to the family section of the Cathedral to give his condolences. Uncle Pockets remembered him after 15 years. He looked worn out but had a grin when he saw his badge and said out loud, in church "Holy Christ, Flanagan stole a Cop's badge!" They hugged, they laughed, and Flanagan flew home.

Chapter 21 "MY VERY OWN FAMILY"

*Some of Flanagan's alcohol-induced meanderings, written to his son.

"And now comes the most painful truths of my life. The truth of your Mother, of myself, and of you. I met your Mom when I was still a Police Officer. It was my final job as a cop. I was reduced (due to my drinking) to working for a five-man police department. Your Mom was a Police Dispatcher for an adjoining police department. Through the general course of my duties, I was at your Mom's department on a weekly basis. Your Mom was very professional, knew her job, and was a better dispatcher than anybody I had ever worked with, even in the big cities. Your Mom was also a very nice person. She had an infectious smile; and the prettiest, whitest teeth I'd ever seen. Your Mother was also shockingly beautiful. I met your Mom when I was married to Sandy and I was still deeply in love with my wife.

The officers your Mom worked with were my friends. We backed each other up on hot calls (bar fights, man with a gun, gang fights, and things like that). As a cop you develop a lot of trust and respect for each other. Being small town cops, (Mom's department was a 20-officer department) you never wanted to drink in a bar where you had to knock the shit out of someone the night before. So, as cops do, we drank together at each other's homes or at out of area bars. Your Mom was at a few of those gatherings and was always a lady.

I had an occasion to be at her department on a Saturday morning for training. As I was leaving, your Mom said that she put her phone number in my jacket pocket that was hung over a chair. As I walked out of the station, one of her department officers' said that he told her of my broken marriage. She told the officer that she was going to put her number in my pocket in case my wife and I split up. I put her phone number away, thinking that if I do become single, I would like to get to know her.

175

A few months after, my wife Sandy left me. I ran into your Mom at a house party (cops only). From that night on, your Mom and I were a couple. We were married on February 1st, 1985. She was a beautiful bride. We had already decided that we wanted a baby right away. We believed that you were conceived on our honeymoon. A month after our wedding, your Mom was having severe back pain and she finally went to the doctor. The next day, I was napping on the living room floor. Your Mom got a phone call from the doctor's office. Suddenly, I was awoken with your Mom sitting on me! She had a big smile on her face and tears in her eyes. She said she was pregnant. I was happy and terrified at the same time. Happy, of course, that we were going to have a baby together. But this story isn't about happiness. It's about terror.

I could not tell your Mother. I could not, and never did, tell anyone of my life's greatest heartbreak. With your Mother being pregnant, I couldn't speak of it. I couldn't speak of my family shame. The shame that caused my parents to treat me as they did. The shame that caused me to treat the women I loved so very poorly."
*End of Flanagan' notes.

Flanagan believed his daughter Saundra's death was his fault. He suspected she died from the same blood disorder that his older brother Donnie had died from. Their disease was hereditary. Flanagan had that same blood disorder also. He never told anyone he had it. His daughter, Saundra, was full-term but had only one lung, a hole in her heart, and was totally blind. He was afraid that his son, too, would be afflicted, if not born dead. He hated himself for that.

Now it's time for a bit of family history. At 61 years of age, Flanagan was the oldest surviving male on his Dad's side, ever. Supposedly, his Grandfather on his Dad's side came to the U.S. from Northern Ireland. He was a coal miner and reportedly a member of the 'Molly Maguire's.' The 'Molly Maguire's, protested against the coal companies for mine safety and pay. The 'Molly Maguire's' were formed as an underground organization. When a miner died from a cave-in or preventable accident, the 'Molly Maguire's' would beat and burn the house down of the mine boss.

Flanagan doesn't know of any particular incidents that his Grandfather was involved in. They were held as family secrets. One story that he was told was that his Grandpa came to the U.S. at the turn of the century, had four children, and he died at 45 years of age of Black Lung Disease. His Grandpa lived in Chicago and his history is shrouded in protective secrecy. Flanagan had asked his aunts and uncle (Dad had two sisters and one brother) on several occasions, of Grandpa. He only got bits and pieces. Another story was that Grandpa was an Irish mafia boss and was murdered in the bedroom of his Chicago mansion. Besides the rackets, Grandpa owned a large brewery in Chicago, and reportedly, he also owned one of the larger construction companies in Chicago. Flanagan had seen photos of his Dad when he was five years old wearing a tailored suit, standing with the house staff and chauffeurs with limousines and a mansion in the background. His Dad's Mom went insane after Grandpa was shot to death. Grandma spend the rest of her life in an asylum. Dad's uncle and aunts put him in an orphanage in Stanford, Wisconsin.

Flanagan doesn't know why or how his Dad ended up there. Flanagan's Mom and Dad met in the orphanage as little kids. Flanagan's Mom's parents were divorced and neither wanted the kids. His Mom and her two younger brothers were put in the orphanage. When his Mom turned 15 (we assumed she got kicked out for being too old) she left the orphanage, taking her two younger brothers with her. Flanagan's Mom worked two full-time jobs to support the three of them. There was no welfare then. Simply, if you didn't work, you didn't eat.

His, Dad was taken from the orphanage at age 13 by his Great Aunt 'Abbie' and was raised in northern Michigan, where he had several cousins. Flanagan didn't understand the cousins' deal

177

or how his Dad's sisters and brother avoided the orphanage. It was puzzling but not important enough for him to pursue. His family dynamics were strange at best. In knowing of his childhood, you must be wondering how his parents could be so cruel. He has told you of his truth, now you must also know their truths.

And the truth is this: Flanagan's Mom and Dad were no more equipped to raise children than he was to do brain surgery. Look at where they came from. Dad's Father was murdered; his Mother was thrown away by selfish parents; both in an orphanage during the Depression. How much love did they receive? There was not any of that 'you are a snowflake' bullshit. Be assured that feeding them was about all the attention any kid got in an orphanage in those times. Now, add the fact that both of his folks dropped out of Jr. High School to work and they never went back to school. They had a small boy who was constantly gravely ill, with a hereditary blood disease that came from the father. Their child had to live for two years in a hospital bed, 150 miles away.

What could that have been like for them? No, it doesn't excuse them from the way they treated young Clinton. Nothing could ever make that right. But knowing that truth brings Flanagan to a greater understanding. Without an understanding, he cannot become willing to forgive them. Forgiveness does not mean approval, but it is the only way for him to make peace within his own heart. Mom and Dad were so deeply racked with their own life pains and the 'death watch' lifestyle. They couldn't leave the phone; they had to put all their money into medical bills and to keeping the car running. There was no joy, no peace, and no future. His Mom turned to prescription drugs, lots and lots of them. His Dad turned to alcohol, and lots and lots of that too. It's understandable.

Chapter 22 "EMBRACING THE END"

It was August 25, 1985 (the anniversary of the day he buried his baby girl, Saundra, in 1967). Flanagan had set up his hunting camp early for the upcoming bow-hunting season. He got drunk to quiet his hurting heart over losing his baby, Saundra. He was projecting how he would fail his unborn son. It was clear to him that with his drinking and mood swings, that he had become his Dad. He couldn't live with the idea that he would do to his unborn son what his father had done to him. Not the physical part; no, not ever that. He was fearful that he would poison his boy with his toxic negativity. That he would steal his boys' childhood innocence, that he would cause him to become a waste of humanity. Like himself.

In his drunken stupor, Flanagan tore off a cardboard box lid and used a pencil (stubby golf course type) to tell his unborn son why "Daddy had to say goodbye." He was going to say goodbye to the world that day. He was going to write to his boy and wife, and when the high country sun faded into nightfall and the first stars started to twinkle, he was going to shoot himself; to protect his family from him. It was his son's only chance to live free of his bondage. He had to say goodbye. He had to.

The next morning, he was startled awake. He was laying on the ground, shivering from the morning frost. There he laid, at 11,000 feet, in only in a t-shirt and shorts. His face was caked with dirt and burning from the tears of his drunken sorrows from the night before. He knew he must have passed out and fell off the log that he was sitting on. His mind was dizzy, his guts full of acid, the taste of vomit was in his mouth, along with the self-disgust of his losing his nerve to end it all. He was convinced that he was a pathetic pile of gutless shit.

He would like to tell how he hunted hard, took a massive racked bull elk, and a monster mule deer buck. But in truth...he sat in camp for five days. He forced himself to eat a bite of food every four hours, he poured out his bottles of vodka and the two cases of beer. He sat in the bone-chilling creek for an hour at a time, trying to detox. He was saturated with alcohol, even after several 'creek sits'. He could still smell the booze oozing from his pores. He vomited for the next two days but kept eating. During the third day the self-loathing started to subside. Then a thought came to him. "I could change, it's not too late, you are not even born yet. I'll stop drinking; Karen and I will go to counseling. I'll go talk to a Priest, ask for help from him and God. It's not too late. If I can just heal myself, we will all have a good life together."

On the fifth day, he started to formulate a plan. He wouldn't stop for a 12-pack on the way home. It would be the first time in many years that he would drive anywhere without an open beer. He hoped he could do it. He would not drink in front of Karen and he would act as if it was no big deal. Maybe she wouldn't know just how bad-off he really was. He couldn't imagine life without alcohol. How was he going to do it? How was he going to drink without her knowing it? Nah, a priest isn't going to do it. That God stuff is for little kids, old people and the handful of phonies that don't have the guts to take life head-on. Shit, I don't have a plan, I don't believe in anything. I'm screwed."

Flanagan made the three-hour trip off the mountain without a stop at a liquor store or bar. He was half-heartedly proud of himself but he knew it wouldn't last. As he pulled into the driveway, Karen ran out to greet him. She hugged him for a long time, took his hand and said dinner was ready. Over dinner she kept smiling at him (it made him uncomfortable). She said he looked rested. She was glad to have him home and looking so good. She asked him all about his hunting trip. She wanted to know about each day.

How could he tell her? How her loser, snot-slinging, drunk, asshole husband had been so stupid drunk and sick that he never left camp? Does he tell her that he threw up blood and bile for two days? Does he tell her how much he needs a drink right now?

How he wants to just drop his fork in his plate and run out the door to get a drink somewhere? Does he tell her that he needs to go away, right now, so he doesn't ruin her and their baby's lives forever? "God damn it; I should have shot myself!"

It broke his heart to sit at that damn table. His favorite meal in front of him and next to him was the most precious person ever in his life, with her perfect porcelain complexion and radiant smile. He could see the depth of her love in her eyes. She was wonderful and he knew he was going to lose her. He just didn't know when. But he was most certain that he would.

As he looked at that amazing woman, who kept smiling and patting his arm all through dinner, his only thought was "At least she is close to her family and they will be a great comfort to her." For him, he thought he didn't need anyone. But the truth was, he didn't have or deserve anyone. His entire life was a train wreck. He just stomped through people's lives, breaking sacred vows, breaking hearts, and breaking lives.

After dinner, Flanagan showered and shaved. They sat on the couch to watch T.V. Karen cuddled up to him, and as always, it was a perfect fit. He wanted to push her off the couch and holler at her to grab her car keys and drive away as fast as she could. He wanted to tell her that he was the devil; that he would consume her and steal her soul. God, she was so pure, so wonderful. She loved him and he was an emotional barbarian. He didn't want to be. He just didn't know how to get out of it. In truth, he wanted to tell her how he needed her help. How he wanted to change. How empty his soul was and how lost, how terribly lost, he was. But as before, so many times before, he couldn't admit his truths, not even to her.

Flanagan went a few weeks without drinking. Every day after work he would pick up some silly little trinket for Karen. He kept gift wrapping and tape behind the seat of his pick-up truck. He would wrap the trinket like a little kid would, give it to her, kiss her cheek and tell her "This is from your son." They would walk after dinner each night holding hands. It was close to time for their baby to be born. Karen was getting big; she was so radiant that she almost glowed. She was beautiful. He had to look at her for long periods of times to soak in all of her beauty. God, he loved her. She would be the perfect Mother. She already was the perfect wife.

Flanagan actually liked not drinking, his wife liked it too. In the past she would get a jolt as he hugged her. She would tense up in his arms at the smell of that sickening stale booze odor. Now, there was no hesitation, she would come into his arms, no pause, no tensing. That felt good. It felt real. He felt real. It was short-lived.

When the day came, it was 1:00 am when Karen woke him. Of course, it's the snow storm of the century, they had only 30 miles to drive and it took 1-1/2 hours to get to the hospital. When their baby was delivered it took the doctor a long time to get him to breathe. The terror was coursing through Flanagan's veins. He didn't know if he was going to pass out or vomit. When the baby finally started to cry and his color came in, it was then, as it is today, the happiest day of his life. Flanagan named his son Dillon.

They cleaned him up, showed him to his Mom, put him in his father's arms all wrapped up, and told him to take his baby to the nursery. Flanagan went back to his wife's room to see how she was doing. Karen was tired but she was happy. He told Karen that he was sleepy and had to go home and rest. The truth? Only in part. He needed to get away from everyone to have his own celebration. He had to cry, he had to get drunk. He went to a liquor store, got booze and beer, drank on the way home with tears running down his cheeks saying "Thank you God, for letting him be alive." Over and over again he kept saying "He's alive, he's alive, he is alive." He couldn't tell anyone of his fears. Flanagan's fear was that his son would be born sick; he feared that he would have to suffer as his brother Donnie did; he feared that his baby would die as his daughter, Saundra, did. He knew that they were not out of the woods yet. There were still a lot of tests to be done. His fears went to a whole new level. Now that the baby was born and seemed healthy, he could breathe a bit easier.

Flanagan's baby was colicky as a newborn. When Karen couldn't settle him down, she would give the baby to him. He would hold his son against his cheek and let him feel the resonance of his voice. He would talk and sing softly. In just a matter of a few minutes he could feel his baby relax and fall asleep. It worked every time. It was their special time. But here comes that double-edged sword again. He could not bathe or change his son, not even once. It would be too intimate. He couldn't trust it; he couldn't look at his son's face directly. He couldn't look into his eyes. He was afraid that it would be his last memory of his baby.

When Flanagan would read to him, he held him in his lap so he could not see his face. When he rocked his boy, he could only look at the top of his head. Karen never knew of Flanagan's deep fears of being too close to his son. He would make a face when the baby needed a diaper change; He would tell Karen he was squeamish, had a weak stomach and would probably vomit all over the baby. Karen never knew how many times he had reached into a person's guts to close a bleeding vein or artery to keep them alive.

As for bathing and tucking the baby in at night, it was all Karen's deal. He saw to it. He convinced Karen that it was 'private time' just for the two of them. For him, it meant he could avoid those special moments that he secretly longed for. Mornings were the worst for him. He would stay up late, long after Karen went to bed. He would shower and shave so he could dress, brush his teeth, and be out the door for work before Mother and child awoke. Flanagan feared hearing his wife scream when she went to wake the baby, fearing that he was dead and he wouldn't be able to revive his own son. Fear and heartache from his past owned him, and he couldn't find the courage to talk of it, to anybody.

Flanagan had been an emotional coward all of his life. If he had ever done just one thing to absolute perfection, it is that his smile, his wit, his kindness and compassion disarmed people so they couldn't know him. He knew hundreds of people's secrets

183

and their weaknesses; they knew none of his. He championed others; engaged them with a warm handshake, showed them the twinkle in his eyes and closed the deal with a quick wink. Through that type of orchestration, they knew that they were safe with him, they know he will hold their confidence. They can tell him their truths with comfort, without fear or ridicule or being harshly judged. His genius was to engage them, make those few moments just about them, empower them with hope and keep them away from him. If there's ever been a supreme phony, it is him. Flanagan's supposed 'genius' of keeping people at arms' length had rendered him lonely and void of the love he so desperately and secretly craved. His whole life had been a lie; he couldn't tell his truths. So he hid in emotional exile, somehow thinking that he was safe. Now it's the time to tell you of the 'more about that later.'

Flanagan was a 'black-out drinker.' He rarely remembered the night before; where he was, what he said, or what he did.

Flanagan's boss, Jim, came into his office (him and his boss drank at and after work every day) and poured them each a fresh drink. Jim asked him what he could bring for dinner. Flanagan asked Jim what he meant. Jim said "Karen called me this morning and invited me and my girlfriend for dinner tonight at your house." Flanagan acted as if he already knew that; he told Jim not to bring anything, it was all taken care of. He called Karen and told her he thought that was sweet of her to invite his boss for dinner. He asked her if she needed him to stop on his way home to pick anything up or if she needed him to come home early to help her with dinner. Karen said "No, everything is good, just be home on time." As always, they said "I love you" as they hung up.

An hour before quitting time, he needed his bosses' signature. He went to Jim's office but he had already left for the day. When Flanagan got home, Jim and his girlfriend were already there, sitting on the couch enjoying a drink. He went to the kitchen to say "Hi" to Karen and give her a bouquet of wild flowers he picked up for her on his way home. He leaned over to kiss her hello; she stepped back, grabbed the flowers from his hand and threw them across the kitchen saying "I'm not going to take it anymore." Those were her very words. They still ring through his mind, even now, thirty-three years later. He still hears her voice and the inflection of the tone of her voice. He knew he had just lost her. For good and forever.

He stood flat-footed and dumbfounded as his wife brushed by him. He stood in shock, looking at his boss and his girlfriend, silently asking "What the hell just happened?" Karen raced up the stairs to the bedroom. He was again shocked as Karen was coming back down the stairs in less than 30 seconds of her going up. And here she came, with a diaper bag over her shoulder and the baby dressed in his snow suit. She didn't say a word. With her car key's in her hand, she walked out the door and he followed. He was speechless. Karen had the baby in his car seat in a blink. He knew better than to try to stop or even touch her. He just said, in a weak and defeated voice "Please don't leave." She had a hard look of resignation, it was the first time she ever showed him that face. It was the face of hatred. He watched her drive away, the fourth time, the fourth wife, with him standing in the driveway watching them drive out of his life.

As he tried to dry his eyes and steal himself to go back in the house, he looked down and saw one of the baby bottles laying in the driveway. He still sees it today and he gulps back the tears.

When he came back in the house Jim thrust a drink in his hand saying "I think you need this." He told Flanagan to take the next few days off and gather himself-up. Jim said that their invitation for dinner was an obvious 'set-up' so she could get away from him without an incident. Flanagan knew he was right.

This now brings him to another truth. The real truth. Yes, he was rude, inconsiderate, demanding, demeaning, sarcastic and...Flanagan was a batterer. He battered each of his wives, including Karen. There is no, and can never be, an excuse for beating a woman. But he did know why he did that. When the charm tarnished; the cuteness, the shield of cool shattered, he stood naked and vulnerable. They didn't like him anymore. When he

185

felt all respect and admiration was lost, he used fear to keep them. He hated himself for doing it, he was overwhelmed with the fear of being alone again. He tried to force them to submit to his self-indulgence. He all but took them hostage. The demons of desperation, the sickening panic of being abandoned, were the vehicles that drove his madness. He had become insane. Perhaps it was from his early years that he brought forward to today. The patterns are clear through these writings. The truest definition of insanity is when one continuously makes the same decisions, but yet, is expecting different results. Changing women has never worked for him. Changing him was his only salvation.

That night, as he walked his boss and his girlfriend to the door, he grabbed his truck keys and drove to a liquor store. With his mind still whirling he bought enough booze he hoped would carry him through the next week. He was afraid to go home, to feel that all too familiar aloneness. He didn't want to cry. He was afraid that he could never stop if he started. He went to a bar. He sat in that bar for six hours. At last call they took his drink. He was about to face it, face him and face his being alone. He was again going to be that little scared Cub Scout, hiding in that abandoned cold shed because he didn't have any cookie money and nobody liked him. He was going to be all alone and he was going to cry. He wanted to kill those mean boys from the past. They were his demons of today. His memories were killing him. His spirit had left him, perhaps some time back, but it felt fresh. The lifelong hole in his belly, just became bigger than his belly itself. The void was immense.

As he drove home from the bar he reviewed his thoughts of the night. When he broke the threshold of that bar, his bewilderment instantly became rage and before he finished his first beer he brought himself to an unbridled hatred. He wanted to punish everyone he saw for their seemingly good lives. "Fuck you, fuck all of you. You're going to all suffer. I'll fucking make you suffer just like I am." He looked hard, real hard at every man in that bar, just daring them to make eye contact. None did. The devil himself was sitting at the bar that night and they all knew it. He thought about Karen leaving and taking his son with her, and he had that same arrogant thought as before. "Ah hell, she'll be back." She had left him before, she always came back. He stiffened himself with the belief and idea that "She needs me." In truth, he wanted to drop his head in his hands and cry his eyes out. He knew that she was gone, and this time, she was gone for good.

Flanagan didn't go to work for six days. He drank, passed out, came to, and drank more. He didn't want to think, he didn't want to feel, so he just didn't. Late at night on the sixth day he came to, laying on the floor next to his baby's crib. He had his son's stuffed animals in his arms and all around him on the floor. He decided that tomorrow morning "I'm going to get my family back." Flanagan drained the water heater several times with hot showers that night. He was sick but mostly sober when he walked into work that morning.

Flanagan was the General Manager of the business. The business was a very large and successful gift/variety pharmacy. His boss, Jim was the owner. They had several employees. He was good to them and they were good to him. As he walked through the store to his office he could see it in their eyes. His boss had told them; he could see they hurt for him. He wanted to run away.

Karen had left him three other times. She had spent a few nights at her folks', came back home, then they both said they were sorry and all was well. But not this time. This time it felt different.

Flanagan loved flowers and so did Karen. They would often send or bring each other flowers on special occasions. Many times they would bring home flowers for each other on the very same day. It was a cool deal. It was unique to them, their special thing. It lightened their hearts and they always smiled.

At 11:00 am that morning, his Assistant Manager knocked on his office door. When he called out to her to enter, she came in beaming with moist eyes and a dozen long-stem red roses. She put

187

them on his desk, smiled at him, patted his shoulder and quietly let herself out. The card read the same as his battered Seiko watch, dated 2-1-85, "All my love, Karen." (Flanagan has worn this watch for the last twenty-four years, as a reminder of Karen's love and the love of the good women throughout his life. He hopes that after his passing, his son will want that watch. Not as a memento of him, but as a tribute to all loving women; past, present and future. It is all that speaks of his time on this earth).

Flanagan sat at his desk looking at those roses, drinking in their beauty, filling his nostrils with their sweet fragrance. His heart was full again; those roses were a sign of her forgiveness. He was so happy. It meant to him that his family was coming home tonight. He was going to kiss his baby and wife until his lips were chapped. He was going to change everything about himself. This time, it was going to be different. This time, he was going to be different.

He called Karen at work. He tried to calm his excitement so he could put a few words together that would make sense to her. He told her how wonderful the flowers were and especially the sentiment behind them. She sweetly said "You are welcome" (his heart nearly left his chest). Karen's voice started to quiver as she told him he was also going to get another delivery later that day. Divorce papers.

Flanagan didn't remember the end of the conversation or even hanging up the phone. He called his assistant manager and told her he was expecting a second delivery and he must receive it in person. Other than that, he was not to be disturbed; he was out of the office and he wanted no phone calls. The process server came at precisely 3:00 pm. He had a blank look on his face but Flanagan could read the thoughts of the process server as he glanced at the quart bottle in his hand; "You poor drunken bastard."

Flanagan thanked him, signed the papers and took out a $10 bill from his shirt pocket and told him it was a tip. The process server blanched as Flanagan said to him "One of us deserves a decent fucking day."

He couldn't bring himself to read those papers that day. He just sat and stared at the framed picture of his family on his desk. He sat there until 10:00 pm when he was sure the building would be empty and he went home. For the next few weeks he was on auto-pilot, went to work early, left late, and kept to himself; drinking himself to sleep each night.

Karen called several days later and said she had been staying at her folks' house but had found a house for her and Dillon and wanted to know when he wouldn't be home (she didn't want any trouble) so she could come and move 'her' stuff. He told her that he would hire a truck and movers to bring her everything that they had, everything in the house. He told her that he wanted his family's comfort more than anything else. He told her that he would have the movers call her, for her address to make the delivery and he would stay out of it. He honored that.

Flanagan's house was empty. All he had left was a framed wedding picture and his son's hospital birth photo. It was all that he needed. Through the courts, he got a 60-minute visit once a week at the daycare provider's house and he could take his boy for a six hour visit every other Saturday until his son was four years old. Then Flanagan could have his boy overnight, every other week.

Flanagan had become a stranger to his son. He could feel his boy's discomfort and confusion. His son was reluctant to leave his Mother's arms and he would dive for her when Flanagan brought him back home.

The pickup point for their visits was at Dillon's Grandparents' house. They lived in a rural farm area on a dirt road. Supposedly, power poles are placed approximately 100 feet apart. Flanagan would count the power poles after he dropped Dillon off, to see how far he could go until he broke down and that damned lower lip started to quiver. He never got past four power poles before the stinging tears were running down his cheeks.

Flanagan had a new girlfriend who had two teenage

daughters. Those girls adored little Dillon and he loved their attention. Every time Flanagan picked him up, Dillon would ask if he could go play with the 'big girls.' Dillon wasn't two years old but he remembered and called the girls by name. Flanagan started to notice how Dillon would fake sleeping on the way back home. It was his son's way of decompressing, going back to Mommy, and saying goodbye to Daddy. He could see how that was screwing up his baby boy. He told his girlfriend that he was thinking of not seeing his son anymore so Dillon wouldn't have to go through all that turmoil. She was upset that he would even think of that. She was very forceful in her opinion that "You never give up a child or ever give up on a child." She was right, of course.

Every time Flanagan picked Dillon up from his Mom, she would get teary-eyed and say "Please bring my son back." He would always say "Of course I will." Finally, one day he asked her why she would always say that to him. Karen admitted that she had a paralyzing fear that he would kidnap her baby and leave the state with him and she would never see him again. At first it angered Flanagan that she would even think that he could ever do that to his son or to her. Shortly after, he realized that none of that was about him; it was about how deeply he had hurt her. He hated himself for instilling that kind of fear in her. But he understood it. It was of his own making.

During that same period, Karen started dating a fellow who they both knew before they were married. He was a guest at their wedding. He became Dillon's new Daddy. Flanagan liked him, he was a decent man and a nice guy. He was happy for Karen and Dillon when they got married. For him, he was crushed. Flanagan had been secretly hoping that Karen and he would get back together and they could all become whole again. Having Karen and Dillon was only the second dream that he ever dared to dream in all his life. Two for two, another shattered dream.

That brought on a crippling depression that he couldn't shake loose of. He went to counseling, took anti-depressants and went to AA meetings, but still drank heavily. He couldn't find the strength to get out from under that oppressive thick cloud of heartache.

When Dillon was about to turn four years old, Flanagan picked him up for their final 6-hour visit. As they were driving to his house for their final bi-monthly visit, Flanagan was trying to tell Dillon (in little kid terms) that "The next time Daddy comes to pick you up for a visit, you can sleep at Daddy's house and we will wake up in the morning and we will have blueberry pancakes for breakfast and watch Scooby Doo." Little Dillon shook his head back and forth and said "Oh no, Daddy, I cannot do that, because Mommy says that if it gets dark outside, that you will be mean to me."

Flanagan's heart sunk. There it was. What he knew and what he feared the most. Although he had never used a harsh or loud word with him, his son was afraid of him. Flanagan's life had just come full circle. A little boy, cowering in fear, taking an oath of kindness and love, becoming a man, only to terrorize his own son with these very same fears.

That day he fought back the tears. They spent the day with his girlfriend and her two daughters. It was great to watch his boy and the big girls play together. They were all so fond of each other. Flanagan stayed quiet, steeling looks at his baby, trying to lock those moments in his mind, as he had decided that this day, was the last day that he would ever see his baby boy.

Flanagan knew he had to stop the cycle of bewilderment, of fear, of rage, of isolation and of loneliness. He had to let his baby go, so he could be free. "None of this can be about me. This can, and must be, only about you and my hope that you would never know of my kind of darkness. You must be removed from the insanity, my insanity. You deserve to have a real chance. As my final act of love, I will see to it."

When Flanagan took his son home that afternoon, he asked Karen if they could talk in private. She was a bit reluctant but willing. He asked her if she and her husband had ever discussed

191

him adopting Dillon. She looked shocked and said they had talked about it often. Flanagan told her to talk to him again, right now, and when he got home he would call her.

The lower lip trembles came before he left the driveway, no counting power poles this time. He wanted to have his wits about him, so there was no drinking on the way home to stave off the tears. He's got to take this one on the chin.

He called Karen and told her that he wanted to let Dillon's Stepdad adopt him. He didn't tell her of their car conversation or his knowing that Dillon's only chance for a normal life was for him to remove himself. Flanagan told Karen to have her lawyer draw up the papers quickly, before he changed his mind. He hung up the phone and packed to go spend the night in the mountains. That night he laid in his tent knowing he had made the right decision. He was at peace. He was at peace, with a gaping hole in his guts.

On the following Monday morning, Flanagan signed the adoption papers. The staff at the law office all seemed to understand. He never told them his reasons but they somehow knew. As he signed those papers, the lawyers commented on witnessing the bravest, unselfish, loving act that they had ever seen. Yes, he was brave, he was unselfish, but mostly it was his only true act of love, in his entire lifetime.

It was the right choice for his boy. It was the wrong choice for him. He had just said goodbye to his heart. The void came instantly. He drove home with a smile on his face and tears in his eyes. "I have hope for you, son. You've got a chance. You're going to make it."

Flanagan's girlfriend went nuts. She loved Dillon, her daughters loved Dillon and he took Dillon away from them. She saw him as selfish and irrational. There was no comforting for him in that household, he was left to be alone. Telling his Mother was a challenge. She too thought he was overreacting. He knew that what he did was right. Karen always sent Flanagan's Mother photos of Dillon each year and on occasion, his Mom spoke on the phone with him. Flanagan's Mother was always trying to convince him that he should see his son, especially the year when he became of age. Flanagan's answer was always the same. No!

Throughout his life, Flanagan had taken the liberty of calling Dillon his son, which does not belong to him. He knows he has no right to try to step into his life. And he most certainly cannot take credit for who Dillon has become. The day he let his boy go was the day he realized his dream came true, for the both of them. Oftentimes, people will ask him if he has any children. His answer: "No, I do not." That's not to hide his shame. It is to avoid having to listen to someone say "I'm sure he will look you up when he gets older." He has heard that far too many times. He didn't want to try to convince those well-meaning folks that he couldn't be happier. His dream did come true. He got what he wanted. His son got what he deserved.

O.K.; part of that is a lie. Flanagan so often and so desperately wanted to see his boy. In talking with Karen a few years back when Dillon was in high school and playing baseball and football, Flanagan did tell her that he just wanted to sit in the bleachers to watch him play, just to get a brief look at him. Flanagan asked Karen and her husband for permission to do that. Flanagan gave his word that Dillon wouldn't see him and he would not try to contact him. They both said that it would be fine with them. Karen gave him the dates, times, places and the numbers on his jerseys. Flanagan lost his nerve, he couldn't bring himself to do it. It already hurt too much. It still hurts today. He must trust God that all is well with his son today. He will always be grateful for the people that Dillon's parents are. Yup, he will call it a win.

Chapter 23" FREAK DREAMS"

Flanagan's second premonition came as a dream. As he awoke he knew it was more than just a dream. A lot more. A whole lot more! He was so thoroughly convinced of this 'dream,' taking place, that he told his pal Sean about it in great detail. Sean was his next door neighbor. They held court and solved all local and world troubles on his patio, each afternoon and well into the evening. Yes, vast amounts of alcohol were consumed and they both got smarter as the night went on. Sean was the managing editor of the local area newspaper.

Flanagan's dream came to him on a Tuesday night. On Wednesday afternoon he laid out his dream to Sean. He told him that this upcoming weekend, most likely Sunday, and during the late afternoon, there was going to be a hostage situation and a police standoff, in a business setting. Flanagan will know both parties, both the hostage and the hostage taker are in some kind of business venture, a bar or liquor store. He could see bottles of alcohol very clearly, but most of them were empty bottles. The hostage would be bound to a chair. He saw knife blades and short swords. The hostage would be cut, but not badly. There was going to be an S.W.A.T. call up and shoot-out. Someone was going to die. He wasn't sure if it was one of the cops or the suspect that was going to be killed, but someone was going to die, very publicly in a large hail of gunfire. He was leaning more toward the suspect, who would be a friend of his. He saw the man's body hit the ground as his family looked on. There was going to be a huge public outcry of gun-happy cops and threats of retaliation and lawsuits. He saw a cop with short red hair.

Sean thought he was nuts. Sean jokingly said he would put the weekend news reporters on alert and issue them all flak jackets. Flanagan's only statement was "You just fucking watch, I know what I know."

On that Sunday, in the early afternoon, Sean knocked on his patio door. He had his hand-held radio and was talking to a reporter who was on the scene at a hostage standoff at a restaurant/bar. Sean said "Grab your jacket, you soothsaying son of a bitch." As they were about to pull into the strip mall where the incident was taking place he heard Sean's radio crackle as they heard the same gun fire, with their own ears. Flanagan knew he heard at least one shotgun blast. The on scene reporter said "Holy shit, they shot the bad guy, they just blew him to pieces!" With Sean's lettered press vehicle, his credentials, and his being well-known by the cops, they were let into the area of the crime scene. They stood within 15 feet of the face-down body. Blood was starting to run in the street gutter. The police were just starting to string up the crime scene tape. There was a woman and a few teen and pre-teen kids screaming horrifically. It was the wife and children of the dead man. They just saw their husband and father being shot to death.

Ken Waters was a friend of Flanagan's, they were drinking buddies. Flanagan had just seen him the day before. Over a few beers that day, he told him of his anger over a failed business venture and how he was screwed-over by his partner.

During the lengthy standoff where the police negotiator, even allowed Ken's wife to talk to him, begging him to surrender, Ken still refused to give up. He continued to tell the cops to kill him or he will kill them all.
Ken exited the bar and charged the cops with a long blade knife. The police opened fire with shotguns and pistols.

The police immediately entered the restaurant and rescued the hostage. The hostage was Ken's business partner, and did have minor knife wounds on his arms and legs, he was bound to a chair. They found full and empty booze bottles placed on the floor, in the front of the doors and windows as an early warning alarm system, in case the cops rushed in.

195

Flanagan and Sean left the scene just as night was falling. Sean and he didn't say much on the way home. They didn't sit on the patio that night. Flanagan sat on his patio alone, in reflection. A lot of Ken's family and friends had gathered, they were angry, swearing at the cops, calling them killers and all the kinds of highly charged statements of the broken-hearted. He knew there were going to be pickets and protesters at the police department. The following days would spawn condemning letters to the editor saying "The cops overreached..." The common bullshit of the uninformed.

Flanagan sat at his dining room table late that night, and penned a letter to the editor of the local newspaper. He was in a state of sorrow and rage. Flanagan was well-fueled by his many past nightmares and experiences, and a twelve-pack of beer. There were a lot of tears. When his wife, Steph, woke up the next morning she saw his grief from across the room. He showed her his letter. Steph said she would take it to work and type it, so he could give it to Sean to publish. She didn't even read it but she knew of the importance of it; not just to him, but to all involved. She said she would call his boss and tell him he was sick. Steph, walked him to the bedroom, and tucked him into bed, as you would a child. He slept for eleven hours.

As projected, the following days were filled with death threats towards the officer's and their families. Protesters, letters to the editor, and fund-raisers for a lawsuit fund. And again, other assorted bullshit. Ken had a large knife and charged the Cops shouting "You fuckers better kill me or I will fucking kill you." If Flanagan's own Mother would have charged him with a knife shouting those kind of threats at him, he would have blown her away!

Flanagan's letter to the editor was published on the following Sunday. Sean held it back until then, as Sunday was their top sales delivery day and he wanted the dust to settle so as to have its' full impact to distill the threats of violence against the police. Following is that article, taken from the newspaper with

196

the, "Lincoln County Daily Call" masthead.

Sunday, October 15, 1989

OPINION
    At the scene: "Violent death is painful for everyone involved"
By: CLINTON FLANAGAN

"I was at the scene of last week's police shooting which resulted in a death. I overheard two witnesses talking. They appeared to be angry and were somewhat belligerent. They were mad at the police. One of the witnesses called the police, cold-blooded murderers. That accuser left the area, and I found myself talking with the other witness. The witness vented his anger for some time and then began to settle down. He said he didn't blame the police. "They really had no choice." As we talked further, he said he wished it just never had happened, or, at least, that the police could have been able to somehow grab or tackle the subject or maybe just shoot and wound him. Both of the witnesses were friends of the dead man. In continuing the conversation, the witness said that if he were a cop in the same situation, he would have done the same thing. After that statement, he became very calm, almost lethargic and somewhat, 'shockey'. I asked him if he had someone to be with tonight. He said he had a family at home. I suggested he go home and talk it through and try to unwind. We shook hands and said goodnight. We never did exchange names.

    I walked over to an area where my friend, a media representative, was standing. There was a man in a suit talking to three uniformed police officers. As I listened to the conversation, I realized that the suited man was reading the three empty-holstered police officers the long form of the, 'Miranda Warning' (standard operating procedure in a police involved shooting). The empty holsters told me that these three police officers were actually

197

involved in the shooting and they had each fired their weapons. It is also standard procedure that the weapons be taken from the officers involved at the scene and be put into police evidence for future investigation.

The three involved officers were being led through the yellow, police barrier, crime scene tape. Obviously, they were going to be taken to the police station to give their statements to the shoot team. The three young men walked right toward me; their faces were grim, bland, and without expression. Their facial features were weak. They wore death masks. Their walk was, 'herd-like,' an amble without direction, but with great effort. The horror they had just experienced and the shock they were presently feeling would have been obvious to the most casual of observers.

I saw three men in transition. All three had just stepped beyond the point of no return. Their lives had just changed, forever. Although I wouldn't be able to recognize any of them tomorrow, I will never forget their faces.

The young officer walking closest to me looked directly into my eyes and I held his gaze. As he got next to me, I nodded my head and said "I am sorry." He stopped and responded "What did you say?" I dropped my head for a second, looked back into his eyes and said "I said hello." He nodded his head and walked to the waiting police car. Actually, I wanted to reach out and put my hand on his shoulder, even give him a hug.

The man under the sheet was an acquaintance of mine. We had shared light conversations, a few funny stories and a few drinks over the years. He was a likeable guy, always gave a friendly "hello" a smile, and always had a joke or two. He had a warmth that always made you feel comfortable. He is dead now. I don't feel comfortable.

I feel a deep pain for all the people who were involved at this scene of everlasting heartache. I understand all too well, for I have been to several violent-death crime scenes, and many more, over and over in my mind. I have seen many bodies under white sheets. Some of these bodies were suspects and some were my

198

friends – fellow police officers.

I left police work a few years ago. I could no longer look at the widows and the children of my fallen brother officers. I lost the strength to put the black tape over my badge, to give a farewell, white-gloved salute to a flag-draped coffin while Taps was softly being played in the background. I know that pain, all too well.

It is one thing to armchair a football game, but it is another thing to be there and have to decide, in parts of a second, to take a human life. The officers could not risk trying to wound him. He was attacking them with a deadly weapon. They had to shoot to stop the man from making contact with them. They had to shoot in self-defense. It was kill or be killed, or so it seems.

It must be understood that the warm, friendly man that died was not shot for who he was in life. He was shot for his life-threatening behavior.

I worry that the public will not understand – the witnesses will become victims of their trauma. I worry about the involved officers – their fear that people will think they are trigger-happy. I worry about those three and their fears. They will someday ask themselves "Did I overreact? Was there something else I could have done differently? Could I have said something differently? If, in the future, I had to do it again, could I do it? Will I hesitate for fear of my fears? Will I be killed or cause someone else to be killed? Will my fellow officers still trust me?" And then the big question "Did this really happen?"

At any police academy, a recruit is told that an officer-involved shooting is proper if there is imminent life-threatening danger, as long as the officer uses "reason and prudence."

The truth is, that there is no, 'hard-and-fast rule.' You simply better be right. But, right will not lesson the horror that these officers are about to experience. The horror will mushroom and reach far beyond the few, 'on- scene' people. No one will walk away unscathed. The horror will change their lives and the lives of the people they are close to.

My heart goes out to you all, but I carry a special warmth and sadness for the involved officers.

I hope that the public will look upon these officers with knowledge and appreciate these fine men who, that evening, changed their lives forever while doing their job "To serve and protect." May God touch and keep all of you whole.

Clinton Flanagan

END OF NEWSPAPER ARTICLE

On that following Monday afternoon, Sean called Flanagan from work. Sean said he just got off the phone with the Chief of Police. Sean said "The Chief wanted to know who you are and he wants to talk to you." Sean gave him the Chief's private phone number. Flanagan called the Chief and the Chief invited him for lunch the next day. When Flanagan pulled into the parking lot of the restaurant he saw a lot of police cars. He assumed (and was right) that the uniformed officers were there to protect the Chief in light of the many death threats that were made in the last week.

The Chief's first question was "Who do you write for?" At first Flanagan didn't understand his question. He was like "Huh? Who do I write for? What?" The Chief said he was a hardcore reader and spent his last twenty-five years as a cop and has read every officer-involved shooting report published in the police journals. The Police Chief said he had never read anything as mentally and emotionally accurate. The Chief told Flanagan that he had reached into the heads and hearts of those three involved officers. The Chief said the officers found more peace and understanding from his small article than all the shrinks the officers had to visit with, in the last week. The Chief told him that he wanted to forward his article to the "International Chief of

Police" magazine for consideration of publication.

Then he again asked him who he wrote for. Flanagan told him he was just a former cop who knew the deal. He told the Chief that he was a stand-out cop that couldn't find his way out of a bottle. As far as the article, he just spoke from his heart. He knew they would all need it.

Flanagan gave the Chief his verbal permission and mailed him a letter, later that day attesting to the same. In his letter he stated that he wanted to waive claim to any revenue or rewards. Any and all parties may use this article and if there were any monies to be realized it was to go to the "Widow and Orphans Fund, for Fallen Police Officers." He didn't know if the article was ever reprinted. It served its purpose. That's all that matters.

Flanagan received a few letters of appreciation from some folks but the most profound letter he received was from a Mother of one of the shooting-involved police officers. This officer's Mother (her son had short red hair) said that he was going to resign and turn in his badge until he read his article. The Mother thanked him for humanizing police officers, and giving her son a perspective that cleared his head and his heart. Flanagan got to meet the officer with short red hair and his Mom and Dad. They were all very nice people. Over the years he had run into Officer, 'Red.' They both nodded and smiled at each other. They don't need to say anything. When their eyes met, they spoke volumes.

Chapter 24 "ATONEMENT"

In 1990, Flanagan took on a project that was well beyond his scope of abilities. His thought was "If I could just find and do something good, (smacks of his childhood, doesn't it?) for someone else, maybe I could find the courage to face life sober." He needed to do something good so he could believe in himself. It's not that he didn't have plenty of chances. A lot of good people tried to show him that he was worthwhile, he just never believed it. Cal Thompson, Tom the Watkins man, Mac the shoe guy, Lurch, Fuzzy Mc Thirst, six wonderful women, their families, and the list goes on. He was never ok with himself.

One early morning, Flanagan was at home, reading the local newspaper. There was a story on how a church had bought a piece of property to develop. There was a city landmark that the church was willing to sell for a dollar to anyone who was willing to remove the building. The building was made of corrugated heavy gauge tin. It was built in the 1930s and was used as a five-stall auto repair shop. It had been abandoned for several years. The man that owned the building was known as 'Cheaper Charlie.' Old Charlie owned an auto parts store called 'Cheaper Charlie's.' Charlie allowed the people of the city to use the building as a community billboard. The building was located on two heavily traveled cross streets. Charlie let it be known, that anyone could paint their messages on the 'Cheaper Charlie's shed,' as long as it was tasteful and there was not any profanity. Thousands, literally, thousands of people from the area went to the 'shed' to post their birthday and anniversary wishes and professed their profound love for their mates. The messages were changed almost daily. You couldn't drive by there without seeing someone with a paint brush and pail. Oftentimes you would see a whole crew, painting the entire building with a base coat of white paint to better display their messages. It was common, 'water cooler' conversations as to the latest messages on the 'shed.'

Flanagan's fifth wife Steph, her two girls and himself, had painted wishes on that very, 'shed.' He thought it was sad to lose such a big piece of that heartbeat of the city. Later that morning as he drove to work and passed the shed he found himself saying, "No, God damn it! No! I am not going to let this happen!" He went to work, called the Pastor of the church that was going to tear the building down, told him that if the building was still available that he had a dollar to buy it with. They met later that day. The Pastor got a buck, Flanagan got a building. Before he could say "Oh, shit, now what?" It all came. The ideas came fast, faster than he could take notes. It was a grand plan (don't tell him there is no God). It was also mind-boggling. "Yeah, it's brilliant, but how am I going to pull it off? I don't know anyone of influence, I'm not community savvy, or hooked-up. I'm not a member of any of those happy horseshit civic groups. I'm really just a drunk. This can't possibly work, but I have to try."

That night he told his wife, Steph, of his rough plan. She thought he would make a fool of himself. He thought "Fuck you, watch me!" Her lack of support and obvious distaste for him caused him to throw himself into the project with a frenzy. "Not smart enough? Watch me!"

Over the years, Flanagan had met all the big guys at the local newspaper as well as the owners, thru his friend, Sean. He went to the owners with his plan. He assured them that he had a solid plan with newsworthy attentions. They agreed to do a kick-off story, and would follow it up with one or even two published articles a week. Flanagan hired a contractor to disassemble the, 'shed.' He stored the 12ft. by 3ft. panels on the side of his house. When the news story broke, he immediately went to Phase One. He wrote the first press release. It became a front page story with photos. The shed was going to be a vehicle to launch a charity drive to properly clothe indigent kids with proper fitting, warm, winter clothing. He had named the project "Heart Warming" and registered that name with the state. His concept was simple. If you buy a child a toy, you may excite their senses but for a brief

203

period of time. If you clothe a child properly, you may warm their heart for a lifetime.

At first, Flanagan, was seen as a bad guy for tearing down the shed. But when word got out as to the scope and depth of his intentions, the plan was well received. Flanagan took the first front page article to the "Tall Peaks Mall" and meet with the mall manager and his promotions manager. He pointed out that the mall had 80 running feet of space not in use (from a closed store). He wanted to attach panels of the shed on the wall and allow the public to paint their messages for a final time on the shed. He assured the mall that their property would be protected and it would be a large draw to the mall. He promised local and metro news coverage with live remotes and newspaper photos. They actually bought it! He was busy making a lot of promises, but he didn't know how he was going to back them up. But he would somehow, find a way.

Flanagan wrangled a guy into inviting him to speak at a Kiwanis luncheon. The only time he ever spoke publically, before that day, was when he was giving a toast at a bar. He laid out his plan and asked those guys to sponsor the project through them buying a 2-1/2 x 4 foot, vinyl banner that he would hang above the replica, 'tin wall' at the mall. For $200, the banner would be a replica of their business card. He sold four banners that day. They now, at least had expense money! He had no idea where to go to get those banners made. When he did find a banner guy, the cost per banner was more than he charged the sponsors for! His only choice was to offer the banner guy two locations for his banners at no charge, and mention of his name and company name in the next news article to come out the week following. He went for it! He said he would print all the banners for the price of just one. It was a good day! However, the voice in his ear kept telling him he was going to fail. Every time he had an idea the voice asked "Now, smart ass, how are you going to do that?" He was getting too good at this promises thing. When would he get caught?

Things were getting scary. He had ordered a gross of t-shirts that had a color photo of the shed, imprinted on the front and writing that read "I own a piece of the shed." He also had ordered 200 full-color posters of the shed with no money to pay for them. He appealed to a daughter of a member of the 'Yellow Gang,' (the original painters of the message board shed) who were all successful business leaders. The 'Yellow Gang' had a personal and long-standing relationship with 'Cheaper Charlie's shed.' His hopes were to meet with them and ask them to underwrite a personal loan or give a donation to cover the costs of start-up.

Flanagan was phoned by a member of the 'Yellow Gang' and was invited to lunch at the member's home the following day. This home was nice, very nice. He had lunch with the 'Gang' (5 elderly married couples), he told them of his plan, and without his request being spoken, they all wrote checks. They were up and running! They now had product to sell. The only problem was that, 'they,' was just him and his wife. He wrote a press release requesting volunteers to man the paint booth at the mall, and sell panels of the shed, t-shirts and posters. The press releases became big splashy, stories. He got a lot of phone calls that supported the project but no volunteers. Two weeks went by and still no help. His wife and he put up the panels on the mall and they manned the paint booth after work and on weekends. They quickly became exhausted. One day he received a phone call from a teacher at, 'High Peak Jr. High School.' The teacher said he had a group of kids who are willing to help him but he may not want them as they were high-energy and a bit wild. They were identified as "at risk" kids. Mr. Steve Little was the teacher to whom he spoke with. Flanagan, of course, said yes. But Mr. Little suggested that he should first meet those kids so he would know what he was getting into. He went to the school and meet with Mr. Little, two other teachers and the school principal. (Wow, another visit with the past.)

The school staff were all very warm but cautious, and a bit fearful that the kids would let him down. He told them that he too was a troubled kid, and he would like to talk with the class as a

205

group, and with them present. So they all went to the classroom so he could speak with them all. There they were, wearing the same smirks that he wore so many years ago. He could hear their minds screaming "Bullshit, fuck you, you phony prick." He locked his eyes on each of them, one at a time. Those 32 little darlings all sat quietly and listened as he told them, their story, by telling them, his own. No, not all the details, just the part that he so desperately needed to fit in, that he needed someone to believe in him, so he could believe in himself. How he got into trouble by seeking attention by being a smartass and a tough guy, truly just trying to be accepted. He told them the truth. He said that when they (as he pointed at each kid) gave him the finger (mentally or literally) they were saying "I'm lonely." When you say "go to hell", you are saying "I'm already there." When they shoot a 'go fuck yourself glare' you're saying "I'm scared."

Flanagan asked for a show of hands as to who in the class had been given final notice of this being their last chance, at school, at home, with the court, or with their probation officer. All hands were in the air. Flanagan then said "I'm going to give you your first chance. Your first chance to do something right, for the first time in your life. It's all on you. You will only be judged on your own efforts, but judged you will be. No excuses, no yeah buts, no one else's fault, you show any shithead behavior and you're out." He told them that they were going to learn about real discipline, self-discipline, and positive peer pressure. "We are going to hold each other up. If one fails, we all fail. And fail, my friend's, we will not!"

He told them that Mr. Little, would put together a schedule, as they were going to man the paint booth at the mall after school and on weekends for the next six weeks. Just a few kids had questions, but the questions were all the same, 'The police, the mall security, his or her probation officers, his or her parents, have banned them from the mall for fighting or shoplifting. How can we go to the mall?' Flanagan assured them that he would talk to the mall, the cops, their probation officers and the school principal said he would send letters to their parents, outlining the project and their work schedule. He thanked the kids for their time and their help. As he was about to leave the classroom, the kids' grouped up and blocked his path. They all said thanks and shook his hand. As that was going on, he glanced at the teachers who were all standing against the wall, each of them had looks of disbelief and smiles of hope; a bit guarded, but he could see the hope and their pride. He could hear their hearts "Finally, someone is going to give our kids a chance, someone other than us cares about our kids, someone believes in them."

Flanagan walked out of that school feeling like he just won the Super Bowl. He saw himself in those kids. He felt like they all, finally, had a chance. "We are all going to become somebody. We are all going to be good."

That is, except for the promises that he could get permission from the mall, the police, the probation officers and the store managers at the mall that banned at least 50% of the "Peak 2" kids. There he goes again, pushing the odds; putting his ass on the line, making promises that he may not be able to keep. Letting the dream get larger than life, larger than reality. "What the hell, shoot for the stars!" Flanagan found out that he had more guts than brains.

So off he went. The Police Chief told him he was "Courageous"; the Juvenile Probation Officer's said he was "Daring." The mall was willing but wanted to poll their retailers before approving the deal. Flanagan suggested they hold a meeting with all the store managers and their clerks. He plied them with a breakfast meeting (Flanagan begged McDonalds for breakfast meals and they gave him free meals for 70 people). He listened to several voices of descent, but the majority of the group reluctantly approved. Of course, he threw out a bunch of bullshit projections of increased traffic and sales, extensive free media coverage, not to mention all the feel-good stuff from the community. They all gave in. The deal was on!

Things were getting way too big for him. He had no real organizational skills, but sweet ole' Steph did. He got real humble when he told her he needed her help and would follow any suggestions she may have. He asked, she told him. But first, he had to hear how his arrogance was hanging out, how he had gone too far with all this dream stuff and how his promising people was going to make this whole thing fall apart, how he would let down the 'Peak 2 kids' and embarrass her.

After (more than) a few "Yup's" and "Yes, Dears" Steph laid out a reasonable and workable plan. First, a steering committee. Flanagan wrote a press release which again became a feature story. He asked for community volunteers to serve on the, 'Heart Warming,' steering committee. They sat a committee of nine.

During all of this, he was falling out of favor with his boss, the store owner. Yes, they saw a lot more traffic, and a fair number of people would say "I've never been in this store before, but after all the news stories, I thought I would check it out."

The store had only six phone lines and Jim (the store owner) said the phone lines were being tied up by people with interest in 'Heart Warming' and the shed, and the doctors could not get through to order prescriptions for their patients. Jim also said Flanagan was spending too much time away from the store.

The pressure was becoming too great. Jim was pissed and had a right to be. Sales were up at the store but he was not there to manage the day-to-day operation and the employees were slacking. His wife was tired of making dinner and him not showing up. He hardly had time to drink. He kept pushing forward. Things were progressing nicely.

The Career Development Center (C.D.C.) is a high school trade center. High school students learn how to weld, do auto repairs, carpentry, etc. He met the woodworking teacher and presented an idea that was brought to the steering committee, by an 11-year old girl. She and her Mother were steering committee members, with the 11-year old, having a full vote.

The child's idea was to make a Lexan plastic replica of the shed with a coin slot in the roof for donations that would be placed at the, 'Paint the Shed,' booth at the mall. The instructor introduced him to his class and Flanagan gave them a brief overview of 'Heart Warming' and asked the students to build these replica sheds. The teacher said that this would be a graded project. They built eight "sheds" in less than a week.

Flanagan took these clear plastic 6x6x8-inch sheds to a preschool class where the little kids finger-painted the sheds. He put three of the sheds at the paint booth at the mall and the remaining five at the cash registers in the pharmacy. A friend of Flanagan's was a department manager at Wal-Mart. She liked the little replica sheds and told her store manager that they too, should have them at their registers. The store manager agreed, so did three grocery store chains and K-Mart. Flanagan placed forty-eight mini 'sheds' in those stores. The paint booth, t-shirt, and poster sales were a great success. Throughout this period, he had gotten personal visits and phone calls from several of the, 'Peak 2 kids' parents asking "What have you done to my child?" The parents said things like "He's taking out the trash now, without being asked a dozen times. My kid has stopped beating up his brother and sisters. They are making their beds, cleaning their rooms, but the most often heard comment was, my kid is acting like they should. They are more respectful and they don't swear as much." Those comments, in and of themselves, made the whole deal worthwhile.

Flanagan was with those kids every minute of every day at the mall. The mall employees, retailers, and mall shoppers often commented on the kids' good manners and respectful attitudes. Flanagan had open dialogue with the kids about the behaviors of screwed-up kids. How profanity was a sign of ignorance and fear, disrespect was a showing of lack of self-respect. They talked of dignity, family loyalty, trust, and how to gain it. They talked of change and the personal rewards of self-improvement. Flanagan witnessed each one of those kids put their lives together.

They didn't just change (to please others), they aspired to be better people. They indeed, did become better people.

They sold out the posters, all but a few t-shirts (that were donated to another clothing charity), sold most all the tin sections but a few, that were donated to the city museum. Those kids were never late for their two-hour shifts, most stayed well after their shift was over. There was never a complaint as to their behaviors (of which you always hear of, 'mall rats', and never once was the cash drawer short. On the final Sunday of the mall paint booth, every kid, with most of their parents, were there to take down the replica shed, fill all the screw holes, and paint the wall as they first found it.

That's when the real fun began. Flanagan requested a list of needy children (1-month to 15 years old) from the O.U.R. Center (Outreach United Resources) which was a clearing house of sorts that combined all church and denomination's social services programs; kind of a one-stop-shop for those in need. He only wanted first names, age and sex. He was given a long list of names. He assigned two, 'Peak 2' kids to shop for 'their' two kids (1 boy, 1 girl). K-Mart gave them cost pricing and gave them a credit of $25 for each $100 they spent at their cost.

Each kid on the list was to get a parka, snow pants, snow boots, hat, scarf, and mittens or gloves. He let the "Peak 2" kids pick out the outfits. They were mindful of size, warmth, durability, and style. Each of those "Peak 2" knuckleheads used their own money to buy each kid on their list a toy as well. When it was time to check out, they had most of the stores shopping carts loaded up. The store manager was there to override the system to apply the discounts and credits. The store manager asked him where their gift wrap was. Flanagan had forgotten all about it. The store manager sent two department heads to fill carts with gift boxes, gift wrap, ribbon, bows and tape. Then it hit him. He couldn't get all this stuff in his full-size pick-up truck.

Flanagan called the school principal for help. The school principal sent a school bus and offered up the school auditorium as a gift wrap center.

He again, didn't think of where they were going to wrap this stuff. The kids said "No dice. We are 'Peak 2.' We will do it in our classroom where 'Peak 2' lives, where we come from." He couldn't argue that!

Those throw away, disturbed, hard cases brought him to tears on gift-wrapping day. Each of those kids were acting just like kids. They were happy, smiling, laughing, teasing, and helping each other. There, against the wall, stood the same disbelieving teachers and principal, except there were several other teachers, janitors and lunchroom workers. You could see the joy, the pride and the love on their faces. No disbelief, no disappointment. They were watching children in transition. They were looking at their success. They were realizing their professional and personal dreams.

The kids were given citizenship award certificates by the Mayor of the city, during a regular City Council meeting. Each kid's name was called one at a time from the gallery. The first kid was John T. (class clown). He walked down the stairs, walked up to the Mayor and froze. The Mayor had John's certificate in one hand and put out his other hand to shake John's hand. John T. didn't know what to do. His face was red with blush, so he started clapping. Everyone cracked up. The Mayor kept trying to hand John T. his award and John T. just stood there. A teacher (all the teachers from the entire school were there along with most of the student's family's) walked up to John T. and "mimed" what John should do. John T. caught on, took his award, shook the Mayor's hand, and he then, bowed. They all went nuts with laughter. The seated City Council members came from behind the big raised, horseshoe panel desk and formed a reception line to congratulate the kids. You would think they just won the World Series...and maybe they did.

The Local newspaper and Heart Warming's greatest supporter, did a feature story on the kids and put it out on the A.P. wires. It was picked up and printed throughout the country. The

211

Governor of the state of Colorado, called Flanagan personally.

Flanagan was on the sales floor of the store when the office clerk paged him on the intercom "Mr. Flanagan, the Honorable Governor, Mr. Richard Downs' is holding on line four."
The office area faces the sales floor with two-way mirrors. Knowing where she was seated he threw a stuffed animal at the window where she was seated. She came running out of the office and said "It really is the Governor." He said "Bullshit" and threw another stuffed animal at her. He pointed to Jim (his boss) and did the phone sign and held up four fingers. Jim answered line four and started nodding his head like you had just plunked a bobble-head. Jim was waving to him to come to the phone. They were always playing jokes on each other. He thought "Ok, I'll bite, this is going to be good." Flanagan took the phone and said "Yo, Gov, wassup?" He about shit himself. It was the Governor of the State of Colorado!

Governor Dick Downs was an educator and served on several school boards of education. His platform for the governorship was "Kids First." His wife, Becky, was also an educator. The Governor invited him and 'his kids' to the Governor's Mansion for dinner and a movie with him and his wife. Flanagan told the Governor that he was truly honored by his gracious invitation but none of what the kids have done, was, or is about him. This was their deal. He declined the Governor's offer, it would be the Governor, his wife, and the kids. There are not many Rhode Scholars or honor students that get an invitation to the Governor's Mansion in any state. The, 'misfits' were all picked up in limousines, sat with the Governor and Mrs. Downs for dinner, saw a movie in the mansion's private theater where Mrs. Downs started a popcorn fight. At least that's the kids' story.

Flanagan had lost contact with the kids over the years. He had to keep in mind that he didn't do anything for these kids, but they did everything for him.
He needed their help. They came through, they met the challenge. He owes them and their community.

212

The kids, did greatly improve their grades, all graduated high school, and several went on to college. John T. was an honor student with a Master's Degree in Finance. The Tall Peaks Mall won a national award for community service. An art professor at the University of Colorado made a documentary movie on the history of the shed. She submitted her film to the Cannes Film Festival under a new title for graffiti art. The documentary won the Cannes Film Festival in that division.

As for Flanagan, he lost his job for poor performance (no good deed ever goes unpunished.) And no, it still was not enough to let him believe that he was good enough to be sober. After all the awards, the handshakes, the hugs, the smiles, he was just as lost and lonely as ever. Steph was a good woman and a good wife, much better than he deserved. Without her help and direction, 'Heart Warming' would have been a miserable failure. He will always be grateful to her.

Steph was the first woman he got involved with who had children and they were both girls. Someone in that household was always having PMS, their period, boyfriend breakups, pimples, and parties they weren't invited to. "I don't have anything to wear" or "she's wearing my favorite (something)." Continuous crying, screaming, and arguing was the order of the day. Every day!

Flanagan was living in a steaming cauldron of estrogen stew! But he sure loved their Mom. She was a terrific Mother and always found time for him.

Flanagan liked the girls, but never being around kids before (like that), he was at a loss. Their mood swings, selfishness and disrespectful attitudes pissed him off all the time. When he tried to straighten them out, he most often heard "You're not my Dad, You're not the boss of me" and those statements were always punctuated with a slamming bedroom door.

He couldn't wait for those rats to grow up and leave home. The truth? He loved both of those girls but he couldn't tell them, he couldn't tell their Mom. The other truth? He was afraid that they would say "So? I don't care. I don't love you. I hate you."

213

Not much fun. Of course he was a raging drunk. He didn't treat them well. He remembers once telling Steph that just once, he would like to have an argument between just her and him. Their arguments were always about the girls. She said "Because you're always picking on them." Years later he would see how right she was.

Steph had kicked him out, again, and this time she meant it. This time she had called the cops! The cops were cool, but said he had to leave the house for the night, and he had to call the police for a civil standby to remove his stuff the next day. He spent a few nights in a motel. On the third night of his being out of the house he ran into Sandy's (his third wife's) Mom in a restaurant. They were both eating alone. Her husband (Sunday service at the Red Door Tavern guy) had passed away a few years back. Flanagan was drinking with him the afternoon he died. After the divorce (which was friendly), Flanagan remained friends with Mom and Dad.

He told Sandy's Mom that he was still a drunken fool and his wife had kicked him out via the cops. Sandy's Mom said "You can come and live at the house for as long as you want to." He enjoyed living there, they were pals. At the time he had just started a new job, and it sucked. His drinking was so bad that he could smell the stale booze oozing from his pores, his body was saturated with booze, and so was his mind. Every afternoon at work he studied the wall clock as though it were an art masterpiece. At 3:30 pm he was out the door, popped a beer top before he put on his seatbelt, and had it downed and cracked the second beer before he left the parking lot and roared to the closest bar. He was sick of it. He was sick of himself. Three months went by before his five phone calls a week finally worked with Steph. She relented and agreed to have dinner with him. For four days he didn't drink, he showered and soaked in the tub several times a night, he almost wore out a new toothbrush, trying to get rid of the bad booze smells. It was like trying to remove a tattoo; you always still knew it was there.

Flanagan felt like a kid on his first date. Steph was warmer and prettier than ever before. He had to have her back. His life meant nothing to him without her in it. He told her he would change, if she would just give him chance. She said she still needed some time. It gave him hope.

Flanagan backed way off of his drinking. A month later they were back together. Things went well, for a while. As happy as he was, he fell back into the bottle. One day, after an argument and him shoving and slapping her, with his once again weak apologies falling on deaf ears, Steph said "It's me or the bottle. You better decide, right now." He didn't drink the entire weekend. It seemed like forever. He kept hoping that she would go to the grocery store, the mall, anywhere! He needed a drink! She went nowhere. He went to work on Monday. He was sick and shaky. God, he hated his life. He was outside at first break having a smoke. A gal he worked with came to the break table and tossed down her keys. On her key ring was an AA medallion, which signifies a period of time in sobriety. He asked, Trish if she was a friend of Bill W's (are you in AA?) Trish said "Yes, I am, and you should be too!"

Well, he knew he was caught. A subordinate even knew that he was a drunk. Shit, he couldn't get away from it. He couldn't get away from himself. He put out his cigarette, walked back into the building, sucked in a deep breath and went into his boss's office. He told his boss that he was a drunk, he wanted to sober up and needed a few days off to kick the shakes and cobwebs out of his head. The boss smiled at him, told him to take the whole week off as sick time and his job was not in jeopardy.

As Flanagan got up to leave, his boss shook his hand, and said something about having guts and grinned as he said "Why don't you round up a few of these other clowns that work here and take them along with you?"

Flanagan spent several days shaking, sweating, sleeping, and stinking. He went to work on Monday morning. He asked Trish where she went to AA meetings and if there was a clubroom

215

in town. Trish gave him a meeting schedule and directions to the 'Alano Club'. After work he passed out two and a half cases of beer and a few bottles of vodka that he had found in his garage on Sunday. He was surprised to find that much stuff that he had hidden so well. The guys he worked with thought he was crazy to give away all that good booze.

When he left work that day, he felt lost, he didn't know where to go. Can't be at the bar, not the liquor store, didn't want to go home, so he drove to the Triangle Club (AA clubroom). Flanagan walked in and found as many people at the sixty-foot coffee bar as were in most regular bars at 5:30 in the afternoon. All with the same sounds of laughter and conversation. It was strange at best. He didn't want to be there but he knew it's where he needed to be. He sat at the coffee bar and stayed quiet. There was a 6:00 pm AA meeting in the 'Great Hall.' He sat in the meeting with about 40 people. He wanted to bolt, every minute that he was there. They all sounded to be full of shit. They were using words like grateful, honesty, God, joy, peace, shame, personal inventory, prayer, etc. That talk made him want to puke. He just wanted to go home, but something told him that these phonies were his only hope. None of them looked right, he sure as hell would not sit next to any of them at a bar! The dribble they were spouting was sickening. A bunch of look-good phonies.

At the end of the meeting and old guy with a dirty t-shirt using two canes and needing a shave and a dentist, came up and blocked his way out of the room. He said he was, 'Dumpster Johnny.' He told him that everyone in the room was scared of him because of the hateful look on his face. Johnny said "I'm an old, wore out crippled man and I'm not afraid of you, so you can get the hell out of here and never come back or there is a 7:30 meeting that you need to go to. Personally, I don't give a fuck which you do." Flanagan bought Dumpster Johnny a cup of coffee.

As Flanagan walked into a different room for the 7:30 pm men's stag meeting, the first man he met was, 'Red Face Tom.' Everyone, has some kind of nickname as last names are rarely

216

used. Tom had a red face as he has high blood pressure and was usually angry. Tom was over 6 ft. tall and 250 pounds at least. Tom squared up with him as he put out his hand to shake and said, "It can be over. It can all be over, starting right now." For some reason he liked Tom and he believed him. Tom was known as a defender of the 12 Traditions. He pissed off a lot of people with his oftentimes direct confrontations, but Tom was most oftentimes right. They became good friends with mutual respect. The day following the meeting with Red Face Tom he went to his favorite neighborhood bar to contemplate his new and life-lasting relationship with sobriety. He could not imagine life without drinking. "What will I do with myself, if I couldn't drink?"

Flanagan ordered a beer. He took two long swallows of that beer and as he set it back down on the bar he clearly saw Red Face Tom's, face on the label of that beer bottle. He pushed the beer bottle away, got up from the barstool, and with knowing that he was done, done forever, he walked out of the bar. He vowed to get his life right, repair his marriage, and let go of the rage and hatred he had carried for most all of his life.

When he made his new declaration of sobriety to his wife over dinner, she lightly smiled and said "I hope it works for you." He took it as she was saying "Bullshit, you can't do it." At the time he didn't think he could either. It hurt his feelings that she didn't believe in him. But he understood. He couldn't blame her. She had heard him swear it off many times before.

Flanagan laid out his plan as to the number of meetings he was going to attend each week. As the days of not drinking went to weeks and then, months he found he slept better, food tasted better, and his wife and he got along, a lot better. In his fourth month of sobriety the cramps in his stomach left him and he could breathe. He wasn't as angry but he did notice that his wife was more aggressive and confrontational. Steph was more and more demanding and expectant of his involvement with the day-to-day household duties. By his tenth month of sobriety, she was a total bitch! She was in his face all the time, correcting and admonishing him on everything. He told his sponsor, 'Chris' about his frustration with her constant bitching. Chris laughed, while reminding him of all the years of Steph putting up with his bullshit. Chris reminded him of the promises he made to himself in his first week of sobriety. Chris said, "You were never going to hit or shove her ever again, have you?" He said "No, not once." Chris said "You were never going to threaten or intimidate her ever again. Have you?" He said "No, not once." Chris said "You were never going to criticize or belittle her ever again, have you?" He said "No, not once." Chris threw his head back and howled in laughter to the point of tears. Chris said "You dumb shit. You don't get it, do you?" Flanagan was ready to bust his jaw. Chris asked "What have you wanted more than anything in your sobriety?" Flanagan answered "I want Steph to trust me." Chris again called him a dumb shit and said "You got it! You have her trust; she can finally tell you the truth without worrying that you will kick her ass. She believes you; she no longer has to hold back or keep her mouth shut; you got what you wanted! Next time, be careful what you pray for."

Flanagan had made some good friends in the group. There were two guys that he had over to the house several times a week for coffee. The girls (his step-daughters) called them the "Three Muscatels". On his first anniversary of sobriety, Steph and the girls made him a cake, had balloons, streamers, and gifts. They invited every one of his group pals. It was great. It took him some time after, to realize, that they weren't celebrating his sobriety. They were celebrating, their freedom from his alcoholism.

Chapter 25 "PETER"

In 1975, Flanagan's brother Petey, developed the same blood disorder that his brother Donnie and his dad had died from.

Petey, was a strong willed guy. He wasn't the run-of-the-mill cancer patient. Petey wanted answers and a cure. The Flanagan family Dr. was a general practitioner. He treated Donnie and dad, with negative results. The Dr. was way over his head and Petey knew it. Petey was not about to buy into the concept that, 'all doctors were Gods, and are not to be challenged.' After extensive research, Petey found a hematologist that was having good results with blood cancers. The doctor was at the University of Wisconsin Hospital. His name was Doctor Thomas Jonathon. Dr. Jonathon was very aggressive with Petey's treatment. The Dr. kept Petey on his feet and out of the hospital. The Dr. was more concerned with Petey's quality of life rather than using him as a lab rat.

Petey went in and out of remission for several years, Petey was able to ignore the pain and the fear. He lived his live the way he wanted to. His cancer was just an inconvenience to him. He wouldn't let it control or own him. Flanagan always marveled at Petey's courage and determination. Petey was not about to let life pass him by. Petey had a drive and a passion to be the very best at everything he did. Petey attended the University of Wisconsin. His grades were always a 3.8 or better. Before Petey got sick, he was a Cross Country runner and did the initial layout for the now, world famous 'Grandma's Marathon,' held annually in Duluth, MN which is only bested in attendance by the Boston and New York Marathons.

One day, Flanagan, Petey and Donnie were shooting baskets in their folk's driveway, Petey was so much faster and more accurate than Donnie and him, that they had to "cheap shot" him to be competitive. Flanagan hip-checked Petey and he fell and broke his ankle. Petey's ankle never healed right and his days of marathon running were over. Petey took up body building. He and a buddy worked out with free-weights in his folk's basement. All they had was a bench, a curl bar and one straight bar, with less than two hundred pounds of weights. Petey soon became a giant in muscle and tone. Petey was just as chiseled as the guys in his towering stacks of body builder magazines. Flanagan never knew his brother, Petey very well due to their six-year age difference and the paths their life's had taken. They did play softball together on the Rampart Rescue Ambulance sponsored, slow pitch team. Petey was left handed and quick as a cat. He never let a ball get by him, no matter how fast the base runner, Petey always threw them out, from his short-stop position. Every time he batted he was always good for extra bases. Flanagan and Petey trout fished and hunted Partridge together a few times but that was about it.

Flanagan had a well-guarded secret about Petey and even Stevie for that matter. He loved them booth but he also despised them. They were close to Mom and Dad, both of the boys idolized Dad. Mom was loving, affectionate and openly showed her pride in them. Dad had stopped drinking when Petey was two years old and Stevie came along 9 years later. The boys never saw Dad as the vicious drunk he knew, so very well. Dad was the parent to them that he had always wanted to have. He resented the boys for their comfortable and happy lives. Petey was in Boy Scouts and had a complete uniform, Dad helped him with his scout projects. Mom and Dad attended all of his monthly awards meetings. Stevie was a Cub Scout, had a full Cub Scout uniform and always had a pack of cookies to bring to his Den Mother's house when it was his turn to bring the cookies. Dad was the proud and loving father just like the ones Flanagan saw in his 'Boys Life' scouting magazines. Dad and Mom both went to all of Petey's track meets and body building competitions, Stevie was a bookworm, won a lot of science awards and played the cello. Yes, Mom and Dad both went to all of Stevie's school events and award ceremonies.

Mom's father, gave Mom and Dad money to buy a nice house with a big yard, flower beds and a basketball hoop on the garage. The boys didn't have to grow up poor and live in a brownstone flat as he did. They always had heat in the winter and there was no frost on the inside of the windows, no breaking the ice in the toilet. They each had their own bedrooms, there was always plenty of food.

Petey and Stevie and even Donnie, for that matter, never knew of his pains or his fears. Flanagan wondered if Petey or Stevie would have achieved such goals, let alone dare to even dream them, if they had to endure Dad's booming voice that would vibrate against his spine as thou he was being electrocuted. They never had to decide if they were better off to cover their faces with their arms and take the beatings to their stomachs. Flanagan had to choose to protect his nose as his Dad had broken it twice before he was eight years old. Add the cold, the hunger and Mother screaming "I wish I would have never had you, I wish you were dead" and he was most certain that they too, would feel defeated and broken, and then, become that way. The way, he became.

Part of Flanagan understands and even accepts his brothers shared affections with Mom and Dad. He knew he was a threat to the real truths of their pasts. He was a reminder of the times they wanted to deny and forget. He was an outcast and no part of their lives.

As the years went by, Petey became sicker. His remissions were shorter. In the late summer of 1988 Steph and he traveled to Stanford, to visit his family and attend his twenty-year high school class reunion. Petey looked good but was quite ill. Flanagan could see the pain that dulled his eyes, the grimace that most people mistook for a grin. He sensed his fear and he knew he was close to death. He further suspected that Petey was ready to die. Petey had divorced a number of years back and now was in love with and engaged to a neat gal with a three-year-old daughter. The three of them made a cute family. That little girl adored Petey, as he did her.

In 1989 Flanagan went back to Stanford for Thanksgiving and he expected to say his final goodbyes to his little brother, Petey. It was Thanksgiving Day, they had all gathered at Mom's &

221

Pops house for the day.

It was a day filled with idle chatter. Everyone acted as thou the 800-pound Silverback Gorilla was not sitting in the center of the living room. He could see that Petey had something on his mind that he needed to talk about. He told Petey that he had to go to buy cigarettes and he wanted him to ride with him. Everyone got quiet and they all looked frightened. They knew he was going to make Petey talk about the unthinkable. Mother gave him a pleading look as if to say "Please don't ruin our Thanksgiving, don't upset him. We all have cried enough."

Petey told Flanagan that he was glad that he took him for the ride. He just needed to be away from everyone for a while. He said he felt a lot of pressure to pretend he was OK around the family. He felt everyone was walking on egg shells and trying not to say the wrong thing, as they feared it might upset him.

Petey said it bothered him to be studied, with everyone looking at him for some kind of sign that he was in pain, and how they would glance at each other as to ask "Did you see that?" Flanagan told Petey that he understood how he felt. He told him that is a common behavior of people in fear of losing a loved one. Petey told him he was afraid of Mom or Pops having a heart attack from all their fear and sadness.

Petey told him that he was going to go back to the U of W Hospital for a lengthy period and they were going to try an attempt at a 'Hail Mary' cure. He said it was high risk and it could possibly end his life much sooner. He said he was ready for an; all or nothing. He could no longer cling to false hope and he couldn't put his girlfriend or her daughter or the rest of the family thru having to watch him die, a little more, each day.

Flanagan told Petey that he did not have to posture in front of him. He knew he was trying to protect him and the family. The next morning Flanagan and Petey went for a walk before he had to catch his flight back to Wyoming. They struck up a deal. Petey, didn't have to play the "I'm O.K. game" with him and after he returned home they promised each other that they would talk no less than three times each week. They agreed that they would openly talk of their fears, their regrets and their shames. No bullshit, just the truth of each other's hearts. The brothers shed a few tears and a final hug. They said good bye and agreed that they would meet up someday, on the other side.

Later that same day, Petey turned himself in to the University of Wisconsin Hospital. Petey and he talked on the phone every night. Flanagan's Mom called him each morning to give him the current updates of Petey's condition. Mother would tell him each morning how proud she was of Petey's courage, strength, and positive attitude. Every time Mother spoke of her pride of Petey, Flanagan could taste the bile in his throat. He so much wanted to shout at her that she needed to snap out of it. His mind and his gut knew that Petey was dying, they were all pretending to be hopeful so they wouldn't have to see the reality. They were in fact, causing Petey more emotional pain, as he had to play the look good game for their comfort. They were being self-centered, with no regard for Petey's suffering. Flanagan knew his comments would fall on deaf ears and he would end up being the bad guy.

During the third week of January, 1990, Flanagan and Petey came to a peace like neither of them had ever known. Flanagan found himself-saying to Petey, that it was now his time to die. Flanagan told Petey that he could no longer respect his 'taking one for the team.' His valiant struggle, was a hoax. He told him that there was no honor in suffering, and it was time to end it. He gave Petey his heart felt permission to let himself go and to allow God to take him.

Flanagan went on to explain that it was unfair to Mom and the family, to force them to witness his becoming a vegetable, supported by machines and with no hope. They would end up having to pray for his passing and they would all be forced to live in limbo, and how it would just prolong their grief. Petey thanked him for his understanding and insights. They exchanged words of love and hung up. Flanagan sat up all that night, waiting for and

223

knowing the call would come, in the next few hours.

Flanagan couldn't figure out why he said what he said to his little brother. He knew it was his voice and his words but he did not know where it all came from. He had just told his little brother that he needed to die. "Am I being selfish and self-seeking? Am I using a dirty trick so I don't have to feel the daily pain of losing him? Did I place my needs in front of my brothers?" Does Flanagan's continued living remind him of his own short-comings and how he failed Petey and his family? Was it grieving or was it shame? Was it arrogance or soulful love?

Flanagan lowered his head as he said an 'Act of Contrition.' "I was a lousy big brother. I should have been a better friend; I should have spent more time with him. I was so self-absorbed with my own little petty life, that I never saw his needs." All thru the dark of night, he was haunted with his shame and remorse.

The phone rang during the first hour of daylight. It was his youngest brother, Stevie. He said, Petey had fallen into a deep coma and it didn't look good. He told Stevie that he would book a flight and be there as soon as he could.

Flanagan was sitting at the coffee-bar when Steph got up. He was lost in his tears and sorrow. Steph said she had picked up the phone and heard his and Stevie's conversation. Steph said she would pack a bag for him and make his flight reservations, and she would come if he wanted her to. He told Steph that there was no real hurry as Petey, was already dead. She protested, saying that Stevie said he was in a coma. She tried to assure him that Petey was strong and he could come back out of it. Flanagan stood up, took both her hands in his, as he looked her directly in her eyes and told her of his phone conversation with Petey, the night before. He told her that he told Petey that it was time for him, and he needed to die. Steph had a look of horror and resignation, as her eyes welled up and her body started to tremble.

Her face showed her disgust for his hardness and the questionable compassion from his heart. He told Steph, as he had told so many others, so many times before "I know what I know, and I don't know why." He made it clear that he was not going back to visit his brother. He was going to bury his brother. He told Steph that he needed to go and do this alone. She said she understood.

Pops was at the gate as Flanagan came off the plane late that afternoon. They shook hands. Pop's grip and his face told it all. They walked the concourse, picked up his bags and walked thru the parking lot, in silence. As Pops started the truck they both lit a cigarette and while looking straight ahead at the falling snow. Flanagan said "He is gone, isn't he?" As they both put out their cigarettes, Pops squared his shoulders, shifted the truck into gear and without looking at him said, "Petey is on life support but does not have any brain activity. Dr. Jonathon wanted you to have a chance to say your final goodbyes." Other than Pops saying "Your Mother is going to really need your support" they drove to the hospital in silence. Both with their thousand mile stares, both lost in their thoughts, both trying not to break down.

When they arrived at the hospital, Mom and Stevie and Petey's fiancé were in a family consolation room with Dr. Jonathon and two of Petey's nurses. Flanagan said hello to everyone, gave Mom a light hug and Dr. Jonathon told him to come with him. Dr. Jonathon told him that Petey would look much different than the last time he saw him a month ago. As they went into Petey's room, Flanagan was shocked and he even wondered if this was someone else. Petey's body was so greatly ballooned from the steroids and other drugs that he had to study hard to know it was him. Petey was now bald, had a moon face and all of his striking, chiseled facial features were gone. Petey had, had a single, small pockmark on his left cheek, when Flanagan finally saw that pockmark, he then knew it was him. Dr. Jonathon was noticeably shaken. He told Flanagan that he did all that could be possibly done for Petey. Flanagan knew that Petey was more than just another patient to him, a lot more. Dr. Jonathon told him that he and Petey prayed together the night before, he told him that

Petey made his peace with God. Dr. Jonathon said that just a few minutes before Petey slipped into the coma, a Catholic priest, he and Petey had joined hands in "The Lord's Prayer."

So it was on January 26th, 1990, Clinton Flanagan leaned over and kissed his little brother Peter "Goodbye" and he felt ashamed.

Chapter 26 "WHERE SHAME TAKES US"

Flanagan left Petey's side for the final time. He sat with the family while the nursing team unhooked Petey from the equipment and monitors. A nurse came and told them that they could visit Petey now. When they went into Petey's room the ventilator, all of the monitors and leads and IV's were gone, the sheets and bedspread were crisp with the covers pulled up to his neck, he looked like he was sleeping and peaceful. He noticed that someone had put some make-up on Petey's face to hide some of the blue, black from the pooled blood just under his skin.

Flanagan felt the hospital staff's love for Petey and their compassion for his family. It felt pure, simply pure. Flanagan rode home with Mom and Pops. Mother sat in the middle of the bench seat of the pick-up truck. She leaned into him, fainting sleep. He held her for the entire 160 mile ride. Other than the periodic sobs from Mom, the diesel motor drowned out his thoughts.

That night he laid in bed and kept asking himself "Why Petey? Why not me? Why Donnie? Why Dad? They were all better men than me. They all did something with their lives. They were all loved and they all meant something to someone. Dad was sober, a great guy, so admired, so respected. He had changed, he helped a lot of guys and women get and stay sober. Dad was only fifty years old when the cancer took him. His suffering was immense. And Donnie? He had two young sons, was married to his second wife and she loved him dearly. He too was sober and helped several people to put their lives back together. Donnie died when he was only 27 years old. And now Petey? Petey never wronged anyone. He was a good guy, everyone liked Petey. He helped a lot of young body builders with their programs. He was good to Mom and Stevie. He was devoted to his fiancé and her precious little daughter. Peaty was only 37 years old when he died. Here I am, 42 years old and a complete nothing. Why am I left? What purpose do I have? My fifth wife is ready to dump me, I am and I had always been a drunk, I couldn't keep a woman and I couldn't keep

227

a job. Selfish, self-centered, self-seeking, a man without promise or courage. Why am I the one to survive?"

At some point during that late night, Flanagan realized he was being self-indulgent in his sorrow. He spent the rest of the darkness writing Petey's eulogy. It was the least he could do. He got out of bed before Mom and Pops and put on a pot of coffee. As they sat in the kitchen he announced that he was going to be Petey's pallbearer and do his eulogy. Mom said that he should sit with the family and let Petey's friends be the pallbearers and the Priest do the eulogy. For the first time in his life, Flanagan told his Mother, no. He was going to do exactly as he stated. He told Mom and Pops that this is something he had to do for himself, and for Petey.

Mom, was Petey's executor of his will. The day before Petey's funeral, they had to go to Petey's apartment to remove his things, as the next month's rent was due the following day and the landlord was being a total prick about it.

Petey's apartment was a small studio. Very small, but neat. Petey had banker boxes stacked everywhere. Mom sat on the bed and read his will out loud. Mom was so tiny and frail looking, Flanagan thought that any moment she would crumble. Mom's tiny voice trembled, she shook uncontrollably, tears ran down her face but she drove on, handing out items from the steel lock box, to each of them, according to Petey's wishes. When Mom finished reading the will she stood to her full height of four feet four inches, she pursed her lips and said "Let's get to it." He was amazed at his Mother's resolve that she somehow beckoned from within her tiny frame. Here she was, about to bury her second son, and yet she was somehow determined to stay the course and complete the task at hand.

Mom directed him to clean out the closet. As like the rest of the apartment, the closet was full of neatly stacked boxes that went all the way to the ceiling.

Flanagan opened and went through each box looking for things that were expressly noted in Petey's will. After going through several boxes he came across a metal lock box. The same type and size that held the personal willed items. He tried Mom's key for the other box and it didn't work. He picked the lock and as he lifted the lid they all stopped what they were doing and were all frozen in place. As thou they knew what he was about to discover. In his heart, Flanagan already knew, as well. He found 15 glass ampules and 10 syringes pre-loaded with steroids and some other kinds of rapid growth hormones. His heart sank and his blood boiled. Time and time again he asked Petey if he was 'juicing' (taking steroids) as he had gotten too big and too fast to be 'natural'. Petey always denied it. Flanagan repeatedly cautioned him about the all but promised side effects of steroids. Uncontrolled rage, depression, floppy heart and the like. Pete always said no, but Flanagan didn't believe him.

Flanagan, repeatedly told Mom and Pops and Stevie to watch for those symptoms but they denied having any knowledge and swore that they wouldn't ever let Petey do steroids. Over and over again, they assured him that Petey was a "clean and natural" body builder. They all claimed that Petey just used vitamins and natural supplements. Flanagan never believed them either.

They had all lied to him to help protect Petey's secret and his dreams of becoming a world class body builder. They all knew exactly what the contents of that metal box held. He threw the box and the contents against the wall with all of his strength. They had now gathered in a tight cluster waiting for him to explode. All of their faces were blank, other than their obvious guilt. He found a voice that he never had before, as he snarled "You knew, you all fucking knew! You all helped to kill him!"

Flanagan spat threw his clenched teeth as he told them all to go fuck themselves, as he stormed down the steps of the apartment building and out onto the street. He hailed a taxi and he had the driver take him to Mom and Pops house and told the driver to wait while he gathered his bags. He had the driver take him to a

229

hotel and again, had him wait for him while he checked in. He then had the driver take him to a bar. Flanagan plunged into one drink after the other, he had no recollection of the rest of that day.

The day of Petey's funeral Flanagan rented a car and refused to ride in the mortuary, 'Family car.' Flanagan did in fact, do his brother's eulogy and he did in fact, carry his brother's casket at the cemetery. He gave Mom a phony hug goodbye, shook Pops hand and Stevie's too. He left the cemetery in the rental car and left his family to their own lives.

Flanagan went to his hotel, changed his clothes and headed out to confront, his life's mission. He was about to visit his Dad's favorite neighborhood bar, the original 'scene of the crime' if you will. He was going to put all of this dark, ugly, back ally of his soul crap, to rest. He is going to figure out Dad's attraction to that depressing shit-hole. After this night he will be able to erase from his mind the early years that formed his life's past and present. He was going to take charge of his life, let go of his haunting nightmares and never again let any part of his past, define or control him or his future.

As Flanagan pulled up to the side street to park, a strange thing took place, a very strange thing. Everything lost its color. The car, his clothes, the two story, flat roofed brick building and the sign that read 'The Tavern Bar and Hotel.' Things were black and white with defused shades of gray and green. The kind of colors that were used to print the hot rod magazines of the 1950's and 60's. It was as though nothing was fluid, everything was in snap shots, as though he was looking at an old family album.

The building itself was more than 80 years old. The hotel part on the second floor was a flop house that rented rooms by the week. The Iron ore boat sailors, the iron ore minors and the lumber jacks would stay there for their 1 week off after working for two whole months. Most of these men did not have a place to call home. These were hard drinking and hard living men, whose families were long forgotten. Whiskey and other lost souls like them, were their only windows to the world in which they lived.

Just as he walked to climb the three stairs, and open the door to enter the acidic belly of the beast, he glanced back and saw the cars that his dad once owned. They were all parked bumper to bumper. Flanagan saw Donnie and him sitting in each of the three cars. He could see that they had aged with each car. First was the 1951 green Pontiac, the brown Willies Jeep Wagoner. Lastly the 1957 Chevy Nomad Wagon. Dad needed big cars so he could haul the illegal Oleo margarine that he smuggled into MN from Wisconsin. He used to help his dad load the heavy cases each Sunday night. They covered the cases with a big blanket. Dad told him that he could not tell anyone because "We would have to go to jail if the Cops caught us."

So there were the three cars and each one represented a part of his young years. All of these cars were junk-yard rescues. Dad bought them from car lots that were 'Buy here-pay here with weekly payments.' All Dad could ever afford were those 'Last gaspers.'

Flanagan braced himself, threw back his shoulders and cleared his mind so as not to miss any part of this experience. This was finally the day that he would confront the enemy that stole his dad away from him, so many years ago. He partially feared that he would start a fight and take the place apart. The memories flooded back as he paused to adjust his eyes in the entry-way. He remembers all the times his Mom made him call the bar to ask Dad when he was coming home. He was surprised that he suddenly remembered the bartenders and the waitress's names. Bart the bartender was a big man with a heavy voice, Annie the waitress talked hard and used a lot of bad words. As he took a stool at the bar, he looked across the room and saw where Donnie and he used to sit in a booth and drank Nesbit orange pop while they waited for dad to finish his beer's and his game of bumper pool, so they could go fishing. The memories of hearing dad say "I just need to run-in and cash a check, and we will go to the lake" still rang in his ears. He saw the side door where Donnie and he would sneak out of, and walk home.

231

Flanagan sat with his first beer and stared back at his distorted image through the bar back mirror with the elaborately carved mahogany frame. They were heavily fogged from the many decades of cigarette tars and nicotine. The outer edge of the mirrors were lined with faded local union bumper stickers, which were badly yellowed and cracked from age. He tried to visualize the beauty of the wood when it was new, the carvings of each corner showed prideful craftsmanship. The appointments of that back wall had faded, much like the time forgot, in his troubled mind.

He watched the bartender as he server up drinks when he wasn't busy passing the dice cup for the 'shake-a-day.' He wanted to ask the bald, barreled chested bar-keep, if he ever knew Bart or Annie from a long time past. More so, he wanted to ask him if he might have known his dad, from thirty years back.

Flanagan wanted to ask him what his dad, was like, where he sat, what he drank and how much, and who he was friends with. As he sat studying himself in the mirror, he became lost in his thoughts. A scuffle broke out behind him. Flanagan was startled when he realized that he was sitting at the bar with his back to the room. He was a cop and he never left his back exposed to a room, no matter where he was. He always sat where he could observe the entire room and watch the doors. He would grade every person in the room as to the level of threat they might pose. He always made sure he knew where the exits were and what was between him and them and the distance of travel.

As he took his beer and started to get off his stool to move to the far end of the bar, the two drunken combatants bumped into him and knocked his beer out of his hand. His beer was now all over his shirt and slacks. Flanagan instantly lit the fuse, to 'kill those two fuckin idiots.' He pushed them both back away from him. Flanagan didn't remember what he said but he felt the veins in his neck about to burst, and his chest was heaving. The rage of this day had found an outlet. It seemed that the entire room of thirty plus men all froze in place. He could plainly see the fear in the eyes of these rough-tuff union workers. They all knew that someone was about to die, and they postured in their submission, hoping it wasn't going to be them. Suddenly the bartender was standing in front of him with his palms up in an attempt to defuse the situation. Once again, he found himself coming out of a trance and he knew what made them all cower was the 1000-mile stare of a madman. The bartender told him that he would buy him a fresh beer and the next two beers after that, were on the two fighters. Flanagan walked to the end of the bar in the back of the room. As the bouncer sent the two fighters out the front door, the bartender brought him a fresh beer and put down two shot glasses in front of him to keep track of his two free beers that he had coming.

Flanagan found the bar surface to be as heavy worn as at the center of the bar. The bare wood with a raised grain, stood in witness of the many of thousands of lost souls, who sat to drink away their failed lives.

As he sat in thought of those shattered dreams, he shuddered at the thought of examining his own. To push away his demons, he blinked his eyes several times, shut down his brain and studied his surroundings. The faint smell of bleach that he first took-in as he entered the bar now seemed much stronger. The smell of stale beer and whiskey were all in competition with the putrid odors of sweaty body's and stale cigar and cigarette smoke. The place stunk, just as he had remembered.

It was the same smell that was on dad's jacket and in all of his cars. How could these odors maintain their place in his mind and be so clearly familiar from more than 30 years past?

There was a brass rail for an arm rest that wrapped the entire bar. There was also a brass foot rest that was dulled and badly scratched from the many years of neglect. The bar proper sat around 30 people. There were 10 booths and several tables along the far wall. The edge of the booths, where the long ago stained wood met the floor, were caked with the filth of decades of being slapped with a dirty mop. The middle of the room was filled with four bumper pool tables. The back wall had two shuffle board tables. The floor was an old-time barber shop style, with one inch white tiles that were accented with black tiles in a diamond pattern. The grout lines had no indentations and were level with the tiles, and had a brownish/grey, cast from years of grime build up. The corners of the room were heavily caked with wax build up.

This joint was most definitely a working man's bar. Most all of them wore the standard 'Dickies,' blue, or gray work shirts and matching pants. They all wore their union local buttons on their shirt collars or shirt pockets. He suddenly noticed the bar was packed with men. All the pool tables were in use with quarters on the end of each table to mark who was next to play when the game was over. Most all of the conversations revolved around union contracts, grievances, what a prick the boss was, their little bastard kids, and what an ungrateful bitch their wife's were.

During all of Flanagan's graphic observations of this dive, he did notice one amusing thing. Every new patron who came in was immediately greeted by the bouncer who witnessed the, 'Lion roar.' They spoke in hushed voices and did quick head nods in his direction. When they went to the bar to get their drink, they leaned forward as if to ask the bartender if the guy at the end of the bar was really all that scary. The bartender had a look of caution, as he nodded his head. Flanagan felt good to have these guys be afraid of him, it reminded him of the days at the Corner Dairy Bar and when the kids made fun of Mac. He enjoyed sitting in that shit-hole with a fresh haircut and shave and well dressed. He locked eyes with every man there. None of them had the guts to hold his gaze. He found himself wanting a "good ole roaring, ass tearing, dust-up." It felt good to be in the middle of their pathetic boy's club and to show them that there was not a fucking thing any of them could do about it.

Flanagan tried to telegraph to these losers that he was better than they were. He wanted to kill them all, and they knew it. Nobody spoke to him the entire night, he hated these assholes for doing to their family's what his dad did to him and his family. He tried to pick out the wife beaters. The guys who knocked their kids around, the guy who was playing the big shot by buying his friends a round of drinks, while at home, he had a family with no heat and no food. He was glad that he left his gun in the hotel room. This bar, as so many others, just keep playing re-runs of horror. The only difference, was time. The bartender flicked the lights and announced last call.

Flanagan was startled to realize that he had been in that joint for the last seven hours. As he ordered a final beer, he asked the bartender, "How many beers did I have?" He said "This one makes 15." The bartender leaned his massive forearms on the bar and thanked him for not tearing the place apart. The bartender told him he held his liquor well and he hoped that what was troubling him would soon be over. He grinned as he said he was going to enjoy the stories that came from this night for the next several weeks. He asked him what he did for a living, Flanagan told him he was a cop that enjoyed a bar fight and punishing guys who reminded him of his dad. The bartender shrugged his shoulders and walked away.

So there it was, the truth he can no longer ignore. Flanagan's eyes started to tear as he realized he had become his Father. He was all the guys in this bar and bars everywhere. Late at night, with no hope and feeling so terribly, all alone. Wondering what had caused his life to go so tragically wrong. "Why had God forsaken me and the devil taken my soul?"

Chapter 27 "MY BOYS"

In early Sept of 1999, Flanagan meet two remarkable young men who would, and have, change his life forever. It was late afternoon during the Wyoming Elk and Deer Archery Season. He had hunted hard the last several days and on this day he was worn out. He didn't have the energy to stalk game so he was driving the U.S. Forest Service fire/logging road looking for animals. Dark thunderheads were building and it looked like a heavy, rain storm would set in before nightfall. He was driving less than 10 mph when he saw a green Chevy pick-up truck coming up behind him, fast. He sped up until he could find a place to pull over and let them by. As the truck roared by, he saw the bed of the truck was loaded with camping gear. He was guessing those two boys were watching those same storm clouds as he was, and they were in a hurry to set their camp before the storm came in. He resumed his slow driving. 15 minutes later he came upon that same truck with the two young men with a topo map spread across the hood of their truck. Since he had hunted the area for more than 20 years, he thought he would stop and try to help them out.

Flanagan pulled past them and parked. The map they were looking at, was several generations old. After introductions, he told them that he had a current map, and asked if they would like to see it. They said yes, so he went to his truck and pulled out his map and spread it out on their truck hood. They told him they had never been to the area before and were looking for a place to camp and hunt. He showed them a place just three miles ahead and told them to take the right fork. He showed them the elk and mule deer routes and the morning and evening bedding areas. He told them to keep the map as he knew this area like the inside of his refrigerator. They showed surprise that he gave the game information and map so freely. They thanked him several times and were respectful. As he drove away they waved a genuine farewell. He thought they were nice fellows; it was nice to meet two humble young men. He was glad that he could help them out

Flanagan went on to hunt for the evening, he was about 2 miles away from where he suggested those fellows set their camp. But less than a quarter-mile away (as the crow flies) and all down-hill thru heavy dark timber and a maze full of tangles and blow-down trees.

He saw four, nice mule deer bucks together, all 4 points (western count) or better. Nice big animals, all still in velvet. Of course they were on that steep hill and they did not know he was there. He had to close a distance of 40 yards before he could take a shot. He slowly crept towards them. When he got to 30 yards of the deer he nocked an arrow, drew and released on the biggest and closest buck, he shot high and the deer did not move. He pulled another arrow from his quiver, nocked it and as he was about to draw he saw a strange movement to his right, and about half the distance between him and the deer. He saw the movement again and saw a blond/tan color of fur, kind of twitching. As it came to mind, what it might be, the mature Mt. Lion stood up. He obviously was crawling on his belly to stalk the same deer, as Flanagan was. The Mt. Lion looked at him, jumped about 6 ft. in his direction and snarled at him. Flanagan dropped his bow and pulled out his belt knife. He knew he could never get an arrow into him fast enough to stop him, so he thought his chances would be better with his six inch, fixed blade, 'Buck knife,' if the Cougar came for him.

Flanagan was using a scent cover and animal attractant to cover his human scent. It smelled like vanilla. The Mt. Lion turned facing him, head on. He hollered at it to scare him away but it didn't budge. He had read enough, over the years, to know he shouldn't bend down to pick up a stick or rock to throw at him because the big cat would read his movement as an attacking posture. He also knows not to turn away or run as, Cougars are known to attack just for sport and blood lust. Flanagan started to back up slowly, having to look behind him every step he took so as not to trip on all the windfall trees, and yet keep the Mt. Lion in his sight. He had to be just as careful not to make direct eye to eye

237

contact, as the big cat would see that as a challenge and he would most certainly attack.

The Mt. Lion let him move away about four steps, then he slunk down and made a very stealthy, tentative step toward him. Flanagan knew it was no longer a question of if he was going to attack. No, it was now, a question of when. His plan was that when the Lion sprung at him, he would crouch down, come up under the MT. Lion, jam his left arm under his neck and block him in mid-air and stab him repeatedly in the belly with his knife in his right hand. It wasn't a matter of being brave, he knew that if he failed to stab him he wouldn't get a second chance. He would just be torn to pieces.

Flanagan didn't want to die that way. He thought of Steph, his Grandkid's, thought of the horror they and his Mom & Dad would have to live with. It made him angry and he wanted to kill that God damned cat. He thought if he was found dead and the cat also dead, it would tell the story and they would feel some relief, that in knowing he died fighting. Those thoughts racing thru his mind, made him lose his concentration. He tripped over a log and almost fell backwards, he caught his balance and as he started to rise back to full height, the cat started to growl, and took another step towards him. Flanagan kept backing up and telling himself to keep his head right, and to only think about the cat and keep backing up.

The road was still 50 or more feet above him and the sun was setting, and his truck was still a quarter of a mile away. He kept backing up and yelling at the cat, the cat kept coming forward, every few steps he would snarl and show his teeth, Flanagan could smell his rancid breath. Sweat was running down his spine like a leaking sink faucet. His head band was saturated with sweat and it was dripping down his face and neck. As he stepped onto the road he had to turn to his right to get to his truck. He turned in baby steps to keep the Mt. Lion in front of him. When he stepped onto the road, the Mt. Lion changed his posture and stood to full height, he kept showing his fangs but stopped growling, he was now hissing like a pissed-off alley cat. As Flanagan quickened his pace in the last few minutes of remaining daylight, the cat started to swipe his paws like a boxer would throw a left and right hook, over and over again. The Lion matched him step for step, and most of the time he was within in 10 feet of him. Flanagan kept telling himself to be ready, the next step could be the one that he would explode on him.

Suddenly there was the truck, 20-feet away, the Mt. Lion slowed down and then, he stopped. Flanagan knew it was time, The Mt. Lion was about to strike. Flanagan, was about to become a bloody mess, but he was going to kill a Mountain Lion. As he reached down to get his keys off the top of the front tire the Mt. Lion turned sideways, let out a short screech and ran down the hill.

Flanagan jumped in his truck and almost passed out from his holding his breath for so long. He didn't know the last time he took a full breath, it seemed as thou it took him forever to normalize his breathing. His clothes, his hair and his skin were foaming with sweat. As he got himself under control he realized that those two young men were camped directly below where the cat ran off to. He started the engine and sped down the bumpy road to warn them. When he got to their camp they were not there, just their truck. He started to honk his horn to warn them and hopefully scar off the Mt. Lion. The boys walked into camp a few minutes later in full dark. They lit their lanterns as he told them about the cat. They became as shook-up as he was. The three of them sat up at their campfire all night.

They each had a flashlight lantern and kept shining their lights in the field next to the fire. They heard noises and thought they saw eyes in the clearing. The boys had hand guns and he had a 10-22 rifle. They all shot at the eyes. At dawn they checked for blood on the ground in the area where they shot at the eyes, they found no blood. During the course of that evening the three became pals. The boys came to his camp the following night for dinner, they had a great time. The oldest boy was named Oliver, the younger, named William but went by 'Shaggy' as he greatly resembled the cartoon character from 'Scooby Doo.' These boys were cut from another cloth, by current day standards. They were young men of honor, with obvious dignity and humility. Flanagan exchanged phone numbers with them and the week following they shared a camp and have hunted together ever since. Except for the years that Oliver was transferred (career Army) and Shaggy was stationed in Alaska while serving in the army.

At some point, Oliver told him of his upbringing. His dad was an asshole and treated him poorly. Oliver received very little praise or even acceptance from his dad. Oliver was left to find his own way and raise himself.

One night, in hunting camp (a few years later), Oliver told him that he had missed out on life as a young man, by not having an active dad. And how he wished he had a father to be a Grandpa to his two young boys. He had no dad to show pride in his sons, his family and Oliver's accomplishments, no dad to put his arm around his shoulder and give approval or encouragement. No one to say "Good job son, I am proud of you." Flanagan knew that feeling all too well.

Flanagan told Oliver of a bit of his young years and it brought them closer. He told him of his ruined opportunity's to be a dad and his many, lifelong regrets. He told Oliver that he would be his dad. He could call him Pops and that he would never let him down.

That was 19 years ago. Oliver's family is his family. Oliver's boys are young men now, they treat each other with respect and share mutual admirations. Flanagan adored Oliver's wife, Carla. During Oliver's many army deployments and transfers, it was Carla that held the family together.

Oliver engaged the enemy in several conflicts throughout the world. Carla, was left to celebrate many holidays alone, with just her and their babies. Carla had an inner strength that would not allow her, nor would she ever show the boys her suffering, or her fears of losing her mate to war.

Flanagan could easily see her lying in bed in the dark of

night, and praying that Oliver was alive but fearing that those prayers were too late.

Few, could imagine the terror she must have felt when she heard a car door slam in front of the house, hoping the doorbell would not ring. Hoping against all hope, that her fear of fears would not be realized. No military wife wants to ever see two, 'Class-A' uniformed officers' come to their door, and be handed an envelope from the "State Department" by the senior officer's white gloved hand. There is not a woman he admires and so greatly respects more than Carla.

Flanagan, Oliver, and Shaggy had many great times together. They have filled and enriched his life with wonderful memories. Both of the "boys" called him "Pops"; they share a mutual respect and they will always have each other's back. They talked on the phone weekly and always ended their conversations with, "Love you son, love you Pops."

Who would have ever thought that on that fateful cloudy September afternoon in 1999, three strangers would build a lifetime of friendship, based on a topographical map spread out on the hood of a pick-up truck?

They did not know what a broken and lonely man Flanagan was that day. Those two boys gave him a life he could never had dreamed of. He got two loving sons who he adores. They got.... well, that is their story to tell. But, he can tell you this, thru their being pals, his lifetime of deep sorrows has greatly faded. He is now whole.

Chapter 28 "THE DOORS"

It was a Saturday morning, Steph had left early to have breakfast with her, 'gal pals' then off for a day of shopping. While he was making the bed he noticed a book on her night stand, entitled 'Dump Him.' It hit him hard. He sat on the edge of the bed and flipped thru several pages and found the gist of it to be 'how to' get out of a relationship with a man that you no longer loved or never did love.

Flanagan's belly twisted and his heart ached. This was the affirmation that he had been trying to avoid for the last few years. He knew in his heart (and he had known for some time,) that Steph no longer cared for him. The one time glances of approval, the flashing eyes and grins that said "I want you" were long past gone. The only time they hugged was always upon his initiation. She always blocked full body contact by using her arm between them as thou she had her arm in a sling. She would let him hug her but there was never a mutual embrace. Being the romantic fool he was, he would somehow find a way to overlook the obvious rejection each time and simply hope for a, 'someday.'

There were several other indications that Steph was done with him. The sex was passionless, more like dutiful and very rare, and like the hugs, he had always been the one to initiate it, most times, she said "No."

Steph went on vacations with her sister and a large group of guys and gals (mostly single), twice a year. They would all cruse the South Seas. He was never invited. Steph would also spend several long weekends at mountain resorts with many of those same people. Again, he was never invited, she simply told him that she was going. Yes, he knew she was going to party and even more so, he knew she was going to get away from him. Those nights that she was gone he would lay in that big empty bed and hug her pillow and try to smell the scent of her and hope that, 'someday,' she would return and be the gal that she once was. Being the romantic that he was, Flanagan always knew he was on a fool's mission. At times, he thought he would just get drunk and put a gun in his mouth. His love for her was too great, he could not do that to her.

Steph had somehow developed a painful left shoulder that kept her from lying next to him. She built a 'wall' of pillows down the center of the king size bed. She said the pillows would keep her from rolling on her sore shoulder in her sleep. She refused to see a doctor and it never appeared her shoulder was bothering her while gardening or playing with the Grandkids. "The pillow wall" was the same as the 'arm in a sling' hug. She was saying "I don't want you to touch me."

They both liked to read in bed at night, she would turn off her light first most every night. Often times he would quietly close his book and watch her fall-off to sleep. He would think back to the times that their love was magical. He mourned the loss of their joy of just being together, the days of laughter and silliness, the breath taking passion, the comfort of being pals, the days - she loved him. He would put up his book and turn off the lamp, laying awake, thinking of ways to live with his sorrow until that, 'someday' came.

In just a few short weeks after the construction of the, 'pillow wall,' Steph announced that she was moving into the guest room to sleep. There was nothing he could say, his heart just sunk as he said to himself, "That damn book." Steph had been withdrawing from him for some time. But this felt so final. The door to his dreams had just been slammed shut. Slammed shut and locked! He laid in bed that night alone. There was just a single wall between them, but she was worlds away. With just his thoughts and tears, he knew, he had lost her forever.

Steph and he became more like brother and sister (of sorts) or maybe like friends, he was not really sure as he had never been friends with a woman. There was a slight hug, 'goodnight' and a lite kiss on the cheek, goodbye in the morning, and nothing more. They shared all the household duties. They were simply roommates, with a lot of history. He tried to act like this new arrangement was fine with him but the truth was that he longed for her and still deeply loved her.

Steph's trips, and nights out pained him greatly. He was fearful that there was another man or that she was looking for one. His secret hope was that Steph would see he had changed and that she would someday, somehow, forgive him, see his devotion to her and of course would, 'someday,' fall back in love with him.

From the first night that Steph moved out of, 'our,' bedroom and for several years to follow he would sleep lightly so as to hear her soft tap on his door (if it ever came.) He would lay in bed each night and wonder what that soft tap would sound like. Would tonight be, 'the night?' Every night he hoped and often times prayed that this night would be, 'the night.' He would awaken each morning with disappointment. He would quickly think "Well not last night, but maybe tonight would be the night." That night never came.

'That night' was not about hopes for sex, no, not even close. That soft door tap, was about hopes that all was not lost. It would mean that Steph still cared for him, Steph still loved him and most importantly it would mean, that Steph needed him.

At some point and he didn't know when, he found the strength to accept the fact that his hope for, 'someday' and 'the night,' were his ways of not having to deal with the truth. That hurtful truth, was that he was all alone and the woman he loved, didn't love or want him.

Flanagan made a pact with God, that he would never hate Steph. He knew that her reasons for withdrawing from him were of his own making. He had let her down too many times. She could no longer allow herself to love him, the hurt had gone too deep, and for far too long. He took a silent oath that he would never turn his back on her. If she ever needed a friend he would be there. He would always care about her and pray for her happiness, no matter where his life took him. And yes, he still held out a bit of hope for 'someday.'

244

This was the brother-sister period. He still lived with Steph but without any hidden agendas. Well ... kind of. The nights they would watch T.V. together were the best. They didn't sit together of course, but he would sneak peeks at her, to see her smile with her beautiful dancing eyes and it made his heart smile. Other times, watching chick flicks, he would see her eyes moisten and he wanted to just hold her hand. But he knew he had lost that privilege, to give comfort. He would only sit there and pretend he didn't notice.

Flanagan had no interest in other woman. Secretly his heart still belonged to Steph. Steph suggested that they see and date other people but out of respect, no dates would be brought into the house. He had all the heartache he could take. He saw sex and romance as a trap and a gateway to more pain, and of that, he had, had enough.

Flanagan felt safe living with Steph, no demands, and no expatiations. When he had days off or short days he would make dinner and clean house. He did laundry, mowed the lawn, weeded the gardens and shoveled snow. It was all the same stuff he would have to do if he lived alone. But he did it so Steph could relax at home and have her weekends free to do as she liked.

Flanagan spent several evenings each week attending AA meetings or just coffee with pals. He stayed away from the house to give Steph her space. Steph had a demanding job and she put her all into it. When she was off work she needed and demanded her privacy. The only time they spent together was when the Grandkids came for a Friday night sleep-over. When it came to the Grandkids they were a couple, or sorts. Maybe, team was a better word. It was fun to be with them. The Grandkids were always sweet and loving, with cute personality's. They were a lot of work but a total joy to be with.

Flanagan's greatest joy came from watching Steph play with the Grandkids. She wasn't the kind of Grandmother to sit and watch the kids play. She became one of them. The kids, often times stayed both Friday and Saturday nights. Dinner was always

245

their choice. Their choice was always, 'Snack night!' Flanagan made nachos, mini corn dogs, mini meat balls, Lil' Smokies and 'Papa's Coke.' They spread a bed sheet on the living room floor so they could watch a kid's video, while they ate. After dinner, Steph would blow-up a king size air mattress and they would all lay in front of the TV and fall off to sleep. On Saturday morning, Steph would load the kids into the car and take them to a toy store and let them both pick out a board game and a toy. From there, it was indoor mini-golf or a movie at the mall. In the summer they would all walk to the irrigation ditch and catch Crawdads. Steph would teach the kids how to play card and board games. They did a lot of arts & crafts. He admired her character and her loving heart with those children.

There were times that he would observe Steph, her daughters and their husbands interact with the Grandchildren. Flanagan had never spoken of it but he did wonder how he would have turned out if he would have felt like a wanted child with loving and supporting parents and a remarkable Grandma like Steph. Of course, there is no way of knowing but he was most certain he would have grown to have been a much, much different man.

There is a second, 'door story,' that also affected him greatly during his years with Steph. This door story, was about terror.

Each night Flanagan came home from an AA meeting or just out for coffee with his pals, that all too familiar feeling of impending doom would wash over him. Admittedly, he used AA meetings and his pals as a diversion to avoid feeling the loneliness and depression that weighed so heavily on his heart. Each time he pulled into the driveway his chest would tighten, his stomach would knot and he could feel and hear his heart banging in his chest. As he got out of his truck and found the house key on his key ring, he would steel himself to face the end.

That end, was his house key not working in the lock. Each time that house key worked he let out a quiet sigh of relief and whispered a thank you. A thank you to God, to sobriety, to Steph. That house key meant that he had a reason to keep on living. Steph had been done with him for several years. He hung around with hope that, 'someday,' she would come to forgive him for his many transgressions and misdeeds. He needed her forgiveness even more then her affections or attentions. The last two years of their living together, he found himself, looking for little deed's to do for Steph to say, thank you. He was like a little puppy who just did a simple trick in anticipation of getting a treat or pat on the head. It sickened him to be such a weak weiner.

The door key working, meant that he still had a friend who still knew and cared about him. It meant that he still had a connection to the step-daughters and most importantly, the Grandchildren. Without these things, without the key working, he knew he would cave into his depression and end his life. This family was, 'his everything.' To lose them all at the same time would be just too much for him, he knew he wouldn't go on.

Chapter 29 "THE CALL"

Flanagan got the mid-morning phone call on May 26th 2009 and saw on the caller I.D. that it was his little brother Stevie. He knew that either Pops or Mom had died. Stevie and he only talked once or twice a year. They were not close, and they didn't know each other very well. Flanagan didn't even let him say hello, he just asked "Which one?" Stevie answered "Mother."

Flanagan's heart of course sank, but not for the reasons some may think. He was glad that Mom's suffering had finally ended. He had only $6.00 in his pocket, and no money in the bank. He could not attend his own Mother's funeral. He earned a good wage but he sunk most all of his money into inventory for his small collectables business. This business was for his retirement which would generate additional revenue when he retired. But at the moment he was flat broke. He feared that his truck would not make the trip. He first went to a friend who was financially well off. His friend loaned him money for the trip. He next went to a friend who loaned him his new car. He called Steph at work and told her of his Mom's passing and that he was on his way home to pack for his trip to Wisconsin. Steph said that she was sorry for his loss and told him to travel safe. He instantly realized that Steph had just cut the cord. She had closed and locked the door. He knew he was totally alone in his sorrow and in his life. It took him less than an hour to pack his bags. Steph's job was only ten minutes away and she was her own boss. She could have come home for a few minutes to comfort him. He needed her to hold him, at least to hug him. She did not come home. She was done with him.

The mind numbing 1,180 miles were filled with sorrow. In two short hours of Stevie's phone call, he was confronted with the truth that he had no one left who cared for him. He had lost his Mother and the love of his life. His best friend of twenty-five years was no longer his friend. Nobody needed or wanted him. He felt like that little boy that he once was. He had no one to turn to.

As Flanagan drove that never ending stretch of I-90 his

only companions were the hundreds of billboards advertising Wall Drug, the Corn Palace, Mt. Rushmore and dozens of other tourist traps.

Flanagan, did a searching moral inventory of how and why he so poorly failed as a son, a man, and as a husband to Steph, and those other four wonderful women. He felt the loss of each of them. He felt the pain that he brought to each of them. He was ashamed of the life he had lived.

As he drove all thru the night he thought of Stanford and all the sorrow that was still waiting for him. His entire 28 years there, were fresh as though he was watching a documentary – and it was ugly.

Flanagan had forgiven his Mom for his childhood years, without them ever speaking of it. They never talked of the past. They, or at least he, needed to leave it behind. He had to stop hating her for his own good. He came to realize (during that drive) that hate has never served him. Hate has only darkened his soul.

As he got back into the car after fueling up he took a deep breath with the thought that he still had to grind out another 400 miles, "Shit!" He knows that all that past sorrow was still waiting for him. There were only two potential bright spots on this trip. He could try to find Heather (his long time forbidden love) and maybe they could visit for a while. He had always wondered how her life had turned out. He secretly prayed for her happiness ... every night. He visualized her to have a happy marriage, that she had a really nice guy that adored her and a couple of good, well mannered, teenage kids. That was always his hopes for her. He hadn't seen or talked to her for several years. He had visited his family 5 times in that 20 years but never tried to contact her. He knew he must leave her alone.

There are two very distinct parts to Flanagan. He is a gracious, considerate, honorable man. He is also, a self-serving, opportunistic, needy bastard.

That second part of him, is the guy that wanted to find Heather in extreme turmoil, he hoped she was broken and desperate. He

249

hoped she would fall into his arms and beg him to rescue her, so he could keep her forever ... all to himself. As in his other last five visits he knew he had to again, leave her alone. This time, as the other times he must be a man of honor and pray that she is safe, as he looked back thru his rearview mirror and whispered "I have never forgotten you, you will always be in my heart, no matter what." He knew he must return home, to an unfulfilling life and that, would just have to do.

Flanagan's best pal Toby was his only other hope of peace on this trip. Toby and he had been inseparable since they were in their early twenty's. They hung out together almost daily, and spent a lot of quality time in bars. They hunted or fished almost every weekend. Toby and he were closer than most brothers. One or both of them would proclaim that they finally found 'Ms. Right.' After a few weeks of blessed love, they would be back in the bars consoling each other until the next 'Ms. Right' came along. Toby was his best man when Liz and he were married, that damned guy even got him arrested once.

It was a cold, late fall night. Flanagan and Liz were sound asleep when the phone rang. It was Toby, and he was in a drunken stupor, and he was not making much sense. Toby said he just piled up his new car on the interstate and had to run before the Cops got there and found him drunk. Flanagan kept asking him "Are you hurt, (sometimes a head injury will cause people to be incoherent and have slurred speech). Did you hit your head? Are you bleeding from your face or head?" Toby said he thought he might be bleeding, "A little bit." Flanagan told Toby to hide in one of the stores recessed doorways until he got there. Toby told him the name of the store that he was standing in front of. Flanagan quickly dressed and raced out the door. He was afraid that Toby might have a head injury because he rarely drove drunk, especially with his new 1973 Plymouth Road Runner. Flanagan was driving thru 30 mph city streets at 50 & 60 mph., fearful for Toby but at the same time thinking "You better be hurt, you son of a bitch, I just left a bed with the most beautiful gal in the city lying next to me. If you're not hurt, then I'm going to fuckin hurt you!"

There were several blocks of retail stores and bars, it was close to "last call" so he knew there would be plenty of Cops in the area. Toby was not where he said he would be. Flanagan didn't want to shout Toby's name and draw any attention, so he trotted past all the store fronts looking for him. He found Toby two blocks from where he said he was. He was sitting on the ground with his knees drawn up and his head down, in a recessed doorway. Flanagan had to shake him awake. Toby lifted his head up with his patented shit-eating grin. His forehead, cheek and neck were bloody and he could see his hair was matted with blood. Flanagan told him not to move and he was going back to get his car.

Toby was unsteady on his feet as Flanagan walked him to his car. Yea, he was plenty drunk, alright. He put Toby into his passenger seat and reached into his glove box to get a flashlight to check the source of the blood coming from his head, Flanagan heard a loud, sharp, commanding voice say "Police! Slowly put your hands in the air. If I see anything in your hands other than just fingers, I am going to blow your fucking head off." The cops, and there were a lot of them, handcuffed them both.

Toby ran a line of bullshit, of how after just two beers he left a bar down the street and as he was getting in his car two guys jumped him. They hit him on the head with a pipe wrench, and knocked him out. When he came-to, his car was gone, so he went back into the bar, and called his best buddy to come and get him. While waiting for his buddy, he had several shots of whiskey and a few beers to get rid of his headache. Flanagan had to chew the inside of his cheeks so as not to start laughing but he was proud of the smooth bullshit Toby was putting out.

As one of the cops went back to his car to run their, I.D.'s for 'Wants & Warrants' a sergeant told them an undercover cop was watching Toby as he was going from doorway to doorway thinking Toby was the 'lookout' for a burglary in progress. Several squads came into the area quietly and were hidden and waiting to pounce. When they saw Flanagan pull up and then jogging down the sidewalk looking in each doorway they figured he was the pickup or transport guy. They all got a good laugh out of that.

That is, right up until the cop who was running their IDs came back. This cop had a bigger shit eating grin on his face than Toby had a few minutes before. The cop said "Good news and bad news (pause)... and worst news, boys. Toby, we found your car. Bad news is the officer who found it says it's demolished. Now for the worst news; Clinton, there is an outstanding warrant for you for an unpaid parking ticket and you're going to jail." The sergeant had an even bigger shit eating grin than Toby or the ID cop when he said "That outta teach you to get out of a nice warm bed, late at night, to help a friend." Toby, being the smart ass that he was chimed in with "You outa see the chick he sleeps with! Hell, I would never have come down here if she was lying next to me!" Toby and all the cops had a big laugh; yep, everyone laughed but Flanagan. He was so pissed at Toby that he wanted to crush his fucking skull in. "Screw that little pussy cut on your head, I want to open that cut to the size of a fuckin bowling alley!" As the sergeant was putting Flanagan in the back seat of the squad car, the ID cop was taking off Toby's handcuffs. He told Toby that his cut was not that bad on his head. He could drive his buddy's car home and he could come into headquarters in the morning to file a report on the assault and car theft. Flanagan couldn't believe that they were going to let that drunken prick drive his car home, and he was going to jail. He was beyond pissed.

Flanagan got to spend the night in the drunk tank, handcuffed to a wooden bench. At ten am the following morning, he was bailed out of jail by Liz and Toby. As they walked out of the jail those two asses were giggling and cracking wise. In the back seat of his car was a big box that was gift wrapped, when he asked about it, Toby said it was a peace-offering, and he should open it right now. In the middle of the parking lot of the County Jail, Flanagan opened the box. Inside was a double layer round cake with a rusty file sticking thru it. Those two smart asses thought they were really cute and giggled like little school girls.

The next week Toby's insurance company bought him a new car, it had a $2,000 upgrade from his original purchase price. He paid nothing, what a prick!

The following week, Flanagan and Liz married. During the reception dinner, Toby (as the best man) stood, and taped his glass to give a toast. Toby asked if anyone had ever heard of the sober guy going to jail and the staggering drunk ordered by the cops to drive his buddy's car home. There were a lot of laughs. Next, Flanagan's Mother-in-law stood up and welcomed Flanagan to the family. She held up a long thin white gift box, the kind that long stem roses come in. The box was wrapped with a red ribbon and bow. She held it up for all to see. She said "It took me some time to find the perfect gift for my new son-in-law, but I did, in fact, find that perfect gift." She lifted off the lid of the box and there was a gleaming, two-foot-long file. She waved the file in the air while looking at him and said "Nothing could be a more appropriate gift than this bastard file, for the bastard that just stole my little girl away from me."

In the reception line the guys were slobbering all over Liz (she looked like a top movie star) and he got kisses on the cheek from each gal and each of them put a metal finger nail file in his hand. The pockets of his tux were bulging with those damn things. Toby's girlfriend told him, that they spent an entire day driving throughout the city buying out every stores inventory of nail files.

Toby took it hard when Flanagan and Liz split up. He loved them both. Toby is a great guy. Every time Flanagan came to Stanford, Toby and he got together for a few hours of "guy time." They have spoken on the phone every few months for the last 30 years.

Chapter 30 "FORBIDDEN LOVE"

Flanagan's Mother's funeral was held on a Thursday, in the late morning. This was a huge mortuary with a large commons area. As he was standing in the commons area talking with his brother Stevie, his wife and two of his nephews, he noticed they kept looking over his shoulders. He asked what was so interesting behind him. His sister-in-law told him that "There is a pretty young lady, tall, slender with very long, dark brown hair who has been standing there behind you for some time. She seems to be studying you, watching your every move you make." Without having to look back, he felt his heart leap as he said "Heather." And yes, as he turned, there stood Heather. She was wearing a smart looking business suit, and she was beautiful. As he approached her, she lightly smiled and lowered her head and softly asked if she was interrupting him and if it was O.K. if she was there, as he took her clasped hands in his.

He was startled with her being there. As in the last time he saw her, he saw far beyond her beauty and felt her warmth throughout his body. He could see that her heart ached for him. Her compassion for him, was transparent. He let go of her hands, smiled and opened his arms, she came to him. Never in his life had he felt so safe. Heather didn't just hug him, she held him. At that moment, at that very moment, he knew the truth. The truth that he had hid from himself and the world for all those many years. He was in love with Heather.

As Heather and he visited she told him she was single and had never been married. They exchanged phone numbers and email addresses. He told her that his Pops' was displaying signs of dementia and he would be there for the next ten days to take care of him and he may not have time to see her.

Flanagan glanced at his watch and realized that the social hour would go on for another hour before his Mom's service would start. He invited Heather to join him as he was going outside for some fresh air. As they stood outside visiting, he saw Toby pull into the parking lot. Toby and he, had a hug, Toby knew Heather from around town and as the three of them chatted, his two nephews and his brother joined them. Suddenly, Flanagan realized that Heather and he were standing side by side and they had their arms around each other's waist. It just seemed so natural.

The service for his Mom was nice. He got to do his Mother's eulogy. After the conclusion of the service and most of the people had left, Heather and Toby stayed with him. He could see Pops was worn out and deeply lost in his thoughts. As he excused Pops and himself, he thanked Toby for coming and supporting him. As he thanked Heather for her taking time away from work, she gave him a final hug and a kiss on his cheek.

Four days later, Heather called and said she would like to make dinner for Phil (Pops) and himself. The next evening Pops and he enjoyed Heathers fine cooking and her beautiful home. As Pops and he were leaving, Heather hugged them both, so kissed Flanagan's cheek and whispered "Happy Birthday" as she tucked a note into his shirt pocket. (Yes, it was his birthday, but he thought no one knew, or cared.)

At bed time, he took the note from Heather out of his shirt pocket, sat on the edge of the bed and had to work up the courage to read it. He had a pretty good idea what it said, the tenderness of her kiss, spoke volumes. The note apologized for her selfishness in stating her need to spend some time with him. She asked if he would delay his returning to Wyoming. She said she needed a friend, but more importantly she wanted to be a friend.

Flanagan felt like a self-centered prick for leaving Pop's but he was worn out. He needed comfort, he was hoping to feel loved. At the same time, he was nervous as he drove to Heathers house. He wondered if she had ever forgiven him. It had been twenty years since he last talked to her, the last time they talked, she asked him to marry her. He said, no.

Flanagan felt like a teenager as he rang Heather's doorbell. How did she view him? Was he an old family friend? Were they just pals from a time past? Was she looking for romance? Was she sick, was it serious? Bewilderment and fear filled his shoes.

Heather and her two Papillion's answered the door. It was dinner time for the dogs. He stood at the counter drinking coffee, as she sat on the floor coaxing them both to eat. He was back to being a teenager, he was wondering if it would be ok if he touched her, if he dared to try to hug her, he couldn't even think of kissing her, and the thought of making love with her, was completely off the charts. He was there to spend the next three days with her. Was he going to sleep in another bedroom? Would they sleep in the same bed? He was racked with fear and confusion. He thought that maybe he should just finish his coffee, thank her, and leave. He hadn't felt that kind of insecurity, since he was a child.

When she stood after the dogs ate, he asked her for a tour of her house. The place was tidy and clean, but not just clean, it was spotless! Beautiful house, beautiful furniture, well appointed and orderly. She took him into the office/den. She pointed to a corner shelf and said "I still have your little boys." There sat the Mickey Mouse figurine that he gave her 32 years ago; the day he left Wisconsin for good. He asked her about the other one. She said he sent that to her twenty-five years ago. He didn't remember sending that one, but then again, those were the years of extreme drink. He was a drunk long before he met Heather and he always hid his, out of control drinking from her and her family. He drank even more when he moved out west. He knew that he was drinking to ease the pain in his heart, from leaving Heather and all the other pains of the past.

After the house tour they went outside and sat on the deck, drinking coffee, while looking down on the vastness of the sea port. They chatted lightly as they watched the sun go down and as they petted the dogs on each of their laps. Heather stood up, leaned down and kissed his mouth and said "I'll get you another cup of coffee. Just sit and relax; I'm going to take a shower."

256

The thought of her naked, wet glistening lean body, just a few feet away made his heart race. He still didn't know why she invited him. A few minutes later she came to the deck door with her hair wet and a towel covering her, well, part of her. 50% towel 50% deeply tanned, firm, youthful flesh. She said "Your turn, big boy." She stood there with that same sweet, "snuggle up to his side grin" that he saw so many years ago. Yes, she still had those little innocent brown, fawn eyes and tiny freckles on the bridge of her nose. She handed him a towel and a guest bathrobe. He was confused, bewildered and any other words that would describe the feelings of a five-year-old driving his Mommy's car, on the freeway, in a rain storm, during rush hour.

They became lovers that night, and for the next three days they played tourist. He was with his dream girl and the time they were together was far better than any of his many years of his dreams of being with her.

They spent several hours sitting on the deck with conversation, coffee, cigarettes and lap dogs. Her hair shined, her eyes shined, her skin shined, along with his own heart. He told her of his lifelong love for her, of his struggles of having to leave her alone. He told her of his broken marriages (Not of the partner's parts, but only of his own faults and failures). Heather had never married, had a few long term boyfriends and had been alone for the last ten years. It was painfully obvious that she was broken too. She was loving towards him, but guarded. He could easily see that her caution in discussing matters of the heart was a minefield, he dares not enter, at least for now. Those three days went by far too quickly. He had to get back and go to work. They both had tears and parted with sorrow, she said that she may someday come out to Wyoming to visit him.

Flanagan was heartbroken. He knew that every moment they were together, that he had a firm grasp on the 'brass ring' that he now had to let go of. A final hug in her driveway, the click of the seat belt latch, shifting into drive and pulling away from her and her house to enter his void, knowing his fears, loneliness and broken heart were about to take over his entire being. He once again, had to resign himself to living an unfulfilled life. A life of regrets, a life of self-loathing and shame.

Driving the 1180 miles with a head full of thoughts, and a broken heart for company brought him to again thinking that dying, was far less painful than living. Those overhead bridge abutments became alluring, somehow, it was almost romantic. Hitting one of those big pillars at over 100 mph would instantly stop his lifelong suffering. It would all be over, every bit of it, would finally, be over.

His entire life was of conflict, fear, disappoint and failure. He was grasping for any reason to go on living. The live or die, coin toss, the dash board lights and tear burned eyes occupied several hundred miles of his travel.

He pulled off at several 'no services' ramps to walk and try to shake off his sorrows. He never stopped to eat as he didn't want anyone to see a broken man, who was a lost soul. It was gas and go only. Just east of Sturgis S.D. (on I-90) he topped a long hill and before him was the far distant Rocky Mountains. He could feel the warmth of the sun as it broke thru the early dawn clouds, the warmth was deep in his body. He wanted to live, and he knew he had a whole lot of work to do.

That 'work' had to do with coming to terms with his life. He had more amends to make, to tell face to face, the people he had harmed, that it wasn't their fault. He had to not step, but he had to leap forward, into understanding and forgiveness for those that had hurt him.

Flanagan knew that once he could understand those many reasons he could own his part and he knew his part was much greater than theirs, for the most part. He knew that understanding was the gateway to forgiveness and from that forgiveness, would come the freedom from bondage. "Hell, I just may want to live forever." The last ten hours of his trip home seemed like minutes rather than hours. When thinking of those he had harmed and those that harmed him came a flood of 'yea-buts'. The 'yea-buts' of thinking "Yea-but they did this, and they did that, so fuck-em! He knew that the 'yea-buts' and 'fuck-ems' were a trap. The trap that has, and will continue to own him. He knew that keeping and feeding these resentments would be to his demise. The freedom that he must seek can only come from forgiveness. Forgiveness of others and self. Fully standing firm in the knowledge that forgiveness and understanding does not mean <u>approval</u>! The bad things that happened to him were simply what happened, in a time that was, the ugliness of the past, will not serve him today in his new quest to live happy, joyous and free.

Things suddenly looked alive. The painting of the lines on the freeway looked bright and sharp. The cars that passed him were shiny and clean and glistened in the sunlight. The shape of the trees and their colors were beautiful. Everything he saw was as if he had just now seen them for the very first time. It was as thou he had been blind most his life and suddenly his sight had been fully restored... and perhaps it was!

Flanagan stopped in Gillette Wyoming for gas. As he was pumping the gas he looked at the base of a mountain only a few miles away. Something told him that he had to drive to the base of that mountain or he won't follow thru on his declaration for a new life. Flanagan drove along the frontage road until he found a badly rutted dirt road that came to a cattle guard with an open gate and several "no trespassing" signs. He had always respected the property of others and he had never crossed on to other people's land, but this time, this day, the draw to the mountain was greater than his moral compass. He drove thru that gate. He had to go another few miles before he could get close to the base of that mountain. He parked the car and walked thru Yucca plants, Tumble weeds and chalky, dry alkaline dirt. The wind was blowing hard and kicking up dust devils from his every step. The ground stopped sharply. Before him, was a steep wall of rock that rose up 50 feet or more. As he looked up to the top of that sheer wall he was reminded of when he was a little kid in Catholic school, almost tipping over looking up at the statues of the Holly Apostles.

259

He suddenly found himself kneeling on both knees with his palms pressed together as in prayer. The way he prayed as a child, back when he still loved God. He doesn't know how long he was there or even what happened. He did however, know that something, did happen. As he turned to return to the car he felt lighter and he knew what it was, as his nostrils were filled with the overpowering pungent odor of sage brush. He had just left behind his lifetime of hatred and rage. Did he leave it with God or did God take it from him? It was not his place to answer that question, it is however, his place to embrace the blessing! As he opened the car door to drive home he stood for a brief moment looking at that wall and whispered "Thank you, I will write the book."

As Flanagan drove into the city limits of Cheyenne, everything lost it deep luster, the cars became just cars, the trees just trees, the mountains just mountains. Oh, they were still beautiful, for sure, but they didn't have the brilliance and luster that he saw from his, 'awakening,' from just a few miles back.

He knew what that sudden dullness was. It was the reckoning of his reality, the dreaded reality that he would soon have to face Steph. He would have to finally acknowledge the fact that she had not loved him for many years and he had to let go of the hope that, 'someday,' she would. Flanagan knew that it was just a silly dream of a lonely man.

When he pulled into the driveway, Steph was mowing the lawn. She waved and smiled but did not stop mowing. He got his bags from the car and took them to his room.

Over an early dinner that evening Steph asked if he was ok. He said yes, and he thanked her for the flowers that she had sent for his Mom's funeral. She nodded and said "I am sorry for your loss but I must ask you to move out as soon as possible." He didn't know which fell faster, his fork or his heart. He knew it was her truth that she had to speak. He moved out within the week.

As in the past, his first thought was to find another woman, his brain said yes but his heart said no, never again.

He could not take the heartache of ever again, hearing those soul crushing words "I don't want you anymore."

Was Steph's not wanting him anymore, a blessing? Had she just set him free to love another? Yes, there was of course, Heather but she was out of reach, out of reach by distance of course, but mostly by her own lives conditions. As sweet and loving as she was, and the, 'Disneyland' few days that they were together, he also saw a hardness about her. A hardness born by her allowing herself to be mistreated. Heather was not only emotionally unavailable but worse yet, she was emotionally un-plugged. It was apparent that she trusted nothing or no one. He knows how that condition causes you to be jaded. He also knew how that causes you to be lonely and leads to hopelessness and paralyzing depression. He prayed every night that Heather would find her way, but he knew, he wasn't the answer and, he didn't have the answer. His heart ached for her many sorrows.

Flanagan and Heather spoke a few times during the week and sometimes, for a few hours at a time, on weekends. He loved the sound of her voice.

About a month after returning from Wisconsin, he was having coffee with his pal Tim, one evening. Flanagan had told Tim, of Heather and how he was missing her. Tim said "If you want to see her, now is the time. Go see her damn it!" Flanagan told him, he could neither afford to fly or did he have the money for gas, let alone did he trust his tired old truck to complete the trip. If it broke down, he didn't have the money to fix it, and he would have to abandon it, leaving it to someone for scrap. His friend Tim started to laugh and said "Friend, you do know what I do for a living? I know you do." (His pal was an executive for a major airline). Tim asked if he knew what a "Buddy Pass" was. He did not. Tim said the only thing standing between him and the love of his life was just the cost of the taxes for a ticket.

Tim reached into his briefcase at his feet, and pulled out his laptop, and as he shook his head at Flanagan, he made a few key strokes. Tim looked up at him and said "It will cost you $28.00 for

261

the air fare, roundtrip. If you don't have the 28 bucks, I will give it to you. Get her on the phone, now!"

Flanagan called Heather and asked her if she had time to, and if she would she like to see him. Heather shrieked like a little kid. Tim told him he would only get that rate if he stayed for 10 days. Heather said she had a lot of vacation time accrued and she would love to have him come. Tim turned his lap top so he could see it and said "Watch this". He mashed the confirmed button. Tim said "I will email you your e-ticket when I got home."

Flanagan sold off about 25% of his collectibles inventory so he would have money for the trip. He sold it for pennies on the dollar but it was a loss he was happy to take. He was going to spend ten days with Heather.

Just four days after Tim pushed the confirm button, Heather was back in his arms. For those 10 days the entire world went away. Just her, those sweet little dogs and him. She was everything he dared to never dream of. He was living in the middle of a 'chick flick' of nothing but tenderness, passion, adoring looks and warm touches. He knew he had not smiled that much in the last 15 years, he was in love with the person that he secretly had loved for 37 years.

However, there were heavy undertones of mistrust. They talked about everything, he laid out his entire life. He told her his entire truths. He spoke of his failings, his weaknesses and his shame of his many wrongs. He wanted her to know exactly who he was, in his past and who he had become, and mostly how he became the man he is today. He left nothing out. He told her of his values and how they were developed threw his life's experiences. He spoke of and from his heart. He told her of his two most important values; honor above all else, and honesty. Both kinds of the truths: situational truths and truths of the heart. His rules for life and his rules for sponsoring an alcoholic were both the same. These rules are simple, no lying. An omission of the truth is a lie, a half truth is a whole lie, and a little 'white' lie (regardless of the color) is still a lie. And why do we lie? We lie most often to avoid being judged. We also lie so as not to be seen as weak or vulnerable.

As he told her of his truths, Heather told only a few of her own. He knew he had to put it all out on the table to start clean with her. But he wondered if he told her too much, too soon. No, he knew he had it right. He could not start out with dishonesty and think that could work.

What he did know, is that Heather had not come to terms with any of her past, she did not even speak of her past other than in broad generality's. He found her lack of trust to be unnerving, but he made a silent pact to help her find her truths so she could make peace with her past. The same way he helped countless others over the years. Heather was very guarded in speaking of their future, and he knew at least for now, he had to avoid the topic. The day he left, he felt there were still too many unspoken words and unresolved issues. He wanted a future with Heather, he did not know what she wanted or if there would even be a future, hell, when he got on the bus for the airport he didn't even know if he would ever see her again. They hugged goodbye, and as the bus pulled out for the 150-mile trip back to the airport, she blew him a kiss.

Flanagan leaned back in his seat, locked his jaws to stave off the tears as all of the joy of the last ten days drained away. He told Heather he would call her when he arrived at the airport. He wasn't on the bus for a half hour when she called, she was crying, as she said "It's not the same, it's just not the same. Nothing is the same, without you here." He told her that he would get off the bus and wait for the next one or even hitchhike back. She said "No, it would not help, I will always feel the loss." Flanagan got an instant ice cream headache. Did she not say goodbye, forever, when he got on the bus? He felt confused and lost.

They spoke on the phone every day, he made three more 'buddy pass' trips. The last trip was bad. Heather had to have surgery, he flew out to take care of her. He got there two days before her surgery. She was scared of what the doctors might find.

263

He did his best to console her. Flanagan promised her that he would stay and take care of her for as long as she needed him. The day he brought her home from the hospital after her surgery's, she was quite ill. Flanagan was concerned for her breathing; it was mid-afternoon but well before dark. He darkened the room and tucked her into bed.

Flanagan sat on the floor with his back against the wall and watched her sleep, making sure she kept breathing. She had very little color and her breathing was labored. He got up off the floor only twice that entire night, to feed the dogs and to let them out for natures call. He sat in the darkness watching her. He prayed most all the night when he wasn't flashing back to her early years and thinking of all her cute little ways, their first day at the zoo, her cleaning the entire house in hopes that Liz and he would come over, her first charge account, her leaping into his arms at the hockey game and those pretty little fawn eyes peering up at him on the ride home. Of course he also remembered the times he hurt her as well; when he introduced her to Sandy, when he married Sandy. When he drove away leaving that precious little girl in tears, in that field standing in total defeat, and heartbroken. He also looked at his shame. His motives were not pure in his coming to take care of her. He selfishly wanted to show her that not all people, especially men, always ran away. He wanted to show her that he truly loved and cared for her, no matter the outcome. He was hoping she would realize she could trust him. And mostly he was hoping she would ask him to come and live with her, forever and ever.

Heather healed quickly, all the test results were negative and she was going to be just fine. A week later, he was once again, on the bus to the airport to return home. He did not hear the words he so desperately hoped for and wanted to hear. After his return home, they talked daily on the phone, it seems that he tried each time to convince her that they belonged together. She was not so sure. He was finally able to convince her (more like bullied her) that they belonged together. He said goodbye to his Grandchildren (who he deeply loved) knowing he would never get to see them again. He said goodbye to his beautiful Wyoming, and to the last thirty years of his life.

When he stepped into the front door of Heathers house and felt her embrace, he knew that he had made a mistake. He knew in his heart that she would never be happy with him, she did not want him to be there. Things were so different from the past visits. He tried his best to show her that he was not like all the rest. He could feel the fear and mistrust within her. In a very short period of time she too (as Steph did) developed the arm across the body hug to avoid full body contact. Her fear of intimacy, her lack of desire, and her unwillingness to engage in conversations of maters of the heart, told him what he already sensed. She didn't want him. He asked himself of all the "what's" and "why not's" but he knew the questions and the answers were of no value, simply, she just did not love him and he was powerless to change that. Three months after his arrival he returned to Wyoming.

Chapter 31 "SICK"

Flanagan fell gravely ill in 2010. It started with a nagging cough and chest cold. He was sick for a month, he could feel his lungs filling with fluid. He could not get a full breath, he felt like he was drowning. Then came the severe stomach pain, it would cause him to double over. Each day he became sicker and weaker. He didn't have health insurance and was too proud to ask for county assistance. He was losing a few pounds each day and his body functions were shutting down, he could not eat and could only get a few cups of chicken broth down each day. Then the intense headaches came, and they stayed. The pain was constant, his vision became blurred, often times all he could see was a field of muted grays. He had a friend looking after him. He couldn't work and had no money. He finally had to give in to the pain and weakness. He went to a free clinic that was set-up for indigent aliens with federal tax payer money. He was one of the very few white people there. Most all of the staff, were non-white and English was not their first language. He could feel the hostility from both staff and patients. The rage started to boil in his veins.

Flanagan was furious as he sat into his third hour of waiting to see a doctor, as he watched dozens of people who had come in after him, and had their names called well before him. He wanted to say "Fuck this" and walk out but there was no other place to go. So there he sat; broke, sick and ashamed. He had worked all his life, paid his bills and taxes. He took an oath, and did defend the constitution of the United States and in his later years he made amends for his wrong doings. Now he is being looked at as a second-class-citizen. Flanagan had now become an, 'official looser.'

The only other thing (besides his stubbornness) that kept him waiting there was remembering his friends, Oliver and Kevin's words echoing in his mind. "You paid for it, you earned it, you deserve proper health care."

The clinics Physician's Assistant, finally called him in and took his vitals. His blood pressure was 228/186, from his past experiences he knew he was having a stroke and cardiac arrest was just a few moments away. With his blood pressure readings so dangerously high, S.O.P. was to start an I.V. and call for an ambulance. Not here however, at least not for him. A lab technician came in and did a blood draw. He sat another forty-five minutes waiting to see a doctor. The doctor spoke in broken English and acted as interested in his health as if he was examining a splinter in his finger. Flanagan asked the doctor for something for his headaches and his stomach pain. The doctor told him to take aspirin and antacids, and to come back in three days. As Flanagan walked thru the lobby of the clinic to leave, he could not have possibly missed the line for the pharmacy windows. "And I am being sent home without any medications, what the fuck?" He thought "Fuck this bullshit, I am never coming back here."

The head pain and the severe stomach cramps did not lesson. They became even worse. He had no choice, he had to go back to the clinic. The night before his appointment the pressure on his brain was causing him to hear voices, the voices on T.V. were garbled and everything around him was moving. For weeks he had been dizzy and had a hard time walking, making it to the bathroom was a chore and became very dangerous.

Flanagan returned to the clinic for his blood results and was hoping that more tests would be ordered. The receptionist was rude and looked right thru him and all but said "You don't belong here." Same for the Physician's Assistant, she made little effort to disguise her contempt for his being there.

Flanagan sat and fumed through his three-hour wait. The Dr. came into the exam room with a lab tech. As she was drawing his blood the Dr. said "It looks like you have colon cancer. The headaches, blurred vision, and dizziness tells me your brain is also effected by the cancer. This condition is common with the terminally ill patients." Flanagan asked him for something for the pain. The Dr. told him to stay with the aspirin and to come back in three days with a stool sample, then walked out of the room.

Flanagan got into his truck and drove home, thinking about dying. He woke up from a nap and drove to an office supply store. With the little money he had, he bought several banker boxes. He took them home and wrote the names on the boxes of the five people who he thought would want his stuff. He didn't want Allie or anyone else to have to suffer going thru his stuff as he knew of the sadness they would have to endure. He felt it was the right thing to do, to protect them. He had three days of tears as he sifted thru the memories of his life.

Flanagan had boxes and totes full of all his stuff, with names on each of them, before his next early morning appointment with the doctor. On his next appointment the P.A. was almost friendly and he thought he might have seen a bit of professional compassion. But he couldn't be sure. She said she was going to sit in with him and the Dr. for his consolation. The Dr. came in and said the test results were conclusive, he had cancer, and it was throughout his body and he didn't think he would live past the next two months. He went on to say that they did not do any heroics at the clinic but told him to expect two phone calls later in the morning. One from a cancer specialist and one from a surgeon who may be able to help him and keep him comfortable. The Doctor admonished him to understand "This is going to kill you soon." He shook Flanagan's hand and pointed to the door and said "You can go now. You told me you were an alcoholic in recovery, but it wouldn't hurt you none if you stopped at a liquor store on your way home."

The P.A. told him he had an outstanding balance and to see the receptionist to take care of it. Flanagan stopped at the receptionist's desk, she gave him a bill for $240 and pointed to the cashier window saying "They will take your money" (it was the only service window without a line) Flanagan said "No, they won't" and he walked out the door. It was snowing with a strong wind as he walked to his truck, when he got into his truck he sat back and lit a cigarette. Tears came as he thought of the people he loved, and the fellows he was working with, to help them stay

268

sober so they could put their lives together. How was he going to tell them that he was dying? How do you find the words to tell them? How do you act strong so they don't worry about you? He decided he would wait until he talked to those other doctors that were going to call later that day. As he shifted his weight behind the wheel and reached for the shifter, he thought about the doctor's crack about the liquor store and he said out loud "No fucker, I am going to die sober!"

Neither of those doctors called that day or for the next three days following. He called the clinic and told them he had not received any phone calls from the two doctors who were supposed to call him. The receptionist said she would have to check the records and would call him right back (this was on a Friday morning). No call back. The following Monday he spoke on the phone with the P.A., she told him that the doctor forgot to sign the orders for the two doctors to call him, she said she would have the doctor sign the orders right away and he would hear from those other two doctors yet today. He waited until the end of business on Thursday. No phone calls came, from anyone. Flanagan resigned himself to his fate "I will just sit here and wait to die."

It was time to make those dreaded phone calls. He hadn't told anyone of his diagnosis as of yet. He knew Oliver (who he calls Allie) had to be first. At the time, Allie was living in Tyler, Texas. Flanagan kept getting his voice mail, he left him messages, but no return calls.

Flanagan felt he owed Allie the first truth, so he held off calling anyone else until he had spoken to him. Allie called the next afternoon saying he was in Houston at the V.A. Hospital with a troubled soldier (Oliver was a career Army Sgt.) under his command. He told him he couldn't talk at the time but would call him on his way home later that afternoon. Allie called that evening as he was just leaving Houston. Flanagan didn't want to tell him then, as he had a long drive ahead of him and he didn't want that working on his mind as he was driving back to Tyler. Flanagan asked him to call him the next day when he got off of work.

269

Allie called him that following evening. Flanagan told him to crack a beer and he had some bad news to give him. He didn't remember what he said but they both cried. Allie said that he would take leave the following day and would drive to Wyoming and would be there in two days. It hurt Flanagan to tell him but he felt such joy to know he would get to see his boy, one last time.

Flanagan had fallen into a deep depression with knowing that he was going to die, alone. No loving wife, no girlfriend to hold his hand, kiss his cheek or forehead and tell him it was going to be ok. Knowing that Allie was coming to see him snapped him out of his fears. He suddenly saw his physical-self for the first time in more than a month. His eyes were dark and sunken, triple bags under each eye, gaunt cheeks and his face was ashen. What alarmed him the most, is he realized he had lost so much bulk in his shoulders and chest. But what was the most alarming, was the skin on his hands was almost transparent and very thin. He had no muscle left and a distended stomach.

Next up on his call list was Shaggy. He too was like a son to him. He, as Allie did, called him "Pops." Shaggy and he lost contact with each other in the last few years and Shaggy had changed his phone number. He thought he would have to wait for Allie's arrival to get Shag's phone number.

Next, to contact was his Pal, Kevin. Kevin and he met on an on-line NASCAR card collecting and trading site six years ago. Kevin is a wacked-out Dale Earnhardt Sr. fan. Kevin even had a Vanity license plate on his truck that reads "3 Dale Sr." Kevin and he were both avid (better yet, rabid) NASCAR autograph trading card collectors. Kevin and he talked on the phone daily. Before he became sick Flanagan bought cases of NASCAR cards that he sold on EBay and at collector card shows. He would always send Kevin all the Dale Earnhardt Sr. cards he got from the cases he bought and anything he found at card shows, or on-line for his collection.

Kevin would send him the cards of the drivers he collected, that he found on EBay and at card shows he went to in California. Although they had never met, they became as close as any pals

270

could ever be. Kevin's wife, Bev was a very sweet gal. Often-times Kevin would put Bev on the phone and they would chat for a bit. Kevin and he (like Allie and Shaggy) were much like father and son, and again, much like Allie and Shaggy, Kevin was also a man of honor and dignity. Kevin, again like Allie and Shaggy, always ended their phone calls with "I love you."

Kevin took the news hard. He openly cried on the phone. He said he was too shocked to talk at the moment and asked if he could call him back in a few hours after he settled down. Of course, Flanagan agreed.

Flanagan sat and thought further as to what he was going to say to Kevin when he called back. What he did know was that he couldn't tell him or anyone else, about his secret. His secret was that he was losing his mind. He knew if anyone found out about it, they would call his caregiver and have her take away his keys and have her disable his truck.

Flanagan would suddenly find himself-driving and didn't know where he was going or where he had been. Other times he didn't know where he was, every street, every building he saw was foreign to him. One night he was sitting in his truck in front of a big building that said, 'Walmart' on the front of it. He wondered about all the people going in and coming out of the big building. He wondered what was inside there. When he had a brief Moment of clear thought, he realized that he was, 'cracking-up' and he knew he was in serious trouble with his mind. Flanagan panicked and reached for his phone to dial 911 for help. He realized that he would be locked-up in a physic ward and they would take away his driver's license. He put his phone down and knew he could not tell anyone.

Kevin did call him back and they talked for a few hours. Flanagan spent most of the time reassuring him that he was just sick and other than that, he was just fine.
He did tell Kevin that he had accepted the inevitable and it was simply his time and he was going to let nature take its course. Kevin did not buy the "I am fine" part; not for a minute.

271

Bev called him the next morning and said Kevin is beside himself with grief in knowing that the man who is like a father to him was dying and yet they had never meet him. Bev said she was going to book a flight for Kevin that day, if it was ok with him. He felt like shit. Flanagan knew they didn't have the money for a plane ticket and they couldn't afford for Kevin to be off work. He told Bev to hold off, as Allie would be there the next day for 3 or 4 days. Bev said "Bullshit." Kevin will be arriving next week, I will give you two days to recover from Allie's visit and then my husband will be on your door step." Flanagan felt the love she had for Kevin and the love for a man, she had never met. He felt it right down to his marrow. He felt blessed, the loneliness was again lifted from him. That day Kevin posted on their trading card site (unbeknown to him) of his situation. Flanagan was overwhelmed by the vast number of well wishes via the sites email system. He read Kevin's post and it brought him to tears. Flanagan never thought that anyone could ever think that well of him.

Kevin's writing was so eloquent and smooth that Flanagan carried a smile on his face all day, it made him proud to be his pal. With Kevin's intelligence and his ability to express both his head and his heart in such a kind and loving manor, Flanagan felt honored to call him friend.

Allie called him when he was an hour away so he could have time to get cleaned up. He had never been to Flanagan's house (out in the county) before and it would be dark by the time he arrived. Flanagan told him he would meet him at a nearby restaurant. When he pulled into the parking lot, there stood Allie, with a big shit-eaten grin as he broke into his famous, 'Happy Dance.' They both, laughed and laughed, it made Flanagan's sides hurt, and it never felt so good. After some long laughs and hugs, they went in for dinner.

At one point Allie reached across the table and grabbed his hand. With a softness in his eyes (that he had never seen before) he said "Pops, I came all this way just to tell you I love you and I am not ready to lose you."

As they were at dinner, Flanagan's mind and vision kept going in and out of focus. For the last several days, he found himself coming to, or maybe out of some kind of a blackout. He couldn't comprehend some of what Allie was saying, and he was having trouble staying awake. He thought that maybe it was the excitement that he was there and his fears that put him into some type of mental overload.

Flanagan's bed was covered with piles of boxes and clothes. He had been sleeping on the couch for the last month. He was afraid that if he laid in his bed, that he would die there.

Allie slept on the floor next to him each night. Flanagan would wake up every half hour or less and look at him sleeping. Flanagan knew his back must be killing him and he felt guilty for putting him through that. Allies loyalty and devotion was glairing. Flanagan would fall back asleep with tears in his eyes, so grateful for the blessings that he had Allie to love him. Allie being there, made him feel safe.

The following day Allie took him to lunch at his favorite 'greasy spoon.' It had been his favorite Mom & Pop restaurant for over 30 years. As they got out of Allie's truck he said he had a surprise for him. Flanagan suddenly saw Shaggy walking towards them. Shag's face was a beam of bright light. As he got to him he shook Flanagan's hand lightly as he was obviously afraid he was going to hurt him. Flanagan said to him "I'm not fragile, I am just sick, now give me a fuckin hug!" They hugged and laughed for some time. Allie put his arm around them and all three just stood there in the middle of that parking lot hugging and laughing and crying. It must have been a hell of an experience for the many of people walking by. Flanagan told Shaggy that he had a few special things set aside for him that Allie would send to him later. He looked at them both and told them "No more tears, no more talk about being sick or dying. Let's go in there and be the "Dicks" that we are."

Those three guys were unmerciful and relentless in the way they teased and made fun of each other. They deeply admired and

273

respected one another, they were pals. Let no man dare to speak to any of them, the way they spoke to each other.

You would have thought that they had over extended their welcome at happy hour that early afternoon, in the restaurant. They about pissed themselves laughing the whole time.

Shaggy was the youngest of the three and was easy to get to. Flanagan and Allie were always screwing with him as though he was their little brother. When Flanagan wanted to get a point across to Shaggy he would call him "William" (his birth name). Shaggy always said that when he called him William that it startled him; it made him think that he was about to spring on him, like a rabid dog. He said his tone of voice when he said "William" made his blood run cold.

As they were eating lunch, Shaggy said he wanted to make amends to Flanagan for them not speaking for the last few years. He went on to say his wife, his two little ones and his new job gave him little time to himself. Flanagan slammed his fork onto his plate, the loud sound made them both jump.

Flanagan locked his eyes hard on him, he set his jaws and said through clenched teeth. "William, you finally have what you have always longed for, you have a loving wife, two healthy babies and a good job to support them with. Apologize to no man for your dreams coming true, your happiness belongs to you, there can be no shame for loving your family, ever!" Shaggy sat stone still, blinked his eyes a few times, as his lower lip quivered and then he grinned a wide grin. He said "Thanks, Pops. I knew you would understand."

Some of the people sitting around them showed disdain with their many, loud outbursts. After a while he saw some grins and open smiles. Those people knew they were witnessing a long overdue reunion of true friends. In some of their eyes you could see joy, in others, it was perhaps envy.

The three of them walked to Allies truck and he dropped his tail gate down. They hopped up and sat on the tail gate and swung their legs like little kids do, for the next half hour. Then, it was time to go. Flanagan told Shaggy to thank his wife and kids for sharing him with them today. They hugged goodbye and he told him he loved him as he kissed him on the cheek. Flanagan had to turn his back to Shaggy, as he walked away. Flanagan walked to the front of the truck as Allie remained at the tail gate, to give him his time.

The next morning, Allie shook him awake before dawn. He said "Pops, I have to go now." Allie squeezed his hand, bent down and kissed his forehead. Flanagan sat up and tried to get to his feet. Allie put his hand lightly on his shoulder to hold him back and told him to go back to sleep. Flanagan bolted to his feet and pushed past him to put on his shoes. Flanagan insisted that he stay for at least a last cup of coffee. Allie said the truck was all packed up and the motor was running. Flanagan walked outside with him and Allie's truck was loaded with all of Flanagan's hunting, camping and fishing gear that he wanted him and his two boys to have. There were also a few trinkets that he wanted Carla to have. Not anything of much value but it represented the total sum of his entire life.

Allie gave him a quick hug and all but bolted to jump behind the wheel. As Flanagan watched his tail lights being swallowed up in the pre-dawn ground fog of that chilly mid-January morning. He knew that Allie was every bit, as broken hearted as he was. Oliver finally had a father and he, finally, had a son. Neither of them were ready to have that all taken away. As Flanagan stood there, he was sure that they were matching each other, tear for tear. Flanagan lit a cigarette and said a short prayer. He prayed that their mourning his loss will be brief but their rejoicing their times together will carry them through their lifetimes. As he stepped out his cigarette, he thought "One more to go, Kevin will be here tomorrow afternoon. I don't know if I have the strength to get through it." With the boys, he tried to be stronger and calmer then he felt and acted like he was ok, but the boys easily saw thru it. They were respectful gentleman and left him to his dignities.

The next day, his friend (Flanagan was too weak and slow thinking to drive to the airport and back), drove to D.I.A. to pick Kevin up. At that same time, Flanagan drove to social services to request help to bury him. A simple pauper's grave would be fine. They said they couldn't help him because his social security payments were $30.00 above poverty level and he was not a minority or indigent.

He told that pompous bitch to kiss his ass and said that he would crawl up on her doorstep and die, then it would be her problem. Security escorted him from the building. Flanagan laughed his ass off, on his way back home.

When he walked in the door, there stood his pal Kevin. They had a great, three-day visit. The time went by too fast, for the both of them. On Kevin's last night, Flanagan loaded him up with his best NASCAR driver autograph cards. Kevin was shocked that he gave him all his high dollar cards with him saying, "These should sell well, you can pay for your plane ticket and maybe buy you a new truck." Kevin balked with his statement. He said it was too much. Flanagan asked him "What the fuck am I going to do with them? Dead guys can't scan cards for sale on EBay!" They hugged and both had a hardy laugh. Then Kevin was gone.

Flanagan sat on the couch and stared at the walls for several days. He did tell Heather (recent, former girlfriend) that he was sick. Heather was insistent that she come from Stanford to see him. He didn't want her to see him the way he was, but he wanted to hold her, just once more, one last time. She came for eight days. It was wonderful. They drove to Estes Park and found a peak that he could walk to. They became married, in Gods eyes and in their hearts. She went back home. After everyone was gone and no one else would be coming, he hit a wall of depression that was none, like he had ever known before.

Flanagan had a friend bring him some pain relievers that he didn't need any longer. Flanagan was and always had been, against illegal drugs and illegal use of prescription drugs. He almost never even took aspirin. He picked up that pill bottle and put it back down several times. The thought of taking all of them at once, was continuous. He did not want to have his life end in a hospital bed. Images of Donnie, Petey, and Dad were foremost in his mind.

Flanagan woke from a brief nap, and his mind was clear, the fear wasn't there any longer. He thought of how blessed he was to be loved by such good people. Allie, Shaggy, Kevin and Heather, all left him with powerful messages and loving words of encouragements. Allies words of "I am not ready to lose you," rang in his mind over and over again.

Flanagan had over a 150 Facebook friends. Karen and Steph were two of them, (Flanagan's former wives). One morning Flanagan posted on FB "For so many years I have looked at the mountains but today I actually saw them." Steph commented on his post as to the beauty of the mountains. Allie called him and said he saw his post and Steph's comment. Allie said that he could tell from Steph's comment, that she didn't understand what his post meant. Allie said "You need to tell her. You guys have been together for over twenty years. She has a right to know." Flanagan knew he was right but he did not want sympathy attention.

He called Steph's house and left her a message, simply asking her to call him back. He was sure that she wouldn't call him back. He sent Karen a private message thru Facebook. He told her of his illness and thanked her for her love. He made further amends for the many ways he had let her down. He thanked her for their son and he thanked her for choosing the very best man to marry and to raise his son. He told her that he had something special that he had set aside for Dillon and if she would email him, her mailing address, so when this time came, Allie would send it to her. He added several personal lines to her and her husband. In closing he told her how sorry he was for bringing his pain into her life. He made it clear that their failed marriage was by no means, any of her doing. He didn't expect her to respond. He just wanted to do his duty.

The following morning, he was shocked to receive an email from Karen. She said that she had Dillon and his girlfriend over for

277

dinner last night. Karen said that she let him read his email, and Dillon said he would like to meet him. Karen included her cell number and asked him to call her so they could set a day, place and time. Flanagan was sure he was going to have a heart attack.

Flanagan called Karen. He told her he was anxious and stunned. He asked Karen what was the best way go about this. Karen suggested they all meet (her, her husband, Dillon and his siblings,) for lunch on Saturday. Flanagan made it clear that he only wanted to be known and treated as an old family friend. He assured her that it was not his intentions to step into her family or take any place into their lives. He was just stopping by to say hello. They set a time and place to meet that upcoming Saturday.

A million things raced thru his head. The last time he saw his boy was on his 6th birthday. What do you say to a twenty-four-year-old man that used to be your son? For two years after the adoption, Karen invited Steph and he for a brief after Christmas party and for an after birthday party. Steph and he brought gifts for all the kids, Steph always brought a potted plant for Karen. They never stayed long for those visits. After his 6th birthday party and on their drive home, Flanagan told Steph that he did not think it a good idea to interfere with their family dynamics. "Today is the last time that we see him."

Flanagan was back and forth with joy and anxiety. Than it struck him! It was the hardest blow he had taken in twenty years. His son wanted to meet his natural father, before the man died. That, brought it home. The reality of his impending death became real. He was not ready to die, he had too many people to visit and to thank them for being in his life.

Now, he knew he had to reach Steph. He owed her a final goodbye and a final thank you. It would not be right for her to learn of his passing through the newspaper obits.

He still needed to set a few things right with her. As he told Karen, he also had to tell Steph that she never failed him. Her only fault was to love him. He left another phone message at her home and at her work. He sent her a text, he emailed and he messaged her. He gave no details, he only asked her to phone him. Steph did not respond.

It was a bit devious and maybe even slimy, but he had to tell her. He knew she had caller I.D. on her cell, home phone and direct line at work. So he called the main switchboard and asked for her, he knew he was blind-siding her but it was the only way. If she knew it was him calling, she would ignore his call and message.

Steph answered, he asked her to please not hang up, and asked her to meet him for coffee or an early dinner after work with no strings attached, he added "If you would be more comfortable, please bring along a friend."

Steph agreed to meet with him for coffee after work that day. It was hard to tell her in public but he knew that's the way she wanted it. She said she was sad for him and his friends but showed no emotion within herself. It was the first time he had seen or talked with her in two years. She was indifferent, they spent more than twenty-five years together and she acted as thou they were mere acquaintances and he knew he had caused that.

Flanagan told Steph of his conversation with Karen, and their planned meeting. He asked Steph if she would like to come along and see what kind of man Dillon had become. Steph's eyes welled up, she nodded her head several times. Her chin and her entire body quivered as tears started to stream down her cheeks, she excused herself to the ladies' room. He knew it broke her heart when he let him go. He doesn't think she ever understood why he did it. He most certainly knew that she had never forgiven him.

That Saturday he met Steph in her driveway. She drove as he didn't trust his driving and Steph trusted it even less. As they drove along Steph apologized for avoiding his calls, she said "I just can't allow myself to get trapped with you again." She said she was sorry that he was sick and suffering but she could be of no comfort. He looked over at her and patted her shoulder and said, "I understand, because I do." She patted his leg and smiled as she put on her sunglasses on that cloudy day, and they drove on in silence.

279

When they arrived at the restaurant, Steph stood with him as he smoked a cigarette and tried to calm himself. Steph offered him a breath mint and gave him peck on his cheek, grabbed his hand, nodded at the front door of the restaurant and smiled as she said, "Come on, let's go see our boy." He wanted to marry her all over again.

Dillon's Mom, dad and two siblings were already seated, he was not there yet. Karen re-introduced Steph and him to their children, they all shook hands. It was a long table. Flanagan sat across from Dillon's dad, Steph sat next to him and across from Karen, on the other side of Steph was an empty chair. Flanagan last saw the younger brother when he was four years old and the sister when she was one-year-old. The four-year-old was now a full grown man. He was well over six-foot-tall and a wall of solid muscle, with good looks. Little sister was a beautiful young lady and in college. They were all sharing some small talk when the table became instantly quiet.

Flanagan followed Mom & Dad's prideful gaze as he saw Dillon walking towards them. His movements showed confidence, his walk was cat like, yet he carried a true air of humility at the same time. Little brother had become a big man, but big brother was a beast! He was all muscle without an ounce of flab. He was extremely handsome and far better looking than Flanagan ever was.

Flanagan rose from his chair and shook his son's hand. Steph reached out to hug him and he saw his awkward shyness as he blushed. There was a lot of lighthearted teasing between the family, but he could feel their uneasiness. After they ordered their meals Flanagan, asked for everyone's attention. He said, "We all know why we are sitting here together, we needn't address that 800-pound Silverback Gorilla. I believe that you are a family of no secrets. In respecting that, I must tell all of you of my truths." Flanagan took off his watch and held it up for all to see. He said as he looked at the three kids, "Your Mother gave this watch to me on our wedding day. The inscription reads, "All my love, Karen. Feb

2 1985." Flanagan looked over at Dillon and said, "Your Mother and I believe that you were conceived on our wedding night. I have worn this watch every day as a tribute, to her, for the last twenty-six years. It is a reminder that I did in fact, have all of your Mother's love. And as a tribute to her and to the other wonderful woman who all tried their very best to love me, an unlovable man." Flanagan handed Dillon his watch and said, "I would be honored if you would accept my watch as a gift of honor and remembrance." Dillon smiled and softly said, "Yes I will, to honor you and my family." Karen reached over and took it from him. She read the inscription out loud and began to sob.

Flanagan easily (as surely the rest did too) saw Karen in transition at that very moment. She was finally able to let go of the sorrows and the memories of a horrible past. A huge smile broke thru her tears as she nodded to him and said, "Thank you." The tears all around the table dried up as lunch was served. At one point he glanced at Karen and she mouthed the words, "Thank you." Steph reached over and squeezed his hand and whispered, "Thank you."

Karen and Steph looked across at each other both nodding as they softly said, "Thank you," to each other.

As they left the restaurant, Flanagan asked if he could take a picture of everyone. Everyone broke out their phones and took pictures. He took several pictures of the family and a few with Steph and Dillon and thought it was time to call it good, and be on their way. Dillon walked up next to him, draped his arm around his shoulder and asked him if it would be ok to have a few pictures, "Of just us, together." Flanagan was overwhelmed. After the pictures they shook hands and had a hug.

Karen told Flanagan that he had become a nice man as they hugged farewell. He thanked them all for their kindness and their time. He excused himself as Karen and Steph were chatting. He slipped behind the restaurant to have a smoke and to let his heart bleed.

Steph was waiting behind the wheel when he got to the car. As they pulled into traffic Steph glanced at him and said, "Mr. Flanagan, you Sir, are one hell of a remarkable man." He smiled at her and nodded his thanks, as he wished he had sunglasses to put on. He stayed quiet on the way home. He was trying to process everything that had just happened, he wanted to lock it all in his mind. He wanted his last memories as he was leaving this world to be of his son, putting his arm around him.

Chapter 32 "GETTING WELL OR DIE TRYING"

As Steph and he got back into town they stopped for coffee to decompress, with each of them knowing, they would be speaking their final words to each other.

Steph thanked him for thinking of her and including her in the meeting with Dillon. Flanagan told her that she loved him too, and she deserved to be invited. Steph asked if he got Dillon's phone number. He said, "No, this was a onetime thing, just a visit with an old family friend, no need for phone or email information."

As they arrived at Steph's house, he told her that he had something for her in his truck and if she could wait for a few seconds he would get it for her. He brought out a banker box with her name on it. He told her that they were just pictures of her, her girls and Dillon. He set the box on the porch. He knew that she was not about to invite him into her home. They stood several feet apart and said good bye. They did not shake hands, hug, or have a lite kiss on the cheek. Steph smiled and gave a short, hand wave. Without any words, she picked up her box and went into her house. The same house that used to be, 'our house.' And yes, he still loved her, even thou she didn't want him to.

On his drive home, he accepted the fact that his death would be mourned, but he would, die alone.

Flanagan went home to watch the world go by, hoping that he would die soon. The pressure on his brain was so intense that he was hallucinating, more often than not. During a brief respite of his out of body and mind visits, a brief moment of clarity came to him. He looked down at his hands resting in his lap. They were the hands of a sickly, little old lady. He could smell himself and saw his pajamas were dirty and he felt his several days' growth of beard on his face.

Flanagan became vein in the neck popping, outraged with himself. "How the hell did I let myself become this way? This is not me!" He was always well groomed, his appearance was always top notch, clean shaven, not a hair out of place, and finger nails always neatly manicured, slacks and shirts with sharp creases and without a wrinkle. The Vogue magazine type model, now looked like a homeless Wino. With the self-disgust boiling in his veins, he jumped to his feet and screamed, "Bullshit." His friend (who he was living with and caring for him) was sitting at the kitchen table and came running into the living room to see what was wrong. He told her to grab the phone book and get the address of County Social Services, because after his shower they were going there. She took his arm to help him walk to the shower and he pulled away saying, "I am going to walk a straight line by myself." In the shower he thought of the sadness he saw in everyone else who loved him, and what a pussy he had become. He took an oath in that shower. "I will never give up and the only way I will die, is if someone kills me, and they will damned well know they were in one hell of a fight!"

Flanagan and his friend spent most of the afternoon signing up for County Medicaid. He couldn't get an appointment for twelve days at the 'Peoples Clinic.'

At 3:30 am the following morning, Flanagan was sure that his head was about to explode. He drove to the hospital emergency room. He told a nurse that he thought he was having a stroke, suddenly there was a sea of medical smocks hovering above him. It seemed like they put an I.V. in and were wheeling him in for a brain scan before he had his shirt off. He woke up later in the emergency room as they were giving him a second I.V. with a piggy back of electrodes. There was this beautiful doctor standing over him and she said that she and the radiologist read his scan and had not seen any tumors, bleeds or blockages. There was however, noticeable and extreme swelling. She thought he may have a severe infection in his respiratory system, and she was going to put something in his IV to make him sleep. She said he should wake up about the time the IV was done, they would give him a shot of vitamins and he could go home. As he was getting dressed the doctor came in and told him he had an appointment in three days at the 'People's Clinic.'

She handed him a bottle of 15 Vicodin and told him to not be afraid to take them, "Just not all at once." She smiled sweetly, put her arm around his waist and gave him a side hug. As he walked out of the hospital, he felt like he had a whole new life. He walked a straight line with no stumbling and no foot dragging. It felt good to walk with purpose.

Flanagan was early for his, "People's Clinic" appointment. They took him back as soon as he finished registering. The Doctor and his Physician's Assistant came into the room and sat down. The doctor said, "Tell us everything that has happened since you've been sick, don't leave anything out and take as much time as you need, we are here to listen." It seemed like he talked for ever. Then they played 20 questions but it seemed like a 1000 questions. He was about to get brain overload, when the Doctor called from the desk phone and ordered three cups of coffee. He sat back and said, "We are all going to sit quietly for the next few minutes and rest. I want you to think of your best joke and when the coffee gets here I want to hear that joke, while we enjoy our coffee." After a few jokes and some lighthearted B.S., the Doctor took his last sip of coffee as he said, "We are not going to let you die. My P.A. here, is the best in the business, she will manage your case and she does not miss a trick. Show up for your appointments on time and trust us to help you." He slapped Flanagan's knee and smiled as he said "Keep Grinnin'" and left the office. The P.A. got up and told him to undress, and put on a gown with the front open and she would be right back. In less than five minutes in came the P.A., a Phlebotomist and a tech with an EKG unit. The P.A. said that before he left today he would get all the tests necessary to see what directions they needed to go. After all that stuff and a full body scan, the P.A. gave him eight more Vicodin and said his blood work was already on its way to the best, fastest blood lab in Denver. He was to come back at 6:00 am the day after tomorrow.

On that next appointment, when the Med. tech was finished with his blood pressure she took him to the exam room, the Doctor was sitting on the exam table, the PA and another Doctor were sitting in chairs. The Doctor was grinning over the top of his coffee cup as he said, "Flanagan, you do not have cancer. You have a nasty infection throughout your entire body. The lab reports suggest you might have Lyme disease, from a deer tick bite that you might have gotten when you were in Wisconsin. We will cure that and your headache, your vision and equilibrium problems will all go away in a few weeks or less. I do however think you are in trouble with your colon. This Doctor here, will be doing you colonoscopy in about ten days. He will give you directions as how to prepare, and "Young missy" here, is going to slam fluids in you. She will make you ass feel like a pin cushion. We are going to load you up with injections of vitamins and antibiotics. We have to knock down the infection before your colonoscopy. Take the medications as and when directed. I hope to see you in three weeks to write you discharge papers." The doctor shook his hand and told him to, "Keep Grinnin." The other Doctor gave him the fluids and told him how to mix them and when to take them. He said the P.A. would tell him when and where to go for the colonoscopy, and he left the room.

The P.A. had a huge smile from the time he had walked into the room, right up until the Doctor's left the exam room. He asked her what she was so happy about. She said, "We don't often get such good news on a patient who is, so badly emaciated as you are, and besides, I get to stick a bunch of real sharp needles in your ass! So now, prepare yourself!"

As they were laughing and he was being ass stuck, she asked if he drove there. He said yes. She asked if he had any valuables in his car. He said no. She asked if it was locked. He said yes, why?" She said, "Our courier is waiting for you in the lobby. He is going to walk you outside for a smoke. Then take you to the hospital, they have a room ready for you. You're going to spend the next 4 days there. You will be given medications to make you sleep and constant IV's to hydrate and flush your system, when you are discharged the courier will pick you up and bring you back here for a final exam before your colonoscopy. Flanagan was in the hospital for four full days, the few times he was awake the nurses treated him like he was royalty, hell for that matter everyone involved, treated him like he was royalty.

The Doctor came in the recovery room and told him that he had six polyps with two of them being cancerous and four of them being pre-cancerous, and he had two small lesions that he repaired and he should have no further stomach pains.

A week later, Flanagan returned to the clinic for an exam. The P.A. was still smiling. He had gained four pounds, she told him that they treat the whole person, not just parts of a person. She pushed a button on the desk as she said a Psychologist would be in in a few minutes. It was only a few minutes when a woman wheeled in a cart with a carafe of coffee, two cups, with six donuts and an apple on it. The PA introduced them and she excused herself. The Psychologist was helpful that day with his self-disgust, for giving up so easy. They talked a lot about shame and depression. She gave him some anti-anxiety medication, and told him to take the apple home and eat it as, "Dr. repellant, as in: An apple a day keeps the Dr. away." She was cute.

On Flanagan's final visit the Doctor deemed him recovered. He wished him a good life and told him to come back anytime he needed anything. He handed him several prescriptions telling him he was still severely undernourished. Flanagan told him he hadn't worked for four months and had no money for the $10.00 co-pays. The Doctor got up and said, "That's not a problem, wait here." The PA came in and told him to follow her. She had a cart full of large boxes of protein powders, supplements and bags of vitamins, she walked him out to his truck. She gave him a warm hug and they said good-bye.

Chapter 33 "HEATHER"

Flanagan met Heather when she was nine years old. His wife Liz, worked in the same building as Heathers Mom, Eva did. Liz & Eva became friends. A few times he would have lunch with Liz on his days off and Heathers Mom, Eva joined them. One afternoon Liz called him and asked if he wanted to meet with her, Eva and her husband Tom, for drinks after work. They were enjoyable people and in a short period of time the four of them became friends. Flanagan and Tom had coffee a few times a week. He liked Tom a lot. Tom had a good mind and he was funny. They became good pals. He liked Eva too. She was funny but when she drank too much, she became brash and oftentimes crude.

Tom and Eva had four adopted children. Two boys and two girls. One day, Tom invited Flanagan and Liz to join them and their kid's for a day at the zoo. He and Liz jumped at the opportunity, they both loved kids, (they couldn't have children of their own and it was a great void in their lives.) They meet at the zoo entrance and were introduced to the children. They seemed to be nice kids and well mannered.

The youngest, of the two girls (Heather) was nine years old. She was very shy and seemed unhappy. Not in her actions but just something he felt, he sensed that she felt as though she didn't belong, like no one cared about her. At the very same time he knew she was something very special. They were instantly drawn to each other. He did his best to give each kid the same amount of attention that day but Flanagan found his eyes always falling back on little Heather. Several times he caught Heather sneaking peaks at him. Each time he saw her looking at him she would have a tiny smile and drop her head in embarrassment. With eight people in the group moving through the exhibits, he found Heather wedging her way in, to stand next to him. Heather and he became instant buddies, something told him that they would be buddies for many years to come. There was an undeniable and electrifying attraction

288

between them.

That evening over dinner, Flanagan and Liz, reviewed their day with the kids. Their conversation was mostly about Heather. Liz said that Heather was smitten on him and acted like she wanted to keep him for her very own, like as if she had found a stray kitty. They guessed that she did not get much validation at home, or at least, she felt that way. Liz said that they should make it a point to spend some time each week with the kids but pay special attention to Heather, without the other kids feeling left out. He did not tell Liz that he had already made that same decision. The first moment he looked into Heathers eyes he saw his own heart. Eighteen years apart in age, but they shared a like soul, maybe the same soul, feeling unwanted, unimportant, lonely and without hope. No joy for today, no happiness for tomorrow. Heather, too, was another, lost soul.

Over time Liz and he became the favorite aunts and uncles to the kids. Every week Tom would mention over coffee that Heather had been cleaning all day hoping that you guys would come for pizza or hot dogs. Flanagan always brought the pizza. The entire family liked the, 'everything on it' pizza including Liz. Flanagan, was a 'thin crust, well done, pepperoni only,' guy. Heather instantly decided that she liked, "Flanagan's Pizza" a lot better. Same for hot dogs or burgers. The whole family only used ketchup, Flanagan used only mustard, suddenly Heather liked only mustard. Heather always sat next to him with their chairs all but touching. If they went to the movies, a restaurant, or riding in the car, Heather always had to sit next to him. It was a rule, known to all. He would like to say it was cute and he liked that. The truth however, is he loved it! He loved her special attention, he loved her adoring eyes. Mostly, he loved knowing that she felt special. One evening, over dinner Liz commented on his and Heathers relationship. She said, "When you are near Heather the whole world goes away for the both of you. You both tease and flirt like no one else is in the room." Liz went on to say that, "Heather worships you, she study's your every move, she mimics the way

289

you move your hands, your head, the way you look at people, everything you eat ... she is becoming a Flanagan Jr.! I think it might be dangerous."

Flanagan was ok with that, every bit of it, but he couldn't tell Liz that. He told her that he would invite Tom & Eva for drinks and they would ask them how they saw things. The next day after work the four of them met. When he asked them if they had any concerns with the way he treated Heather, they both laughed. They said Heather has always been quiet and withdrawn. Until she met him, they were very concerned in the way she was always isolating in her room and only came out for dinner. She didn't go out to play with other kids. She just sat in her room on the side of her bed with her hands in her lap, with her head down. They said that they had tried to draw her out, in several ways but after every attempt she would go back to, 'hiding.' They said that Heather would ask every Thursday, that if she cleaned the whole house, if Flanagan and Liz could come over, (they never were too busy to pass up an opportunity to see them). Eva said that Heather came to life when they said you guys were coming over, or they were all going to do something. "Heather would light up like a Christmas tree. You couldn't get that smile off her face. She would sit looking out the front window waiting for you to pull into the driveway."

Flanagan knew all too well, that they were close to losing her, much closer than they thought. He had been toying with the idea of suicide at her age. Heather and he both knew of each other's thoughts without muttering a word. They shared a kindred spirit. Flanagan swore an oath to himself, "I will not let her die."

Liz and Heather had their own attractions to each other. Liz was adopted also. Liz was a very pretty woman, she managed a woman's clothing store. They sold only better to best clothes and none of the common, off the rack stuff. Liz was always a portrait of perfection. Her hair, her teeth, her make-up, her clothes but the true perfection was the way she carried herself. Dignified, but completely approachable. Heather studied Liz too. Heather idolized Liz and it was apparent that someday, she wanted to be just like Liz. Heather baby sat (very mature at her young age) several times a week for neighbors. She had two paper routes and would mow lawns and shovel snow. For a little kid she was very much into money. She needed money to buy the identical clothes that Liz wore. Liz did all the buying for the store. When Liz saw something that she herself would wear she would order the same thing for Heather in her size. One day Flanagan was at their house helping Tom with a plumbing project. The phone rang and it was Liz (who was at work). She was calling Heather to tell her that a new blouse had just come in and it would be perfect for her. Tom and he were working in the kitchen near the phone. When Heather hung up the phone she was misty eyed. Flanagan asked her what was wrong. Heather said, "Liz just told me that a new blouse had just come in, that would be perfect for me and in just my size." Heather went on to say, "I spent all my money on my brother's birthday present and I can't buy the blouse." Flanagan and Tom looked at each other and with a nod and a grin, Flanagan said, "Come on baby, let's go look at your new blouse." Tom and Eva didn't have much. They were the working poor. Their furniture was old, they owned only one old car (and Tom's company car) none of them had much in the way of clothing. There just wasn't money for that.

As Flanagan drove to the store (20 minutes away) Heather was sullen. It was a quiet ride. When they got out of the car, she wasn't her usual new born fawn, high energy kid. She just slid her feet along and looked sad. Liz brought out the special blouse and Heather's eyes lit up, but only for a moment and she was back to the misty eyes. Liz, of course, asked what was wrong and Heather began to sob and went into Liz's arms. Saying "I don't have any money and now I can't look just like you." Liz held her for a moment and dried her eyes. Than Liz said, "Our boyfriend here, is going down the street to the sporting goods shop to look at worms, you and I, young lady are going to my office to have some girl talk." Flanagan wasn't sure what was going on, but he got the hell out of there in a hurry.

291

When Flanagan came back into the store, there stood Heather wearing the new blouse, with a smile so big that he could see all of the teeth in her mouth. She went over to Liz and held her hand and said, "Liz fixed my hair and put some make-up on my face so no one can tell that I was crying and guess what else, guess what else, (pause)? I have a charge account!" Liz and Heather were jumping up and down. Flanagan's heart melted. There in front of him, were his two best gals, both so happy, both so sweet. Heather became quiet and said, "I have to be responsible, with my charge account and I can only use it, if I don't have any money and as soon as I get some money, I have to bring it right down here and pay on my bill."

As he drove Heather back home he found himself wishing it was as quiet, as the ride to the store was. Heather was so animated and speaking so fast that he had to struggle not to bust out laughing. She was bouncing up and down in her seat with hands and arms flying everywhere. He was wondering if this kid was ever going to take a breath.

For 20 minutes he got to enjoy hearing all about how to manage your money and your credit, interest rates, credit ratings, how you can even buy a car and someday a house and on and on and on. He wanted to strangle and kiss Liz, all at the same time. Flanagan grinned as he pulled into their driveway, thinking, "Here yea go Tommy boy, she's all yours." When he went into the house with Heather she started up all over again for dad. Flanagan said, "Baby, give me a hug. I got to go." Heather said, "No, I have my new blouse on and it could get wrinkled, because Liz said I have to take care of my clothes and ... and..." He waved goodbye and ran out the door. He laughed his ass off as he drove home. After every mile he drove, he wondered what part of the, 'credit story' she was in at that moment. He could see Tom nodding his head and trying to act interested while thinking about wanting to kill Liz and him.

Tom and Eva both worked long hours and Tom was out of town at least twice a week. Often times, Liz and he would drive the kids to their school events and even medical and dentist appointments.

Those kid's, were their kid's too, and they loved them. Liz and he both admitted that Heather was their favorite but they worked hard not to show favoritism, in fear of hurting the other kid's feelings. Flanagan and Liz were always at their sporting events, band concerts, plays and Christmas programs.

It didn't take him long to understand his affections for Heather, his affections went far beyond her being a sweet, cute little kid.

Secretly he could not get enough of Heather, the moment he left her, he felt a deep let-down and a sadness come over him, that he could never speak of ... to anyone.

Even in Heathers youthful appearance she strikingly resembled Paula (Flanagan's first wife and the Mother of Saundra.) The glossy brown eyes with green flecks, the facial structure, her unique blended brown and red thin hair down below her waist. Heather looked like he visualized Saundra (his deceased daughter) might have looked like, had she lived. Heather, was Flanagan's dream child.

Saundra was born in 1967. Heather was supposedly born in 1965. The reason he says supposedly is this. It was a common practice for parents of young girls who were fearful that their daughter's lives would be ruined by having a baby so young, and for religious reasons, to let the pregnant daughter go to full term and delivery. The young girl would deliver the healthy baby and the young Mother would be heavily sedated. When the Mother came to a few days later, she was told that the baby had died. The hospital would turn a blind eye and produce a death certificate, the county would validate it and the adoption agency would create a false birth certificate. The new birth certificate would show a different state, county and city of birth as well as date of birth to avoid traceability. Could they have all lied to him? Is that why Paula detached from him so quickly? Maybe it wasn't the shame of believing their baby's death was her fault. Could it be more sinister than that? Did they all steal his baby away?

293

Was that Flanagan's overpowering draw to Heather? After all, she was adopted. Could Heather actually be his daughter? She was so deep in his heart that she had to be his little girl! He had no proof, so he had to just go on being Heathers favorite uncle and that would have to be good enough. In his heart, she was his little girl, either way.

Flanagan was a paramedic at this time. Heather would call him giggling and say she saw him on the news on T.V. Tom told him that she told all the relatives, neighbors and her playmates that her Uncle Flanagan was going to be a movie star because he was always on T.V.

Flanagan also worked a part-time job at an ice hockey arena as the rink-side attending paramedic. Every Wednesday and Friday night he was working at the ice arena for, bar league, hockey games. The arena was in in another city, 60 miles from home.

When Heather found out he was doing this, she suddenly developed a passion for ice hockey and just had to go to all the games with him. Flanagan had a pick-up truck and Liz had a Mustang. Tom's company car was the only vehicle big enough for them all to ride in. Flanagan paid for Tom's gas and bought hot chocolate for them all. The other kids didn't care for hockey, so it was just Tom, Eva, Liz, Heather and him that went to the games. The lady's sat in the back seat. Tom, Heather and he in the front seat. Heather sat in the middle but always leaned toward or on him, during the ride.

Flanagan sat with the players in the box to have quick access to the ice for potential serious injuries. One night a player collapsed on the ice. The 35-year-old player was in full cardiac arrest. Flanagan did C.P.R. started an I.V. and pushed several drugs into him with negative results. When the local volunteer ambulance arrived (15 minutes) the patient was still in full arrest. The ambulance crew was still in training for their E.M.T. certification. Flanagan retained control of the patient and rode in the ambulance, continuing CPR. When they arrived at the hospital, the E.R. team put leads on the patient and he was flat lined. After the second defibrillation he showed some heart activity. After a few minutes he showed a heart rhythm, not normal, but he was alive. If he survived the next 72 hours he might live. Pneumonia and brain damage was now the greatest concern.

The hockey arena was located in a cluster of smaller towns. Hockey was a way of life, almost, a religion. There were more people at the hockey games than at church, that's all the churches combined! The entire area is known as the, "Iron Range," for the iron ore deposits and the huge mining industry. The iron ore is shipped down the great lakes to make steel. The iron range is a close knit and closed society. They did not like outsiders, none of the players (from any team) so much as said hello to him. He was an outsider but they had to have an on-site paramedic to play organized hockey, by state law.

As Flanagan walked out of the trauma room there was a cop there and he said, "I'm your ride back to the arena, they can't play till you get back, so let's go." The cop turned on his lights and siren to drive to the arena only 6 minutes away. Flanagan laughed his ass off. The cop said he was off duty, so Flanagan invited him to sit with him in the player's box for the rest of the game. As they entered the arena he got the chills. The ice was empty, there was a puck on the centerline, and both teams were in their boxes, no one was speaking. The 2,000 fans were hushed. After all, they all just witnessed a man die. A man who most all of them knew, or knew his family.

As Flanagan and the cop stepped out on the ice to cross over to his seat the crowd spoke in hushed voices. As they got to the middle of the rink they stopped and gave them, a thumbs-up. Those people went nuts. You would have thought that they just won the Stanley cup.

That night, Flanagan became one of them. The guys in the box all went out on the ice and lined up to shake his hand, so did the other team. After the game they half dragged, half carried him to their locker room. They changed and they all went to the local bar. He didn't remember the rest of that night, other than the vast sea of beer bottles in front of him.

On the way home that night, Flanagan was grateful that Heather had a parent teacher conference that night, so the 'gang' didn't come along. He didn't want her to have to witness that kind of horror.

The next game the 'gang' came to, was three weeks since the heart attack game. He never told his wife about it. It was what he did for a living. Doctor Long, taught him not to take credit for a save, some time ago.

Tom drove, with Heather and him in the front seat and the wives in the back seat. When they arrived at the arena the parking lot was jammed full. Several cops and firefighters were directing traffic. They could not find a parking spot, (all the other nights the parking lot was less than a third full.) Flanagan rolled down his window to tell the cop that he had to get into the arena as the game will start in 15 minutes and he was the game paramedic. The cop looked at Flanagan's uniform and told Tom to pull up to the front entrance and park in the fire lane and leave his keys in the ignition.

The crowd was massive, they had a hard time getting thru the crowd. Heather was sad that she could not sit with him in the player's box. As Flanagan said hello to the players he took his seat. He noticed a wide red carpet laid on the ice at the center line, it ran the whole width of the rink. After the national anthem the arena announcer, a handful of photographers and a family walked out on the red carpet. There was a man, a woman and two little girls. They each had a long-stem red rose in their hands. A few more people walked out, obviously the Police Chief, the Fire Chief (both in uniform) and a man in a suit. There were also the games referee's on the ice.

The arena announcer held the microphone up to the lead referee's mouth. The ref. blew his whistle as he pointed to both player benches and announced, "Gentleman take your positions on the ice." The players skated onto the ice forming equal lines on both edges of the red carpet, like a receiving line. The announcer introduced the family and held the microphone for the biggest little girl. She said, "I want to thank the doctor-man for making my Daddy be alive and I want to give him my flower and give him a great big kiss."

The Police Chief and the Fire Chief walked over to Flanagan and escorted him from the players' box. He was embarrassed, like never before. No one told him this was planned for tonight's game. He got kisses from the girls and Mom, and when he shook Dad's hand, Dad gave him the rose and a hug. The arena exploded with cheers, and hundreds and hundreds of red and white, long stem roses, were thrown onto the ice.

The man in the suit was the President of the local mining company division. (Most everyone that lived on the iron range worked for the mines.) He announced that his company was going to buy five, 'Life-Pak 5' portable defibrillator units for fire-rescue and ambulance Units. The company was also going to pay for the recruitment and the hiring of five certified paramedics and pay their wages for the next three years. The Fire Chief announced that all fire and police dept. personal would receive advanced first-aid and CPR training and certification in the next 18 months. The Police Chief gave Flanagan a certificate and a plaque, proclaiming him an, honorary 'Ranger' (what the people are called on the iron range.)

As Flanagan walked off the ice and stepped into the box (with a lot of cheers and clapping), he saw Heather bounding down the arena stairs two at a time, she vaulted over the player's box and threw herself at him. He held her for a moment, and as he was putting her down she said, "You will always be my hero and I love you." He let her sit next to him in the box to watch the game. She snuggled into him and just kept smiling up at him with those little fawn eyes. The hockey players rolled up the red carpet then skated around, picking up all the roses from the ice. Heather put her hand out and asked one of the players if she could have the roses in his hands. He grinned at Flanagan, they both nodded at each other and he dumped them in her lap. He skated over to the other players that were all picking up the roses and pointed back at Heather. Heather became covered with roses. People were laughing their heads off, as each player covered her up, like she was in a leaf pile.

As Flanagan sat thru the game he felt no internal joy. Rather than feeling happiness for the family, for the community, even for Heather sitting next to him, he only felt sorrow. Sorrow for the ones he couldn't save. Sorrow for their families. He was lost in a deep depression and had been for some time, maybe all his life. He couldn't tell anyone of his sorrow, he just had to wear his, 'nothing bothers me,' mask. He knew his life was a lie and he hated himself for it.

As they were pulling out of the parking lot after the game, with a trunk full of roses Heather said, "Dad, it's ok if we get into a really bad car crash because Flanagan will save our lives and we can give him roses." They pulled onto the highway for the 60 mile ride home, Heather took his wrist and lifted his arm around her shoulder. She snuggled into his side with her head on his chest. In a few minutes she was asleep, curled up like a kitten. They all spoke in hushed voices, so as to not wake her. At one point he looked down at her and he saw her peering up at him with those soft, fawn-like shiny eyes and her angelic grin. She was wide awake but fainting sleep all the way home.

The gang came to several games after that. Heather always sat next to him in the box. One night before the game started, the referee skated over and handed her a new puck, and told her that she could keep it. She was thrilled. Another night a ref. skated over and said, "Hi Heather, I see you brought your boyfriend tonight." She smiled and giggled all night.

As they got into the car that night Heather announced, "The man in the striped shirt, with the whistle said that Flanagan can be my boyfriend." As the other nights, Heather feinted sleep, snuggled into him, and smiled the entire ride home as they all spoke in hushed voices, as not to wake her.

When Flanagan and Liz broke up, Heather took it in stride by saying to her parent's, "I like Liz a lot and she was always real nice to me. But now Flanagan can come and live with us and as soon as I get bigger, we can get married!"

Chapter 34 "YOU MADE ME CRY"

Four months after Flanagan's break up with Liz, he brought Sandy, to Tom and Eva's house to introduce her to the family. Heather came over to him and held onto his waist. When she realized that Sandy was his new girlfriend she started to cry and ran to her room. She would not come out of her room the rest of the night. He tapped on her bedroom door to tell her he was leaving and he needed a hug goodbye. She did not answer but he could hear her sobbing. It broke his heart, to know that she was so hurt. Tom called him a few days later and said Heather refused to go to school (she loved school) and would not eat or leave her room. She just sits on the edge of her bed and cries.

Sandy said she would pick Heather up after school the next day, take her to their house, fix dinner for them and have a visit. After that day Heather became a different person. She was still a sweet little girl, but not as attentive. He, never again, would see those adoring, little fawn eyes.

Over the next few years Flanagan and Sandy both, got fed up with the brutal Wisconsin winters and they decided to move out West.

Heather was than 13 years old and she was becoming a young lady. She was also becoming more aggressive with her affections towards him. It deeply saddened him to know that he had lost his little adoring girl. She would now intentionally brush up against him and give him that, 'come-on look.' It made him uncomfortable and he felt dirty.

Flanagan would never let anything happen between them. Protecting her innocence was of the greatest importance to him. He felt trapped and the only thing he could think to do, was to avoid her. Avoid her and avoid his truths. That truth that he loved her. He had been secretly pretending that he was her Daddy. Heather was his, 'Forbidden Love.' He had to ignore what was in his heart and take that truth of his, 'secret and forbidden love,' to his grave.

Flanagan and Sandy sold most all of their furniture and needed only a small size U-Haul trailer, for their move out west. The night before they left, they had a pizza party at Tom & Eva's, with all the kids. It was apparent to everyone that Heather was heartbroken. She sat in her chair with her head down staring at the slice of pizza that they all knew she wouldn't eat. He looked at Tom, Eva and Sandy with a pleading look asking, "What are we going to do?" Everyone had a glum, and surrendering look on their faces. Sandy suddenly stood up and went over to Heather, put her arms around her and said, "Come on, you and Flanagan and I are going to go for a walk. Heather lit up and they left the house. With Heather between them, the three walked hand-in-hand. It was a warm evening and they walked a few blocks to a corner store to buy ice cream. Heather was quiet but Sandy used soft, assuring words and promised to take good care of him for her. They all had more than just a few tears. It was hard to say goodbye to everyone, they had all become family.

As they were leaving, he leaned over to Heather and kissed her on the forehead and told her that she was his special little girl and ... and he loved her. He promised that they would come back to visit in a few years.

Flanagan could feel her heart breaking, as he could feel his own.

Flanagan and Sandy lived in a rural area with lots of farm fields between houses. The next morning as they were loading the U-Haul, they heard a car coming down the road, they looked up and saw it was Tom's car and he had Heather with him. Flanagan thought, "Shit, I can't take any more of this, I have all the hurt I can take, I can't say goodbye to her all over again."

Heather came running over to him, wrapped her arms around his waist and gave him a big hug. Tom said he thought they would come by to see if they needed any help with loading the trailer. He had a sheepish look on his face, as thou he was asking for forgiveness. Sandy and he both knew that it was Heather that made her dad drive there, to see them, one more time.

301

After gently prying Heather's grip from around his waist, they did help pack the trailer but it took less than 15 minutes. He noticed Heather looking into a box marked, "Mickey Mouse," (he had a large Mickey Mouse collection). Flanagan asked her what she was looking at and she pointed at a large brightly painted Mickey Mouse figurine. She said it was cute. He took it out of the box and told her he wanted her to have it. He told her that she could put it in her room and when she was sad, she could look at it and feel safe and be happy, and know that he was safe and happy too.

They all said their final good-byes, got in the truck and they could see Tom and Heather waving goodbye in the driveway as they pulled out onto the road. The dirt road was heavily rutted so he had to drive slowly with the trailer behind. Suddenly, Heather was running alongside of them in the field, her pretty brown hair was flowing behind her like a horses' mane. Tears were streaming down her face. He sped up. As they got to the corner, Heather stopped running. She stood with her head down, her shoulders rolled forward, and her arms dangling at her side. She looked completely dejected.

Sandy said he had to stop and go talk to her. He did not stop. He could barely see the road thru his own-tears. He turned onto a road in the opposite direction they should have taken. Sandy asked what he was doing. He said, "Once we get over this hill where they can't see us, I'm going to stop and go for a little walk." He pulled to the side of the gravel road and told Sandy that he would be just a few minutes.

Sandy said, "Fuck you, I love her too, we will walk together." As they walked in tears, Sandy took his hand as she said, "We don't have to move. I know you love her. Tom and Eva have said that you love her even more than they do. We (Tom, Eva and I) have all noticed how you so drastically change when you're around her. Your voice softens to almost a whisper, your eyes shine and they turn a much different shade of green. You become lite hearted like you're a kid, everything is about Heather, and you

302

fall all over yourself, trying to be attentive to her every word." Sandy stopped and she stepped in front of him and put her hands on his arms and said, "Look, you have to come to terms that Heather, is not Saundra. Saundra is gone, it's not fair to Heather or to you. You have to let them both go, or you will never have any peace. You buried Sandra several years ago, she must stay buried. Heather has to find her own way. Trust Tom and Eva to care for her. I need you to care for me and yourself." They moved to Colorado.

Heather would call them each week. She would say, "Hi', they would hang up and he would call her right back, so Tom and Eva didn't get a huge phone bill. Each time they called her back she acted surprised and always said the same thing. "Thank you for calling me back, I am afraid that you don't like me anymore, I'm afraid that your trying to forget me." It was hard to console and reassure her, that he would always have her in his life. He felt the depths of her fears and the void in her heart, as they were the same within him. He hated that all of his attentions to her healing and trying to draw her out, may have actually damaged her even further. Each time they talked she seemed more depressed. She was sinking. He told her that he was sending her a very special and important letter, and he wanted her to pin it to her cork board in her bedroom and look at it every day. She said she would. He called Tom and told him he was fearful that Heather was slipping away. He was afraid that she might kill herself. Tom and Eva took her to a psychologist the next day.

Flanagan mailed a long hand, and lengthy letter to Heather. He asked her to promise him that she would never hurt herself. He told her of several calls that he had been on with young teen suicides, (not the gore) and how the families of these kids hurt so deeply because that they couldn't save their child. He told her of his loosing Saundra and how it had hurt him all of his life. He told her that she was all he had left. He asked her to not break his heart. He told her that he needed her. He told her that she was his only beacon of light. And when he was sad or scared he would think of her and it would make him feel safe.

Tom called the day after his letter arrived. Tom said that the night before, Heather insisted that he take her to the mall to buy two more cork boards. Tom said that the day the letter came, she rode her bike to his office and told him to make copies of the letter. He was laughing as he said, "Heather always asks sweetly for something she wants, but this time, she told me, I had to make copies for her." She said that the copies were for her book bag. She said she would never go anywhere without her letter from her best friend.

Five years later Flanagan and Sandy traveled back to Wisconsin to visit his family. He called Tom and told him that they were only in town for a few days but would like to see the family. Tom chuckled and said, "How about tonight?" Tom went on to say that, "Today is Heathers 18th birthday. I won't tell her you're coming, be here at 7:00 pm and don't ring the bell, just slip in, we will be at the dinner table." Flanagan said, "We will be there."

When they tiptoed into the dining room, Heather froze in disbelief, (for a moment) she then shot out of her chair, she came at him in a blur (like at the hockey arena.) She flattened herself to him. Her warmth was all but suffocating and she clung to his neck like a wrestler. He had to pry her arms from around his neck and stood back a few feet and said, "Let me look at you." In front of him stood a mature woman. She was no longer a scrawny, knock kneed little kid. She was a beautiful, trim but full bodied young lady. He was so lost in her that Tom had to clear his throat several times to bring him out of his trance. He was embarrassed to realize that he had yet to greet the rest of the family. He felt like a dork. It was warm hugs all around. They spent about two hours with the family. Heather landed on his lap and stayed there. She had a constant smile and clung to him, like dog hair on fleece.

On the way back to his parents' house that night, Sandy took his hand and said, "You do know that she is in love with you, don't you?" He tried to play it off as just a teenage crush. Sandy disagreed, saying a woman knows when another woman is in love.

Sandy suggested that he call Tom & Eva and ask if he could take Heather for the day to put her straight on her infatuation with him. She said if they left without doing it, poor little Heather would pine for him and would carry a void in her belly, the rest of her life.

He knew that Sandy was right. When it came to affairs of the heart, Sandy was always right. He called Tom and Eva that same night and told them of Sandy's suggestion and asked them what they thought. They both agreed that it was a good idea.

As Flanagan left his parents' house the next morning, (they were pissed that he had just got there and would be gone for the entire day) Sandy walked him to the car. She told him to be careful, that Heather was vulnerable, and everyone, could hear her hormones screaming last night. That pissed him off, for a moment, but he knew she was right. He told Sandy that he would never hurt Heather that way. Sandy knew that he meant it, and so did he.

Flanagan pulled into the driveway at 8:00 am to pick Heather up. She came out the door before he could take his seat belt off. Her hair was flawless; her makeup was perfect. She wore a stark white, snug blouse with white, skin tight, heavily creased jeans. She walked down those stairs with the posture and elegance of a princess. She was stunningly beautiful.

She came up to his door and kissed him on the cheek with her glossy, full, pouting lips. Heather opened his door and put her hand out to him and said, "Come inside with me, there is something I want to show you." Flanagan could not catch his breath, he couldn't think, he couldn't find his voice. As they walked up the stairs hand in hand he could hear Sandy's warning and his own oath of just fifteen minutes ago. He knew Heather was about to give herself to him . . . and he wanted to take her. Part of him hoped that the other kids were home, part of him didn't. As she opened the front door he saw and heard the house was quiet. Heather did not break stride when she said, "We are going to my bedroom." She opened her bedroom door and pulled him in. She stopped in front of three framed cork boards hanging on the wall, mounted edge to edge making one board. The thumb tacks held his

305

hand written letter to her from five years ago. She squeezed his hand and with tears in her eyes she said, "Your letter saved my life, thank you for loving me." She turned and pointed to the Mickey Mouse figurine on the shelf of the headboard of her bed. She told him that every night as she got under the covers she kissed her two fingers and touched them to Mickey's forehead and say, "Good night, I love you." They stood side by side, holding hands for a few minutes without talking. She wiped her tears and said, "Let's go eat, I'm hungry."

At breakfast, she sat across from him with adoring eyes that he tried to ignore. They walked thru the downtown area and went through a few shops. He tried to buy her a few things that she showed an interest in, but she wouldn't let him. They went down to, 'Pine Point' and waded in the water along the sandy beach of Lake Superior. They skipped rocks in the water, found little pieces of driftwood and kept them for mementos. All during this time Heather kept trying to put her arm around his waist, but he told her, she could not do that. Several times she tried to talk about her and him, as if they were a couple that had a future. He would side-slip her conversation and ask her about how school was, who her friends were, what her future plans were, but she kept going back to wanting to talk about them. He knew it was time to level with her. They sat on a log and looked at the still water as the seagull's squawked all around them. He first told her he had no interest in a romantic relationship with her, (he could see the hurt in her eyes). He told her, he deeply loved Sandy and he was committed to her and her alone. He admitted that he saw (Heather) as his little girl and him, as her Daddy.

Flanagan apologized for his selfishness, in using her to fill his void of not having Saundra to love and to love him. He was startled when Heather said, "I know about your little girl, I tried to be her for you, I tried real hard." They hugged and cried a few tears as they gazed at the water surface.

As they walked in the sand on their way back to the car they held hands and she told him he was a good Daddy and a good man. She always felt safe and loved being with him. She said she would look for a man just like him and would not settle for anything less. He opened the door for her to get in the car and she asked for a last hug. They hugged and she kissed him, full on the lips. She said, "Thank you for not trying to seduce me, but I wanted you to. I'm glad we didn't."

All he could do was shake his head and marvel at what a wonderful, young woman she had become.

They pulled into the driveway and as he reached down to unbuckle his seat belt she said, "No, don't get out. She hopped out and skipped in front of the car, came to his window, patted his arm and said, "I don't care what you say, you will always be, my boyfriend." She turned and ran up the stairs. As she got to the front door, she turned back and blew him a kiss, he saw the tears in her eyes.

Chapter 35 "SHE LEFT"

Flanagan came to be with her, as she is his heart. He deeply longed (and has for so many years) to be with her, for now and forever. From gangly legs and knobby knees to a shockingly beautiful woman, she is statuesque but timid.

As she was leaving for work that morning, he held her but for just a moment. Her warmth radiated into his chest. The softness of her hair on his cheek was soothing and the smell of her perfume was intoxicating. He told her, "I love you," and she left.

He poured a cup of coffee and went out onto the deck, to enjoy the warmth of the morning sun. He sat and looked down upon the vast bay of Lake Superior. He lit a cigarette and as he exhaled he felt a sharp chill come over him, but the temperature had not changed. The view of the bay with its deep, dark, dirty waters makes him feel insignificant and lost. Some days, most days, he felt adrift in the middle of that bay, in a small leaky, old wooden boat. With sharp, choppy waves, crashing over the bow, he wondered if the next wave will be the one to shatter his little craft and put him to the bottom. He is floundering, bouncing around, being pulled by multidirectional currents. He has no motor, no ores and no one knows he is there. The chill he felt was not from his looking into the abyss, it was of his looking, into his own soul.

Heather will not speak of her heart or of her emotional needs. Her past life's events and her personal decisions have rendered her an emotional cripple and she has become a recluse, he is not enough, he can't reach her. His dark of night, tears tell him that he has failed her. She is guarded, even rigid when he tells her, "I love you." She responds with, a passive, "Thank you."

She keeps him at arms lengths but he refuses to quit on her. He wants so much to rescue her from her self-doubt and depression. He wants to show her what true joy is, he wants her to know comfort in her own skin. He wants to teach her to believe in herself. It is just what he wants, however.

During those times of his frustrations, when he can't reach her, he just looks at her striking beauty and smiles. Her physical stature takes his breath away. Her inner beauty causes him to all but gasp. He does know, who and what she is, he sees her warmth, her kindness and sensitivities for others. At those very same times he sees and feels her many pains of the past. Heather has felt she was abandoned all of her young life. As an adult she has never known any true validation, just countless broken promises. And yes, of course, he knows her adult life is of her own making, but he knows how fear and self-doubt cause us to settle. "We somehow believe we don't deserve any better. We surrender our dreams and accept a life we don't want and we simply call it, good enough."

Thru all of this, she has endured, and even prospered. She fills her heart with love of her dogs, her home, her job, but little else.

Flanagan's fondest memories of Heather, was when it was time for bed, the last words of the night were when he told her, "I love you, as he lightly kissed her forehead. Upon awaking the next morning, his first words were, "I love you," as he kissed her gently on her forehead, as he set a cup of hot, fresh coffee on her nightstand.

As Heather was walking out the door that morning, she said over her shoulder, "I put out a fresh towel for you." She has now been gone for several hours, he still hasn't showered. He doesn't want to give up the faint smell of her perfume.... his memories.... his dreams.

Flanagan spoke from his heart. He told her his truths, all of them. He bared his entire soul. He was living in a lie. The lie he told himself was that she truly loves him. However, the longing suggestive looks, the deep passionate kisses have been replaced with kisses on the cheek and matter of fact hugs only if they are initiated by him. "Yea it's over, the next morning would be more of the same." As she left he said, "I love you." She said, "Thank you." Flanagan packed his bags and he left.

309

Flanagan's cell phone started to ring at about the time Heather would be home from work. It rang over and over as he drove thru the night. Each time it rang he looked at the caller ID and each time it was Heather, she left a message with each call. He dared not take her call or listen to any of her messages. He knew he would cave in, his heart wanted to go back but he knew he had to stay the course. To continue living in the lie and the false hope, would kill him. His spirit was all he had left, and that was hanging by a thread. He could only hope that the note he left for her would be comforting, as he drove on and spied those big round bridge supports as his only solution to end his failed and shattered life.

Heather and he spoke after his third week back in Wyoming. They were both sorry for the hurt they brought into each other's lives. They made a pact that they would always be friends and most importantly they both vowed not to take their own lives. He then became sick and he was facing the end. He did not want to die but in the same vein, he was looking forward to the relief from his life's pains.

Flanagan recovered from his illness and returned to Wisconsin, to be with Heather, forever and always. They lasted for only one and a half years.

Heather and he agreed that it was time that they part. They set the date of July 22nd as their final day together. She would go to work as usual, while he packed and loaded his truck. He would shower and wait for her to come home from work. They would have their final cup of coffee on the deck, while they held hands, as they say good-bye to their dreams.

They finished their coffee and it was time for him to leave. They walked hand in hand out to the driveway. They stood apart, facing each other for a few moments, they both knew that their own fears had killed them. There was no blame, no anger, just sorrow. As he took Heather into his arms for their last hug, he said, "I will always want the best for you, I will hope and I will pray that all of your dreams come true." Heather, with moist eyes to match his own said, "I have never had a dream." He lightly kissed her forehead and he drove away.

If there can ever be such a thing as comfort in a broken heart, Flanagan did, in fact, feel comfort. He knew that he had done his very best. He never raised his voice to her, never a dirty look or ever used cross words or profanity. The letter he placed under her pillow on their last day will hopefully set her free.

This is a part of that letter:

"Love has always been elusive for me. I realize we carry a shared and same fear. What if I trust to love and I am still lonely, what then? How do I live then? What if I find out that I'm unlovable, what then? How do I live then?

We are equally lost; we cannot rescue each other. We are in the same storm, going in different directions. We both know we are going the wrong way, but don't have the courage to turn around. So we sit down in the snow with the wind howling, waiting for the bitter cold to overtake us. Uncontrolled shivering and numbness will signal we are close to the end. With a morbid smile we welcome that end, with a lengthy sigh, we both, collectively and individually are happy that we won't ever have to hurt again. We close our eyes and hope to never awaken."

Chapter 36 "THE TRANSITION"

How does a broken man become whole? How does he shed his long worn and tattered, threadbare suit of darkness? How does he become respectable and respected? How does he finally find peace?

Flanagan had been blessed with a soothing and melodic voice. He carries a presence of humble confidence. People are drawn to his easiness and they openly want to share their deepest secrets. People know that when he looks into their eyes, he sees into their soul, they seem to welcome it. They know that they are safe with him, they know they are not being judged, they are being understood. They see and feel the hope he has for them. He has found that in a few short moments of attentive, tender listening, they can remove a lifetime of hidden fears and shame. Flanagan has truly become a man of God.

Last night, Flanagan told the story of his life, to a group of 100 or more fellow alcoholics in sobriety. He has told his, 'story' hundreds of times, to tens of thousands, maybe 100's of thousands of people in the last 23 years, but this night was a challenge. It was the most difficult of all the times he had told his story.

Most often times, the audience is a mixture of all ages and walks of life, ages from 20 to 80 years old. More than half the audience had been sober longer than he had been. This group gives one hour to speak and has many college age members, the majority of them are woman. He was honored (as he always is) to be invited to speak, but he was also troubled by the request. For six days he wondered about how he could impact a group of 20 something, fresh faced kids. "How, can this old dinosaur, be seen as a vital source of knowledge, pertinent to this day and time in their lives?"

The answer came to him at 3:30 am the morning he was to speak, as he was sitting at the kitchen table. He will tell them of his fears and his past hatred of God and God's cruelty's in his life and the lives of so many others. He knew that when he spoke of God he understood that it would make him vulnerable to his, "rested" heartache and confusion of why God had punished him. He knew that at some point in that one hour or more, he would stand before them, naked. He would bare his soul, the tears wound come for him and for them. Perhaps when he shared of his break-thru in recognizing Gods presence that they too, could find the courage to allow or become at least willing, to embrace God's love in their own lives.

As he sat on a raised platform, sharing a small table with the meeting chairperson he looked out at all of these faces and felt an uneasiness that was uncommon to him. The meeting started with the standard readings and the recognition of sobriety birthdays. As he sat there his mind went entirely blank. He started to panic and his shirt became damp with sweat. His mind raced but he couldn't find anything to lock onto. His mind was like a never stopping roulette wheel, it just kept spinning. Suddenly, his old pal Carl, came to mind. He remembered Carl's council from many years ago. (Carl is a world known AA circuit speaker and a very successful published author, with several books to his credit.) Carl was a good friend of his dad's. Carl would always say, "You and I, are here to comfort the afflicted and to afflict the comfortable." Carl always shot it to you straight, no bullshit, ever.

Flanagan and Carl were guest speakers in Montreal Canada nine years ago. It was the Canadian National Annual AA, Banquet. Flanagan was the speaker for the Friday night dinner, Carl was to be the key-note speaker for the Saturday night banquet. There were more than twenty-thousand people in attendance.

Just before Flanagan was to take the stage Carl nudged him and said, "Scared shitless aren't you." Flanagan nodded as Carl put his hands on his shoulders and turned him to face him. He said, "I knew your dad for several years, he was a powerful speaker. He could make the earth move. He had the ability to change people's lives in just a one-hour talk. You are your father's son; God has given you that very same ability.

313

Flanagan, close your mind, open the doors of your heart, and trust God to guide you, as you bare your soul. Tell the truth, and maybe these twenty thousand drunks just might let us out of here alive."

This is the talk Flanagan gave with those one hundred plus, fresh faced youngsters:
"Good evening, my name is Clinton Flanagan and I am an alcoholic. I have been associated with Alcoholics Anonymous for 54 years. I first must start with saying that I am not an authority, nor am I a representative of Alcoholics Anonymous. I am simply a grateful and humbled member.

I further must state that I am no less an alcoholic today, than I was the last day I drank on August 7th 1991.

If you have come this evening to hear a lengthy 'drunk-a-log,' you will be sorely disappointed. My life today, is not about falling down. My life, today is about getting and standing up, and I hope yours is too! My story is about the loneliness, the fear and the pain brought to me as a child. My story is also about the loneliness, the fear and the pain that I delivered to those who dared to love me, as an adult.

My ego would like to report to you all, that my alcoholism is not my fault. I want to believe, and even more so, I want you, to believe that I became a drunk because;
I did not get a, "Radio Flyer," wagon when I was four years old.
OR . . . because I didn't get a, "Schwinn-Stingray," bike when I was eight years old.
OR . . . because I didn't get a, "Red Ryder" BB gun when I was ten years old.

If you believe any part of that dribble, then I have a whole bunch of swamp land to sell you. Some, want to believe that they became alcoholics because there was heavy drinking in their home as they were growing-up.
OR . . . my Grandpa was a drunk.
OR . . . my Kitty ran away.

If you need to believe your Alcoholism came from a life

condition, you certainly may. I am sorry for your suffering, but I stand here now to tell you that it may not be your fault but it sure as HELL is your responsibility to manage it.

For me, I strongly suspect that I, 'caught' my alcoholism somewhere between a liquor store and a bar stool. To believe anything else is pure, unadulterated bullshit.

For me to search for the root cause of my alcoholism, is for me to look for a reason to believe that I can be a controlled, social drinker. Entertaining that belief, most assuredly, will kill me.

Over the years, I have had the distinct honor of speaking to several social, church, educational and professional groups, on the topic of alcoholism. During the Q&A periods I have been repeatedly asked to define what an alcoholic is. My answer is always the same:

An alcoholic; is an egomaniac with a low self-image.

An alcoholic; is a person who is emotionally immature.

An alcoholic; is a person with shattered dreams and a broken heart.

If any of you here tonight, want to shout to the rooftops that you don't suffer from shattered dreams or a broken heart, I would like to inform you that you have yet to confront your truths.

Our shared sameness is about our perceptions of realty, which is not always accurate as to our actual realities. Whether our troubles are real or imagined, those troubles have brought us all together, in the fellowship of Alcoholics Anonymous.

I am well aware that some of you sitting here tonight, don't like me. I am, 'old school, AA.' I am direct and don't give, any part of a shit, of how you may feel. I do care and I am willing to help you do something about, how you may feel. I don't subscribe to modern day attitudes, where some people want to believe their needs are special and unique. Their situations are special and unique. I assure you all that none of you are special, and no one in

315

this room is a 'snowflake.' To honor my old family friend, Carl, and his signature statement, "I am here to comfort the afflicted and afflict the comfortable." I will tell you, that if you believe, "You got this," your sobriety is in great jeopardy and your life, is in even greater peril. Over the past several years, I have witnessed many men and woman spiral into the ground and even some die. Arrogance mixed with a lack of humility, is a deadly cocktail.

Many of us Alkies' tend to minimize our misdeeds. We want to claim we only hurt ourselves, and we weren't all that bad. We want to liken our drinking behaviors and our effects on others, to tossing a tiny pebble into a very large pond. Hardly a ripple. In truth, at least for me, I liken my drinking and my effects on others, to dropping a dump truck from a helicopter into a tiny, pristine pond in the high mountain wilderness. That pond will never be the same!

I grew up in a cruel, violent, abusive, alcoholic household. In 1957 at the age of 9 years old, my dad became sober. He attended AA meetings on a regular basis. I attended Ala-teens. I knew there was little hope for me, even at that tender age. The damage had been done. My fate, was cast in stone. I believed that I did not belong. Anywhere. I wasn't good enough and nobody liked me. I believed these things about me as many of you may have believed about yourself. That, in-part, is again, why we all sit here in the fellowship of Alcoholics Anonymous on a Friday night in Fort Collins, Colorado, sane, safe and sober.

My alcoholic drinking started at age 14. I drank as much and as often as I could. I found trouble and plenty of it. By the age of twenty-two I had to face my greatest demon, I was losing the will to live. I knew I was a drunk. I knew I had to get sober, I didn't want to, but I knew I had to.

Yes, I knew AA was my only hope but I feared it wouldn't take. AA is based on faith. To achieve sobriety, you must entertain a belief or at least a willingness to believe in a higher power. Without a God of your understanding, little good can come of your efforts. I maintained my sobriety for four years. I got as sick of

316

living sober, as I did as living as a drunk. I went back to drinking for another eighteen years, with fully knowing what I was and I didn't care. For a short period in 1980 I decided to try sobriety again. Well of sorts.

I did not try to stop drinking. I tried to find a way to believe I could stop drinking. When I was absolutely sure that my wife would not come home and, "catch me" I would climb my ladder in the garage and take down my "Big Book" that I had hidden in the rafters (much the way a drunk hides a bottle). I would desperately read to find an answer. Maybe I was simply looking for hope? I don't know.

I was a police officer at the time. When cops go out drinking together we called it choir practice. I attended choir practice on a very regular basis. There was a time period of approximately two months, when twice a week, I would shower & dress to go out for choir practice, leaving my wife to think I was going out to drink, gamble and chase women. When in fact, I was driving forty miles out of town to attend an AA meeting. My dirty little secret was never found out. If I told her of my "Big Book" and my AA meetings I feared that she would expect me to stop drinking. I knew I couldn't stop drinking and she would see me as a looser and leave me. Strange how the alcoholic mind works, isn't it?

My day of reckoning came on August 5th, 1991 at approximately 4:00 am. I came out of an alcohol induced blackout. My face was burning as though it was in flames. I had a terrible, caustic taste in my mouth. I then realized I was holding my duty weapon in my mouth. That, 'caustic taste' was, gun oil. I don't know how long I was like that, but it took several days for the burn marks on my face to heal. Those burns were from my tears. I told myself that I was done drinking, done for now and done forever.

Then the sheer terror set in. The terror that I was about to face was even worse than my almost blowing my brains out. The terror of having to accept or be at least willing to accept God in my life.

I knew my contempt of God would kill me, and now I will tell you why.

When I was 7 years old I loved God. I had memorized the, 'Lord's Prayer,' the, 'Hail Mary,' and the, 'Act of Contrition.' I said the, 'Rosary' and did the, 'Stations of the Cross,' every day, several times a day. I went to Parochial school. I walked the 10 blocks to school early each day so I could pray in the church before Mass. (Mass was mandatory before school each day). I went back to the church to pray after school. I spent most Saturdays and Sundays in church, praying.

I prayed so we could have more food, but God; said no.

I prayed so we could have fuel oil, for heat, but God; said no.

I prayed so Mommy and Daddy would stop beating me up, but God; said no.

I thought maybe I was praying the wrong way, so I tried to pray really slowly, but God still; said no.

I tried to pray real fast, but God still; said no.

I tried to pray more, I prayed in bed until I fell asleep.

I prayed from the Moment I woke up.

I prayed while I walked to school, with my palms together and my head bowed.

I prayed and I prayed and I prayed.

No matter how I prayed, God always; said no. I prayed like that, for over two years with the same answer, always the same answer. No! I stopped praying.

When I was 15 years old, I prayed that my two oldest brother's fighting in Viet Nam would come home safe. They were both killed in action, 4 days apart. God, had said, no.

When I was 17 years old, I prayed that my sick baby girl would live, but God, had said, no.

I prayed that my other brothers and my dad would survive their cancer, but God, had said, no.

I never prayed again. Now, at 43 years old, I have to find a way to stop hating God? How can I forgive him for all the pain, all the sorrow that he made me suffer through? How do I believe in any kind of a God, when I was forced to witness the carnage of broken bodies from disasters, the savagery & cruelty that man bestows upon his fellow man? How could God allow me to hurt the women in my life that I so dearly loved? I was convinced, that there is no God. And if there was a God, he hated me.

I somehow made it thru four years of sobriety, but as the last time, I hated it and I hated myself. I mumbled my way thru four years of saying the Lord's Prayer, after each AA meeting, (of which there were 1,000's). I read the 'Big Book,' several times where God, higher power, and spiritualty, were mentioned on every other page (or so it seemed). I sat thru meeting after meeting with all that God dribble and it sickened me. My sponsor would say, "Don't worry about the God deal, it will come in time. Just don't drink between meetings and go to lots of meetings."

My Pops (with 26 years of continuous sobriety at the time) called me one afternoon with the greeting; "Hey punk, how you doing with God?" 'Punk', was his term of endearment for me. I suggested he go and reproduce himself. We both laughed, he then went on to tell me that he had a solution, to my not trusting in God.

Pops told me to go out my front door. Get down on all fours, hike my butt up in the air, like those Olympic runners, hold myself up with my finger tips and take off running, like they just shot a starters pistol. He told me to run as hard and as fast as I could toward that cottonwood tree at the corner of my lot. He said, "Just before you get to that tree, lower your head and hit that sum-of-a-bitch with your full force. Head on! If you ever do wake up, look up at that tree and realize, that you, have just met, a power, greater than yourself!"

That was it! I had just had, a spiritual awaking. Those words from my Pops, (a simple man, with simple ways), had just set me free. He took the hate and the fear that I carried for so many years and told me I didn't need those things any longer. I suddenly felt neutral. I could allow there to be a God. I didn't need to seek or understand him. I just needed to be willing to allow there to be a

God. I need not describe him, I needn't give him shape, form or definition. I just had to allow him. To allow him into my life. My Pop's saved my life that day.

I have been married, I have been married a lot. I was married to five wonderful women. They were all smart, independent, self-sufficient, loving and affectionate. Each of them adored me. I was their sun and their moon. I was also . . . their nightmare. I think I chose strong women because I knew that they would be able to hold themselves up, when the inevitable came. I knew none of my marriages would last.

I knew from the very beginning that they would end. Because I knew myself. The only thing those wonderful Gals' ever did wrong, was their trying to love an unlovable man. I have made amends to them all, face to face. We shared a few moments of tears and smiles. All in the presence of their mates.

My Mother died four years ago, it was simply her time to go. I was grateful that her life long suffering was finally over, for her. Mom had 32 years of continues sobriety when she passed. She was well known in the AA and Al-anon Community's. I traveled back to Stanford Wisconsin, (my home town) for Mom's funeral. My Pops was heartbroken; he had just lost his mate of 30 years. Pops had 42 years of sobriety at the time. I arrived in the early-morning, Pops and I swilled pots and pots of coffee that morning until it was time to leave for the noon, AA meeting. All during my 1,180-mile drive, I tried to think of what would be fitting to honor Mom's life and her passing. Mom did not like or allow cut flowers in her house. She loved live flowers. She thought it cruel to kill a flower, just so we could enjoy its beauty. Flowers were out of the question.

As I walked into that AA Club Room my answer stood directly in front of me. There was a book case filled with AA 'Big Books' and 12x12s, (the 12x12 is the 'cliff notes' for AA). I told the Club Manager that I wanted to buy all the books she had.

I paid for them all, but donated three of each book back to the club in my Mother's memory and to supply newcomers free of

320

charge, until they could replace their inventory.

The next morning, I got on the highway early, I covered 350 miles and visited 9 cities with AA clubrooms. I bought all the books each club room had, and as in the first club room, I donated three of each book, back to the Club Room. It was my silent way of honoring my Mom. I got the giggles with looking in my rear view mirror and seeing nothing but cases of big books, blocking the back window. The trunk of the full size car was jammed with big books and 12x12's. I could not see out of the passenger window either. As alcoholics, we all know that more, is better.

The mortuary was colossal in size. The fellowship area was huge. The morning of Mom's service I got there early and stacked those books like the great pyramids.

Of the hundreds of people that attended my Mom's funeral, very few people were non-alcoholics. As I was doing my Mother's eulogy I asked if anyone may have noticed the small stack of, 'Big Books' and 12x12s in the fellowship area. That brought a lot of laughs. I asked each of them to please take a, 'Big Book' and a 12x12 as they left the building and put them in the trunk of their cars. When they were in an AA meeting and a new-comer was present, to go to their cars and retrieve their, 'trunk books' and give those books to that newcomer, in honor and remembrance of my Mother and with the honor and remembrances of those millions, who gave us all, so very much and whose names we don't even know. Tears of gratitude filled the room as I asked for a moment of silence to honor those that have passed and those who are still suffering.

After Mom's service the fellowship hall was full of wide smiles and laughter and tears. We drunks are masters of multi-tasking, we can laugh and cry at the very same moment.

Two years after Mom's passing, my Pops passed away. I again traveled to Stanford WI.

Pops died with 44 years of continues sobriety. Pops too, was a regional circuit speaker, (Dakota's, MN, WI and Canada), Pops had many friends and followers. There was standing room only at his service. I could not afford to do the book thing that I did at my Mom's service. When it came time for personal remembrances, I somehow knew that I had to keep my mouth shut and listen. After 1½ hours of listening to my Pops' pals, I was ready to lose my mind. I had gone more than 2 hours without a cigarette and had drank a few pots of coffee. I had to pee, but I knew I had to keep my seat. My friend Heather was there with me. She squeezed my hand and asked me if I wanted to say something, I said, "No, something is telling me to listen, there is something I need to hear. Besides, everyone in this room knows of my love for Pops, he was my hero."

Most everyone in that room spoke, and suddenly, I knew why I needed to listen.

A young lady, (in her early 20's) stood up and said, "I only have 4 months of sobriety, I only saw Phil, once. There was a lady at my first AA meeting. She went out to her car and came back with what she said, were both a "very special," Big Book and a 12x12. She gave me those books, for free.

The one time I saw Phil, at a meeting, my sponsor pointed at him and told me to go thank him for my, 'special Big Book' and '12x12', that came from his wife. I felt so bad because when I said thank you for my books, Phil started to cry. I don't know why he cried, or why my books are so special, but I do know, they will always be special to me."

A part of me wanted to get up, go over to hug her and tell her why the books were so special, the other part of me said, "No, some mysteries are special too, and need to be left alone." I kept my seat.

In closing I ask you all, to bow your heads in silence, to honor those who have filled these seats before us and have given us direction and guidance, as we all trudge that road to happy destiny. May God, bless us all. Goodnight."

Well, my most darling little boy, I hope I have given you and the others who will read this book, some tools to live your life by. Only you can decide the value it may bring into your heart and to the hearts of those you love. Please know this: some days, hope is all you will have, and every day, hope is all that you need.

So now you know why, "Daddy Had To Say Goodbye."

David J. Brown

To contact David J. Brown:
djbrownbooks@gmail.com

To order signed copies or schedule a speaking engagement, please visit David's website at davidjbrownbooks.com

David's next release
"FLESH OF A FRAUD"
A Companion Book to *Daddy Had To Say Goodbye*
Available Late 2018

56475872R00186

Made in the USA
Columbia, SC
25 April 2019